A Brief History of Brazil

A Brief History of Brazil

Second Edition

Teresa A. Meade

Union College

An imprint of Infobase Publishing

A Brief History of Brazil, Second Edition

Copyright © 2010, 2004 Teresa A. Meade

All rights reserved. No part of this book may be reproduced or utilized in any form or by any means, electronic or mechanical, including photocopying, recording, or by any information storage or retrieval systems, without permission in writing from the publisher. For information contact:

Facts On File
An imprint of Infobase Publishing
132 West 31st Street
New York NY 10001

Library of Congress Cataloging-in-Publication Data

Meade, Teresa A., 1948–
  A brief history of Brazil / Teresa A. Meade. — 2nd ed.
    p. cm.
  Includes bibliographical references and index.
  ISBN 978-0-8160-7788-5 (acid-free paper) 1. Brazil—History. I. Title.
  F2521.M517 2009
  981—dc22   2009033853

Facts On File books are available at special discounts when purchased in bulk quantities for businesses, associations, institutions, or sales promotions. Please call our Special Sales Department in New York at (212) 967-8800 or (800) 322-8755.

You can find Facts On File on the World Wide Web at http://www.factsonfile.com

Cover design by Semadar Megged/Alicia Post

Printed in the United States of America

MP Hermitage 10 9 8 7 6 5 4 3 2 1

This book is printed on acid-free paper.

In memory of my mother, Magdalen Meade,
a great lover of history

CONTENTS

LIST OF ILLUSTRATIONS

LIST OF MAPS

ACKNOWLEDGMENTS

As always I am indebted to my husband and fellow historian, Andor Skotnes, who supported me with his good cheer, wise advice, and more than his share of child entertaining so that I could finish this book. Our mutual interest in Brazil is documented in the many photographs we took during our travels there.

I am grateful to Jane Earley for typing parts of the manuscript and to Emily Wood, Deanna Collins, and Stacy L. Paull for their many trips to the library to track down sources. The staff of Union College's Schaffer Library rendered professional, efficient, and gracious assistance at every turn. Many thanks to Erich Goode, Barbara Weinstein, H. L. Hoffenberg, and Claire Skotnes for photographs.

Claudia Schaab at Facts On File has been an outstanding editor from the beginning to the end of this process. I am thankful to the Brazilian historians Susan Besse, Barbara Weinstein, Mary Ann Mahony, Thomas Holloway, and Bert Barickman for their suggestions and to Robert Conrad for use of his translated documents. Paulo Venancio Filho and David Fleischer provided assistance from Brazil, Zach Levey and Lilly Briger from Washington clarified details and filled me in on recent events. Finally, I want to thank the many historians, journalists, political theorists, travelers, economists, anthropologists, and others from Brazil and other parts of the world for their splendid books, articles, and Web pages. Without their many insights, I would never have been able to write this book.

PREFACE TO THE SECOND EDITION

Since the first edition of *A Brief History of Brazil* was published in 2002, Brazil's economic and political situation has changed markedly. The country's population has increased although its growth has slowed significantly. It is a nation that is today richer, less in debt, more active in international trade, and continuing to offer major contributions in art, music, dance, and, increasingly, film. It is more urbanized and is making better use of its vast agricultural resources. Probably most dramatically, the discovery of sizable offshore oil and gas reserves has meant that Brazil has moved from importing oil to feed its expanding economy to achieving energy self-sufficiency. It is on the verge of becoming a petroleum exporter and is second only to the United States in the production and export of biofuels, which it processes from sugarcane.

When the first edition of this book went to press, Lula Inácio da Silva was attempting to win the presidency for a third term. In the heated and often bitter campaign, Lula ultimately prevailed, winning more than 60 percent of the vote in a runoff election. Two years later, his socialist-inspired Workers Party was installed in Brasilia, as well as in many state and local governments. Also in 2002, Brazil won its fifth World Cup in soccer, a victory marked by a series of brilliant plays from Ronaldo Luís Nazário de Lima (Ronaldinho), the latest soccer sensation. However, by 2006, Lula was implicated in a massive vote-buying scandal and fighting for his political survival, and the nation's soccer team did not make it to the final World Cup match. Scandal sullied Lula and the Workers Party, at the same time that Ronaldinho stood accused of being too heavy and slow to carry his team to victory. The two icons, Lula and Ronaldinho, seemed emblematic of how far—and fast—fortunes can rise and fall in a short time. If Brazilians were disappointed in the corruption and scandal on which Lula's first term foundered, his second has been cause for optimism.

Despite much progress, poverty still enshrouds the lives of more than a third of the population: An estimated 85 percent of adults are illiterate, and crime, endemic corruption, and environmental degradation persist. In 2008, an outbreak of dengue fever sickened 75,000 people and killed 80 in Rio de Janeiro, the country's second-largest city and foremost tourist attraction. Even as the pendulum of progress and prosperity swings, Brazil is a country in the midst of profound change.

In this edition, as in the previous, I have sought to write a lively, informative, comprehensive, but brief, history of Brazil from precolonial times to the present. I have included the stories of men and women, examining the social and cultural context of their lives as well as important political and economic influences. In updating this survey, I have drawn from recent scholarship on social movements, such as the Landless Workers Movement (MST), and the controversy over implementing race-based quotas in universities and workplaces.

Although statistics and other data have been updated in all chapters, readers may appreciate more extensive revisions in three areas. Chapter 9, on popular culture, has been significantly updated, including information on Brazil's growing movie industry. In addition, the final chapter, which appraises Brazil's place within the globalized 21st century, has been rewritten. Finally, readers can find important recent additions to scholarship on Brazil in the bibliography and the suggested readings that supplement each chapter.

I have benefited enormously from the insights, available in print, electronic, and audio form, from scholars and commentators both in and outside Brazil. We share an appreciation for Brazil's history, culture, and people, while recognizing the many problems of the past, as well as the potential and challenges of the future. I hope this book can contribute to that understanding.

INTRODUCTION

The Federative Republic of Brazil, with an area of 3,286,500 square miles, is the largest country in South America and shares a boundary with every country of the continent except Chile and Ecuador. Slightly smaller in size than the United States, Brazil is the fifth largest country of the world. Most of it falls within the Tropics, but the populous industrial zones of the south are in the temperate zone. It is a land mainly of flat and rolling lowlands in the north with some plains,

(Based on E. Bradford Burns, *A History of Brazil*)

hills, and mountains in other parts of the country. Its highest elevation is Pico de Neblina, at 9,886 feet.

Brazil is divided into several geographic regions. The most important region in the early colonial period was the Northeast, mainly the current states of Pernambuco and Bahia. Since the early 19th century the Northeast has been eclipsed by the Southeast, which includes the industrialized regions of Rio de Janeiro, São Paulo, and Minas Gerais. An important area of grain and cattle production is the South, extending from the southern border of São Paulo to Argentina and Uruguay. The North is made up of the Amazon River basin, while the area called the Center-West, encompassing the vast Mato Grosso plateau, stretches from the southern areas of the Amazon basin to the frontier societies along the border with Paraguay and Bolivia. Most of the population is concentrated in the cities of the coastline, especially in the industrialized areas of the Southeast. By contrast, the North and the Center-West comprise nearly two-thirds of Brazil's landmass but only 13 percent of its population.

People

Brazil's population of 198,739,269 makes it the most populous nation of South America and one of the most populous in the world. Nearly one-third of the population is under the age of 15 years. More than half of Brazilians claim to be descendants of European immigrants from Portugal, Germany, Italy, Spain, and a few other countries, while the remaining 44 percent draw their heritage from Africa, descendants of people the Portuguese settlers imported as slaves from the first days of the colony until abolition in 1888. Many today are of mixed-race ancestry, referred to as *mulattos* or Afro-descendant, a term that has gained popularity because it relies on ethnicity and not color to define a large section of the population. Brazil boasts a smattering of other nationalities, from the Middle East and Asia, including the largest settlement of Japanese outside of Japan. Less than 1 percent of the population comprises the indigenous people descended from those who inhabited the land before the arrival of the Portuguese colonists in 1500.

African culture exerts a strong influence on religion, music and dance, literature, food, a wide range of customs, and in the Portuguese language. Whereas 70 percent of Brazilians state their religion as Roman Catholic, it is widely believed that many who profess to be Catholic actually also practice the African cults of *candomblé, macumba,* and *umbanda* that grew up under the tutelage of slaves and their Afro-Brazilian descendants from the 16th century until modern times. Since the 1980s various Protestant evangelical sects have attracted a large number of followers.

Politics

Divided into 26 states and a federal district, Brazil is governed from its capital in Brasília, a temple to modernism built from scratch on the plains of Mato Grosso in the early 1960s. Although the newly independent Brazilian state adopted its first constitution in 1824, several others have been promulgated since, in 1891, 1934, 1946, and 1967. Today, the government operates under a constitution adopted in 1988 when the country emerged from more than 20 years of military dictatorships. Under Brazil's current and highly active democracy, about 20 political parties contend for power and make policy in the bicameral legislature, made up of a Senate with 81 members and a Chamber of Deputies with 513 members elected by majority vote in the states. Eleven justices preside over the Federal Supreme Court. They are appointed by the president, who heads the executive branch, and are confirmed by the Senate.

From the last decades of the 20th century and on into the 21st, the center, left, and moderately left-wing parties have held the majority of congressional seats, as well as state and municipal offices, especially in the urban areas. In October 2002 Luis Inácio Lula da Silva (Lula), a former labor union leader and head of the leftist Workers Party (PT), soundly defeated José Serra in a runoff election. Lula captured 61 percent of the vote to Serra's 39 percent, signaling an end to the centrist policies of the previous administration of Fernando Henrique Cardoso from 1994–2002. Lula's victory in a runoff election with more than 60 percent of the popular vote proved bittersweet when the promised reforms stalled in the face of scandals, charges of corruption, and vote-buying that cost the leftist PT valuable support. Despite the rocky beginning, the PT managed to survive the scandal-laden first term, and Lula won a second term in 2006, garnering nearly the exact same margin in the second runoff as he had in 2002. Lula's second term has been largely free of scandal, and he has benefited from a much improved economy. Although the small political parties do not have the votes to pass legislation on their own, their support is often key to the success or failure of particular initiatives, because Brazil's decision-making process relies on building alliances and reaching consensus among the many parties that span the political spectrum from left to right.

On the other hand, there are many conservative congressional delegates and the right wing exerts considerable influence. The military

MAJOR CITIEƒ OF BRAZIL

City	Population*	Defining characteristics
São Paulo	10,886,518	The largest industrial city; main financial and cultural center.
Rio de Janeiro	6,093,472	A major commercial city, famous for its beaches, tourism, and nightlife. Capital 1763–1960.
Salvador da Bahia	2,892,625	Early colonial city and capital to 1763; famous for ornate Portuguese architecture, African music, dance, and cuisine.
Belo Horizonte	2,412,937	Capital of the mining state of Minas Gerais; a center of industry and transportation hub.
Brasília	2,455,903	Modernist capital founded in 1960 on plains of Mato Grosso.
Recife	1,533,580	Northeastern port city and capital of Pernambuco; shows the influence of Dutch, African, and Portuguese settlement.

Source: Census 2000. *Instituto Brasileira de Geografia e Estatistica.*

* City population. Figures for the "metropolitan area" are considerably higher. For example São Paulo's population jumps more than 18 million if the surrounding area is included, making it the second-largest city of the Americas, after Mexico City.

remains one of the most powerful official institutions in the country. The largest in Latin America, it is very well financed and has many influential allies among the conservatives in the government and in the business community. Although Brazil is not now under military rule, the generals have stepped in on several occasions in the past and there is no guarantee that they would not do so again should they, or their allies in the political and economic arenas, feel that their interests are threatened.

Surprisingly, given the lackluster economic and abysmal political record of the military during its reign from 1964 to the mid-1980s, the military still maintains a following in some sectors. According to David Fleischer's *Brazil Focus,* a weekly Internet newsletter on Brazilian affairs, in a 2001 poll 24.2 percent of respondents ranked the armed forces as an institution in which they had confidence, while the federal government had only a 9.4 percent favorable rating. Probably owing to repeated scandals and allegations of corruption, the Chamber of Deputies was rated favorably by only 3.4 percent of the respondents while the Federal Senate ranked last at 2 percent. Without a full analysis of the poll, one would not want to draw firm conclusions from this finding.

Economy

Possessing large agricultural, mining, manufacturing, and service sectors, Brazil's economy outweighs that of all other South American countries and is expanding its presence in world markets. Even with periodic slow-downs and an unstable financial standing, Brazil has been Latin America's leading economic power since the 1970s. The main accomplishment of President Fernando Henrique Cardoso's administration in the late 1990s was to bring rampant inflation into line. By 1999 it had fallen to 5 per-cent from more than 100 percent in the early 1980s. In 2009, China sur-passed the United States as Brazil's most important trading partner, with Argentina (as part of Mercosul [Mercosur]) now in third place. Because of its size and because both nations compete on the world market as export-ers of agricultural goods and petroleum, the United States maintains a keen interest in Brazil's economic standing. Brasilia closely monitors eco-nomic turbulence in neighboring Argentina, a nation with which it shares a border, strong economic ties, and a love-hate diplomatic relationship.

One key factor influencing Brazil's economic prospects at the begin-ning of the 21st century has been the need to improve the lives of the 31 percent of the population below the poverty line. On the positive side, Brazil has had a steady 5 percent growth rate over several years, which has resulted in a slight increase in real wages. More important, the discovery of sizable oil deposits offshore has bolstered considerably the nation's economic status, while it has moved from a net importer to self-sufficiency in oil. The Tupi oil field has shown sufficient promise to lead Brasilia to announce plans to seek admission to the Organization of Petroleum Exporting Countries (OPEC), a position so far only Venezuela holds among Latin American nations. Meanwhile, Petrobras, the state-owned oil company, has been drilling in Africa and even in Venezuela and the United States, indicating a newfound confidence in Brazil's place among current oil-producing nations.

In terms of trade, Brazil has been active in regional trading groups, including Mercosur, the Andean Community trade group. In addition, it has demonstrated remarkably vigorous trading relations with the Latin American Integration Association, registering a $15 billion trade surplus in the last four years in trade with 11 Latin American nations. With oil, massive capacities in agricultural goods, and the largest industrial might in all of Latin America, Brazil is beginning to flex its muscle as a regional power.

The Land

Many analysts argue that Brazil's potential lies in its ability to exploit abundant natural resources of bauxite, gold, iron ore, manganese, nickel, phosphates, platinum, tin, uranium, petroleum, hydropower, and timber. Nonetheless, Brazil has only recently begun to make use of its most obvious natural resource: land. In 2002, only 5 percent of the land was under cultivation, but by 2008, that figure climbed to 7 percent, and it seems to be increasing as worldwide demand for foodstuffs grows dramatically. Sustainable development of land and other natural resources remains one of the most hotly debated issues in Brasilia, pitting agribusiness leaders intent on clearing vast areas and harvesting cash crops against environmentalists and a powerful movement of rural dwellers who seek to occupy and work the land for the livelihood of

Peasants farming the banks of the São Francisco River. The river is very low during the frequent drought that plagues the Northeast and interior. (Meade-Skotnes Photo)

Brazilians. However, extensive pastures, woodlands, and forests remain unused over much of the territory.

With the exception of some parts of the far South and Southeast, huge tracts of land are controlled by a small number of individual or corporate landowners, who until recently felt little political or economic pressure to utilize their resources efficiently. At the turn of the 21st century, 50,000 people owned more than half of the farmland in Brazil. Irrigation techniques lagged far behind those of other parts of the world, leaving sharecroppers and tenants forced to work with primitive tools on arid patches of land for near starvation wages. Because the vast landed estates enjoy disproportionately high tax shelters, the elite have placed little emphasis on scientific agricultural techniques, crop rotation, and the use of modern implements and machinery. With thousands of acres of countryside left uncultivated, or inefficiently tilled and then abandoned, much of the land has simply eroded in the recurring droughts and floods that plague the interior and northeastern landscape.

While Brazilian transportation networks have been an impediment to efficient distribution networks, the government has placed some emphasis on improving an otherwise abysmal state of road construction. Over the past four years, the federal and state governments have overseen the construction of 141,000 miles of highway and paving of nearly 60,000 miles of old roads. Despite these improvements, more than a million miles of road in the Northeast and interior languish in various states of gravel, dirt, and mud. In the absence of transportation and communication networks, the poverty-stricken peasants of the Brazilian backlands have been left to fend for themselves and eke out a living in the interstices of estates controlled for generations by the same families. In addition, domestic and international corporations have bought huge tracts of unused land to hold as tax write-offs and shelters against profits earned elsewhere. The largest mass movement in Latin America, the Brazilian Landless Workers Movement (MST) has sought to change the age-old balance that has left the majority of rural dwellers without land, but the struggle has been difficult. The MST, unaffiliated rural poor, religious workers, international organizations, and human rights groups have sought to bring about widespread land reform with varying degrees of success. Under pressure from more than 3,000 protesters who camped out in Brasilia in late 2003, the government finally announced the National Plan for Agrarian Reform. The plan distributed land to 400,000 families by the end of 2006, granted legal title to 500,000 more families, and allowed 127,000 others to purchase small farms with govern-ment-assisted loans.

Content and Structure of This Book

This history of Brazil opens with the formation of the great "River Sea," the Amazon River. Home to many of Brazil's indigenous people before the arrival of the European explorers in the late 15th and early 16th centuries, the area has figured more prominently in international discussions of environmental issues than in histories of Brazil. It is, however, of tremendous importance to Brazil and, therefore, this history begins there.

Following the opening chapter's explanation of precolonial Brazil, the story moves to the history of Portuguese exploration, through the early years of the slave trade between Africa and the Americas and the creation of the largest slaveholding society in the modern world. Brazil's history for the first 400 years was a culture, politics, and economy based on slave labor commanded by slave owners. Within those four centuries, however, a vibrant African culture left its mark, joined by influences from European, Asian, and Middle Eastern immigrants. These many forces, as this history shows, have combined to create modern Brazil.

History is the story of men and women, of boys and girls and, more importantly, of their interaction. Human events unfold on a field played with gendered rules. This history seeks, to the extent it is possible, to show that there is more than "his-story." Moreover, the historical narrative is always a complex creation. It emerges out of the views, events, actions, triumphs, and defeats of men, of women, of old and young, of people of many classes and racial and ethnic backgrounds. This history attempts to paint the picture with broad strokes including these many actors from prominent and obscure backgrounds alike. They are all essential to this account.

Structurally it is, nevertheless, extremely difficult to narrate fully everyone's story. The technique in this book has been to include key figures, concepts, historical events, and explanations in sidebars, when they either do not fit with the chronology or when they can supplement the narrative more concisely as an aside. These boxed close-ups, along with charts, works of art, and testimonials from named and unnamed people from the past, show the extent to which the historical narrative builds from many sides. The text of this brief history will introduce the reader to the main contours of Brazil's development. The close-ups, along with suggested readings at the ends of chapters, bibliographies, and appendixes, will supplement the text. They provide the tools for readers to delve deeper into the events and characters outlined in the narrative.

Finally, this history follows for the most part a chronology, although at times events simply have to be explained outside a chronological framework. The text makes quite clear in topic headings or textual explanations when I have been forced to depart from a strict chronology. In the final chapters, however, the book's focus shifts from the chronology so as to include the history of some immensely important aspects of Brazilian life: soccer, television, music, cinema, and the Carnival. These are, after all, some of the major daily concerns of ordinary people, and no history of Brazil, no matter how brief, should fail to include them.

Our story ends where it began: the Amazon Basin. In the 21st century the Amazon figures prominently in the worldwide concern with preserving the planet's resources. As such, the story of the Amazon is more than a trope. It is a focal point from which Brazil entered the world's political economy and from which it yet remains inserted as a crucial player in world affairs. While tied to the sustainable use of the resources of the Amazon Basin, it is the totality of Brazil's political influence, economic strength, and cultural vitality that defines its historical importance.

1

LAND AND PEOPLE BEFORE AND AFTER PORTUGUESE EXPLORATION (PREHISTORY TO 1530)

The history of Brazil began 10 million years ago with the formation of the Amazon River Basin, or Amazonia. Because modern Brazil, and its potential for change, is so intimately tied up with Amazonia, our story begins with the formation of one of the world's great rivers. For 15 million years, the Amazon River flowed into the Pacific Ocean, but when the South American continent collided with another tectonic plate 10 million years ago, the Andes erupted, the river reversed course, and it began to empty into the Atlantic Ocean. Beginning in the Andean Mountains of Ecuador, 18,000 feet above sea level, the river forms out of the inland seas and freshwater lakes in the Altiplano. From there it travels 6,500 miles to the Atlantic Ocean.

Forming the "River Sea"
Ten times larger than the Mississippi River in North America and exceeded in length only by the Nile in Africa, the Amazon and its tributaries provide 25,000 miles of water, much of it navigable by ocean-going vessels. The largest river in volume, containing 16 percent of the world's river water and 20 percent of the world's fresh water, it is well deserving of its nickname, the "River Sea." The depth of the Amazon varies from 66 to 660 feet within Brazil, and its width extends to as much as seven miles wide. The 25,000 miles of water is supplied by 11,000 small and large tributaries, the largest of which are the Negro and Orinoco Rivers of the northern basin. Boundaries on the northern and southern banks force the river into a narrow channel as it reaches

the Atlantic Ocean, creating a daily tidal bore up to 16 feet high and driving the water into the ocean at a rate of 7 million cubic feet per second. In fact, the river joins the sea with such volume and force that the water remains fresh for more than 100 miles out into the ocean.

Because the river drains into both the Northern and the Southern Hemispheres, the Amazon has two rainy seasons, one in February and one in July. Fed from the Andes on the one hand and from the lowlands on the other, the white and dark rivers join at Manaus where they form a noticeable intermingling for more than 30 miles. The river holds a wide diversity of aquatic life, including the highly endangered giant otter, piranhas, freshwater dolphins, giant turtles, manatees, electric eels, and the widest variety of freshwater fish of any body of water in the world. Snowmelt from the Andes Mountains to the west combines with seasonal torrential downpours to form an area with the greatest rainfall on Earth. These two sources cause an upsurge of 30 to 40 feet in the water level, spreading out 12 miles each side of the river, over-whelming the Amazon Basin and engulfing millions of acres of rain forest into a giant sea for half the year.

When the waters recede, they leave behind flooded forest beds, half-submerged meadows, and temporary islands jutting up from the slow moving river sea. It is this flooded forest that accounts for the prolif-eration of aquatic life, since the surrounding land joins the river itself to form a single ecosystem. When viewed over the course of a year, for example, it would be impossible to find a single habitat on land or in the water that is unaffected by its relationship with the other, just as it would be difficult to know precisely where the river proper leaves off and the rain forest begins.

Plant Life

While the river itself is impressive, and home to countless species of fish and water animals, it is the rain forest it feeds that plays such a major role in the world's ecological system. At 2.5 million square miles, the Amazon rain forest is the largest in the world and is home to more than 10 percent of all living species on the planet, including plants, humans, and other animals. From a botanist's perspective, according to Michael J. Balick, research director at the New York Botanical Gardens, "these lands are among the richest and most diverse forests on the planet." (Balick 2000:1). Researchers have identified 300 to 500 differ-ent species of trees growing in plots of 2,000–3,000 acres. Studies of the plant life have uncovered a vast array of species that grow under harsh conditions, with minimal care, containing high quantities of oil and proteins and that have the ability to produce drugs, insecticides, waxes, and a wide range of important products.

The indigenous people in Amazonia have utilized plant extracts for centuries to prevent and cure many illnesses, leading modern-day specialists to assert that the ability of humans to survive and flourish on the planet, as did the Amazonian people, will rely on extracts from the rain forest plant life. It offers a diversity of natural products, including nuts, cacao, coca, guarana, manioc, palm hearts, plants from which medicines are derived, tropical fruits, rubber, spices, and many varieties of lumber and oils.

Animal Life

The animal life of the Amazon is no less impressive and diverse than the plant life. When the rainy season ends and the sun begins to transform the flooded plains into solid earth, the wildlife return to claim their territory. The best-known in Brazil is the jaguar, a name given it by the indigenous people, meaning "He who kills with one leap." Renowned for its stealth and hunting prowess, the jaguar is the largest and most powerful member of the cat family in the Americas. Standing at the top of the jungle's food chain, the jaguar's power was not lost on Jorge Amado, one of Brazil's foremost novelists. In his tales of the Brazilian backlands and coastal jungles, Amado made Manuel of the Jaguars the most feared and unscrupulous of the cacao barons in *The Violent Land, Gabriela: Clove and Cinnamon,* and other stories of the conquest of the Bahian jungle. The jaguar shares its notoriety with the anaconda, one of the longest snakes in the world and by far the heaviest. The jaguar is famous for its crushing jaw that can penetrate its prey in an instant, while the anaconda simply swallows the victim whole, ingesting it first, digesting it second.

Animal life on the ground is matched by a plentiful world of birds and animals in the trees, including eagles, tree sloth, monkeys, ants, macaws, and an estimated 30 million different types of insects. In the forest canopy, as the treetops are called, scientists believe, half the world's species exist, including 500 mammals, 175 lizards, 300 other reptile species, and a full one-third of the world's birds. Moreover, as one of the great paradoxes in which nature abounds, some of the tallest trees in the world grow in the extremely poor soil of the rain forest. Although 99 percent of the nutrients reach less than two inches into the acidic soil, the trees flourish by trapping sunlight on each leaf and turn-

3

ing it into energy-filled matter. An extraordinary abundance of plant and animal life has evolved over millions of years in this region, producing a very fragile ecosystem. Dr. Tom Lovejoy of the Smithsonian Institution has called the Brazilian forest canopy "the greatest expression of life on earth" because it supports so many plants and animals living in an intricate relationship with each other. (quoted in van Roosmalen and Plotkin 2000:1)

Human Habitation

The population that inhabited this rich ecosystem spread over hundreds of years from one end of it to the other. Humans congregated along the rich coastal zone of Brazil, stretching from the current states of Santa Catarina in the South to Maranhão and Pará in the North. Estimates on the decline of the preconquest population vary widely, but the agency responsible for the indigenous population, the National Indian Foundation (FUNAI), states that the preconquest population of 4 million to 6 million fell to about a million 300 years after the arrival of Europeans. Indian decline took place at the hand of the Portuguese colonizers as a result of slavery, forced confinement on Catholic missions, European intrusions into Indian territory to search for gold, land seizures, and, probably most decidedly, the spread of epidemic diseases. When the Portuguese colony ended in the early 19th century, its population had increased to more than 3 million people, but Indians comprised less than 6 percent of that number. Slaves from Africa composed 38 percent, with whites, free blacks, and people of mixed-race making up 28 percent each. In the early 21st century, FUNAI estimates that Brazil has 358,000 Indians, or 0.2 percent of the total population, in 215 different ethnic groups, with 180 distinct spoken languages.

The indigenous population of Brazil has been divided into three main groups: the Mundurucú, the Tupinambá, and the Yanomami. Although they migrated throughout the country during pre-Colombian times and adjusted to a variety of climates and topographies, their settlements have been drastically disrupted since the time of contact with the European settlers. Because the Native Brazilians did not live in highly concentrated city-states with well-defined hierarchical leadership as did the Aztecs, Maya, Inca, and others in Mesoamerica and the Andean Highlands, and because the groups of the Atlantic coast and Amazon suffered such immediate destruction at the hands of the Europeans, it has been harder for historians to piece together a full picture of the preconquest civilizations.

The Tupinambá were the main group of indigenous people on the coast of Brazil. Anthropologists include all the coastal groups under the rubric of "Tupi," which is a part of the larger Tupi-Guaraní family that encompasses more than 40 language groups throughout much of Latin America. In addition to Brazil, Tupi-Guaraní exist in Bolivia, Peru, Argentina, Paraguay, French Guiana, Venezuela, and Colombia. Paraguay has the largest concentration, with 3 million Paraguayan Tupi, followed by Bolivian Guaraní, spoken by an estimated 50,000 people. There are 21 Tupi-Guaraní languages spoken in Brazil, mostly concentrated in the states of Maranhão and Pará in the North and Mato Grosso in the Center-West.

The extensive reach of the Tupi-Guaraní language indicates that there was a great deal of migration by these peoples prior to the beginnings of European exploration in the 16th century. One group, the Guaraní-Mbia, moved from southwestern Brazil through Paraguay and then to the Atlantic coast in the 500 years before the arrival of the Europeans. When the Portuguese landed they occupied most of the Atlantic coast from today's boundaries in southern Brazil all the way north.

Two main groups of Tupi speakers had extended over much of the territory of Brazil. The Mundurucú occupied the area in the Center-West that is today Mato Grosso. The Tupinambá extended over a corridor that stretches for more than 2,000 miles from the coastal regions, beginning in the far south near the current state of Rio de Janeiro, up along the Bahian coast to as far north as Maranhão. Contrary to later stereotypes and the accounts of some of the early colonizers, the Tupi speakers were not disorganized, roving bands. They indeed moved through vast territories, but their migrations seem to have been motivated by war, search for food, mystical goals, and climate changes.

The Mundurucú

The Mundurucú migrated to the area of Mato Grosso near the Amazon River basin nearly 500 years before the arrival of the Portuguese. Studies indicate that they gradually gave up their more warlike ways to live in the forests and tend agricultural crops. A headman ruled the community, having been appointed for his abilities in oratory as well as in warfare. Since oratory often involved communicating the myths and spiritual messages of the gods to the villagers, a headman's role as political leader was closely tied to religion. There were designated religious authorities, or shamans, who advised the headman and leading figures of the community on matters such as hunting, planting, and war. The

5

Mundurucú held to the belief that balance in the universe could be maintained only through a fairly strict system of settling scores among rival villages. They traveled over great distances at times on land and also in canoes to procure a supply of sacrificial heads, since balance, they believed, was maintained when one group captured and ritually sacrificed prisoners from an opposing village.

Known for their skills with bows and arrows, the Mundurucú were adept at both feeding themselves with the largesse of the jungle and with maintaining an adequate supply of heads. They immortalized their hunting prowess in tales that were passed down to the members of the community from the eldest men and used as the main form of instruction for the adolescent boys. The society was male-dominated, and the most skillful hunters resided for periods of time in special houses from which women were barred. The male-only hut was a place where the men gathered nightly to swap stories of their hunting feats, to fashion bows and arrows, and to indoctrinate the young men and boys in the Mundurucú's belief system.

Interestingly, the central origin myth asserted that in the ancient days of the tribe women had been dominant and powerful. Eventually the men outsmarted the women and scared them into submission, supposedly by fashioning a device that made a roaring sound when flung through the air. The sight and sound so frightened the women that they submitted to the men. The myth might indicate that the line between male and female power was viewed as quite tenuous. The very notion that women were at an earlier stage seen as the powerful force within this hunting and warrior-based community, and were merely tricked into giving up that power, might have meant that males saw women as a potential threat to their dominant role. The Mundurucú's understanding of "balance" was circumscribed within defined lines of gender inequality.

Using bows and arrows, men downed jaguars, tapirs, deer, monkeys, and birds, while women and children trapped smaller game, reptiles, and rodents. They added to their meat and fish diet with manioc and vegetables, farmed in fields located on the outskirts of villages. They lived in dwellings made of thatch on poles, shared food communally and, apparently, ate quite well. There is little indication of devastating disease interrupting normal population increase prior to the arrival of the Europeans. Mundurucú villages, generally situated on the tops of grassy knolls from which they could view their fields, spread over a vast territory. They may have known their Mundurucú neighbors, but there is little evidence that they maintained far-reaching trade or communication networks with any inhabitants distant from them.

These were apparently a people who thought of their world as demarcated by supernatural spirits who stalked the lands, and because of the threat they posed, had to be killed if they came into contact with humans. In that regard, as anthropologist Louis C. Faron notes, they were not dissimilar from most of their contemporaries in the world: "The Mundurucú took enemy heads and impaled them on posts in the villages, a practice that occurred, also, in Queen Mary Tudor's 16th-century London and in 17th-century European colonies, like New Amsterdam in North America, probably without the same mystical overtones." (Faron 1993:193) From oral testimony, accounts of European explorers, and archaeological evidence, we can piece together a picture of the highly ritualized preparation of the heads for posting, a process that stretched over three rainy seasons. Since the most successful headhunters occupied exalted positions in the community, head-hunting was emblematic of political and religious authority.

Faron and other anthropologists have reconstructed the accounts of the elaborate head-hunting and preservation rituals. Immediately after taking the head from the victim during the first rainy season, and even before a captured head was returned to the village, the brains were removed and the teeth were knocked out and preserved in a special pouch. In the village the headman oversaw the process of preparing the trophy for display: the head was parboiled and dried, leaving the skin like parchment; it was suspended on a cord that ran through the mouth and out one of the nostrils; the eyes were sealed with beeswax; and finally, specially selected feathers from five different types of birds were hung from the ears as decorative pendants.

Tradition mandated that the successful headhunter, who as a result of his prowess entered into a state of near reverence in the village, was then served and revered by men in the men's house, remained detached from sexual contact with his wives for a period of time, and led the men on hunts, since his mere presence supposedly guaranteed success. He maintained his position through the next rainy season during which time the head was skinned and the skull hung in the men's house, amidst much celebration by the residents and neighboring villagers. Finally, the extracted teeth were placed in a basket hung in the hero's house. After three years, the "taker of the head" returned to normal village life but maintained a more esteemed position, assuming that no evidence surfaced that would indicate he had in any way violated the villagers' trust, such as the pregnancy of one of his wives during his prescribed celibacy. In three years, another "taker of the head" would assume the exalted position.

The Tupinambá

The Tupinambá were another group of Tupi-speaking people. They occupied the area along the coast of Brazil in 1500 when the Portuguese explorers arrived. Possibly centuries earlier they had migrated from the South to the northern coast and settled in communities. It appears that the Tupinambá were motivated to move about both in search of more fertile soil, fish, game, and other sources of food and because in their mythology they discuss the search for a "land without evil." Tupinambá villages were made up of anywhere from 100 to 1,000 inhabitants who were organized according to families, related by blood and marriage. A typical village might have about 30 families, living in groups of about 100, in huge houses more than 500 feet long and 100 feet wide. Within these great houses, families occupied defined units that they delineated by stringing hammocks around a specific space. The houses had a well-ordered assortment of benches, cooking pots, pottery, and other containers, and tables that were arranged in the defined family spaces along a long central corridor.

A male leader who derived his position patrilineally occupied the living area at the head of the long house with his wives, female slaves, and a few boys, all of whom served him. He ate alone, served by his first wife, but consumed the same food as everyone else: manioc soup with boiled fish and mangara leaves. Others in the family ate from communal bowls. All members of the community farmed the land surrounding the village and seem to have followed a pattern of hunting similar to that of the Mundurucú, with men taking on the big game and women and children downing reptiles, rodents, and other small animals.

Despite this apparently docile life, the Tupinambá are known for their warfare. Tupinambá men were feared as expert warriors, who took captives and engaged in ritual cannibalism, against other Tupi groups. Much of their warfare had many of the same rituals and ceremonies known among the Mundurucú, except that the Tupinambá placed ritual cannibalism, rather than head-hunting, high on the list of ceremonies. It was believed that each generation in order to survive had to consume human flesh as a way of absorbing the wisdom and the spirits of the ancestors. On the other hand, war captives and those found guilty of crimes were also consumed in order to restore balance to society and placate the spirits. Finally, anthropologists have found evidence that the Tupinambá used astronomical symbols to guide planting, indicating that they had some knowledge of the sun's rotation, time, and seasons.

The struggle for territory and the lack of strong alliances among the Tupinambá made them vulnerable to conquest by the Portuguese and French invaders. At the same time, the fact that the Tupinambá were warlike meant that they were not easily conquered. They formed new confederations to resist violently the attempts by the colonists to enslave them or by the Jesuit priests to isolate them in missions, called *reduções*. While they resisted colonization, especially enslavement at the hands of the Portuguese, and scattered into the far interior, their numbers were greatly reduced by disease (primarily smallpox and influenza) and continual assaults by the Portuguese. The number declined markedly during the prolonged war led by the Portuguese military officer Mem de Sá from 1557 to 1572. By the mid-17th century the Tupinambá had been eliminated from the coastal areas of Brazil and could be found only in small pockets in the areas of Maranhão and Amazonia.

Although the Tupinambá and other smaller groupings of native peoples have been so dramatically reduced as to have little influence on modern Brazilian life, anthropologists note that all of the Tupi speakers left an imprint on postconquest society. Tupi-Portuguese agricultural techniques remain, words and names were adopted by the Portuguese, and at various times literary and artistic movements surfaced that have drawn on the Tupi as a symbol of Brazilian nationalism, such as the naturalists' movement in the 19th century and the modernists in the early 20th.

The Yanomami

In the area of the Amazon Basin, the best-known indigenous people are the Yanomami, South America's largest unassimilated tribal group. The 20,000 remaining members of this group live and farm today on a 30,000-square-mile piece of land in the Parima section of the Guiana Highlands. The boundary between Venezuela and Brazil passes through the middle of their homeland. Their villages are situated in cleared sections of the rain forest. They live in circular habitations and they conduct their affairs according to long-standing communal principles.

Archaeological research in the region has identified a number of pottery traditions dating to 2000 B.C. and human adaptations to tropical rain forests. Although inconclusive, there is evidence that the ceramics may have come from societies that moved from the lower or central Amazon regions to the northern section. Scientists and archaeologists have analyzed extensively the rich organic soils, called *terra preta,* that cover the region, with the intent of trying to discover if the current

Indigenous river travelers on the Amazon. (Hoffenberg Collection)

Amazon Basin supported larger populations of both humans and animals in early periods.

At the time of the arrival of Europeans in the 16th century, the Yanomami were living in isolated villages based on communal agriculture. They subsisted mainly on plantains (cooking bananas). Different from the Tupi-speaking groups of the Atlantic forest region, the Yanomami successfully avoided conquest and even extensive contact with the European colonists, a fact that helps to account for their continued survival. Very few of the Yanomami have adopted any aspects of European culture. They avoid contact with outsiders and do not often venture away from their settled areas. Since they have developed little resistance to the viruses Europeans introduced more than 500 years ago into the South American ecosystem, they are still vulnerable to epidemics.

Although their material culture appears to have changed little in the centuries since the arrival of the Europeans, the humid climate does not allow for artifacts to hold up for long. Archaeologists and anthropologists have only been able to guess at some of the evolutionary changes in these people. They trace the various groups that have appeared in the historical record since the 18th century under the names Waika, Shamatari, Shirishana, and Guajaribo back to the larger Yanomami community. Living in semipermanent settlements throughout the Amazon region, the Yanomami and related tribes appear to have formed the largest and most stable civilizations at Santarém and on Marajó Island.

In 1991–92 Brazil set aside 23 million acres and Venezuela 22 million acres as "indigenous areas." Although these regions are protected, they have no government of their own and are susceptible to incursions from loggers and farmers should the political situation change. In a way, the Yanomami are caught in the ultimate catch-22. From one side, their survival depends on the ability of modern governments to prevent raiders from taking their land and stealing their lumber. In turn, those governments are held accountable through of the oversight of human rights activists, anthropologists, and an international community dedicated to preserving the Yanomami people. From the other side, however, the more contact the Yanomami have with outsiders, regardless of their good or bad intentions, the greater is their risk of contracting fatal diseases against which they have little genetic resistance.

European Exploration

European explorations of the territory that is today Brazil proceeded from various fronts. By the terms of the Treaty of Tordesillas in 1494, the papal decree that divided the newly explored lands of the Americas and Africa between Spain and Portugal, most of the area that is today Brazil belonged to Spain. Portugal had possession of only a strip along the coast, and initially had little interest in its American territories, favoring instead its long-established, and more lucrative, empire in Africa and Asia.

Portugal was the first European nation to establish a global empire. Its imperial holdings endured for five centuries, beginning in 1415 with the conquest of Ceuta in the Mediterranean Sea and ending in the 1970s with the independence of the African countries of Angola, Mozambique, and Cabo Verde. The Portuguese first occupied a series of islands in the Atlantic Ocean off the coast of North Africa, including the Madeiras (1418), the Azores (1427–52), and Cabo Verde, where they established prosperous sugar plantations. Portuguese explorers were the first Europeans to accurately and repeatedly sail along the coast of Africa and into the Indian Ocean. In January 1488 Bartholomeu Dias rounded the Cape of Good Hope and Vasco da Gama sailed in 1497 from Lisbon to India, returning two years later after having explored much of the land along the coast of the Indian Ocean. In the 16th century the Portuguese dominated the seas, establishing contact, shipping lines, and colonies in Macao, off the coast of China; Malacca, in the South China Sea; a colonial capital in India at Goa, south of Bombay; and major trading centers in Ceylon (Sri Lanka) and on Nagasaki in the Japanese archipelago.

The dominance of the Portuguese in exploration, trade, and colonization beginning in the late 15th century began to wane in the face of attacks from the Dutch and eventually the British in the 17th and 18th centuries. By the end of the 18th century, with the exception of Macao and a few other possessions, Portugal retained only Brazil and its African holdings.

With the exception of the Amazon Basin, much of what constitutes Brazil today was not of great interest to any European power. Indeed the Amazon was coveted by many of the European colonists during the

TREATY OF TORDESILLAS, 1494

Indicative of the absolute control of the Catholic Church and its integral ties to European expansion in the 15th and 16th centuries, in 1493 Pope Alexander VI granted to the Spanish kingdom of Castile dominion over all the lands "to the west and south of the so-called Azore and Cape Verde Islands" that were not already under the jurisdiction of a Christian monarch. Essentially this edict gave all of the New World to Spain and allowed Portugal rights over newly explored (and non-Christian) areas of Africa and Asia. Portugal, however, protested because it had designs on the Brazilian coast. The dispute was settled in an agreement signed on June 4, 1494, in the town of Tordesillas in Spain. The treaty ultimately drew the line between the current marking of 48 and 49 degrees west of Greenwich. With this agreement Portugal gained access to the American continent through the grant of a strip of land along the west coast of today's Brazil.

By the end of the 17th century Portugal held claim to a vast territory extending from the Atlantic coast to the foot of the Andean mountain range; from north of the Amazon River to the borders with Paraguay, Argentina, and Uruguay to the south. They faced little resistance to taking the territory ostensibly ceded to Spain since much of it, apart from the Amazon, was unexplored, was sparsely inhabited by either indigenous or European settlers, and did not appear to be of great worth. Portuguese exploration in the early 16th century stretched inward only a few hundred miles from the Atlantic seaboard.

early conquest era, from the 16th through the 18th centuries. Along with Spain and Portugal, England, France, and the Netherlands all explored the region, established trading posts, and sought to exploit its riches. A Spaniard, Vicente Yañez Pinzón, was the first European to reach the Amazon region in 1500 and 1501, while another Spaniard, Francisco de Orellana, a member of Gonzalo Pizarro's Peruvian expedition, named it. It was during Orellana's ill-fated descent from the Andes into the river valley in 1541–42 in search of the mythical "El Dorado" (Spanish for "the land of gold") that the region got its name. The physically sick and psychologically crazed Orellana reported he was attacked by powerful women warriors like the notorious Amazons of Greek mythology. From this tale the great river basin, whose hidden riches of gold and precious jewels were supposedly protected by fearsome women, came to be known as "the Amazon."

Portuguese Landing

The fleet of 13 Portuguese ships that reached Brazil on April 22, 1500, under the command of Pedro Álvares Cabral, was supposedly headed for India. The sailors were following a route around the Cape of Good Hope pioneered three years earlier by another Portuguese explorer, Vasco da Gama. The landfall on the South American continent had the appearance of an accident, given that Cabral's log reveals that he had set a course far from the African coast in anticipation of catching favorable winds to again round the cape. Portuguese charts nonetheless had demarcated and even named the place where Cabral landed on the Brazilian coast. These notations have led historians to speculate that the Crown may have been interested in formalizing its claim to the western side of the territory it had been granted in the Treaty of Tordesillas six years earlier.

The Portuguese made landfall at a place they named Vera Cruz, or "Land of the True Cross." As if signaling the fate of the rest of the territory in decades to come, the first thing the Europeans did upon disembarking was to chop down a tree, from which they fashioned a cross and under which a Catholic priest celebrated the first mass. This was the site of what was to become eventually the country of Brazil. Warren Dean's masterful account of the destruction of the Atlantic forest notes that the founding acts of the Portuguese should not be lost in the metaphor. Over subsequent centuries they would destroy the forest, take possession of the land, and forcibly convert the natives to their "true faith" under the sign of the "true cross."

The landing took place at a bay about 500 miles south of today's city of Salvador da Bahia on a beach that the Portuguese, according to their chroniclers, found to be idyllic. They gave it the name of Porto Seguro, or secure port. The encounter between the Portuguese sailors and the native Tupinambá comes to us in magnificent detail because the expedition's scribe, Pêro Vaz de Caminha, sent back a long letter to King Manoel I of Portugal describing the land and the people who greeted them.

The first sailor to arrive onshore was Nicolau Coelho, who reported being met by a few men who were "dark and entirely naked, with nothing to cover their private parts, and carried bows and arrows in their hands." (Dean 1997:44) Vaz de Caminha's letter reveals a kind of detached charm that seemed to envelop both sides during their initial interactions. The sailors planted a symbol (the cross in this case), performed a ritual (said mass), and exchanged gifts. It was standard procedure, followed in nearly every case when the Europeans confronted a new land and people. The Portuguese gave the Tupi some hats, linen bonnets, bracelets, and rosaries; the latter gave the sailors feathered headdresses, parrots, bows, arrows, and beads. By all reports the encounter at Porto Seguro was pleasant and even cordial, giving no hint of the momentous, and for some calamitous, transformation in the civilizations of the two peoples that was to follow. They shared food and drink, played their respective musical instruments, danced, and the Portuguese replenished their water supply.

Vaz de Caminha's account of the Catholic mass under a cross portends the terms of later interaction between the two sides in this encounter. The Tupi were apparently quite interested in the metal tools the sailors used to fell the tree and hammer it into a cross. The chronicler's log reported "that they have nothing made of iron. They cut their wood and boards with wedge-shaped stones fixed into pieces of wood and firmly tied between two sticks." (Dean 1997:44) After the cross was completed, Cabral directed his crew to kiss it in order to show the Indians the reverence in which the sailors held it. He then invited the Indians to kiss it as well. Presumably oblivious to any deeper significance that these new arrivals would lend to such a gesture, the Tupi complied, and even assisted at the mass that followed. Again, Vaz de Caminha interprets the Indians' compliance as an embrace of Catholicism. They knelt and stood at the appropriate times in imitation of the Portuguese, and "at the elevation of the Host, when we knelt, they placed themselves as we were with hands uplifted, and so quietly that I assure your Highness that they gave us much edification." (Dean 1997:44)

Whether their indigenous hosts were edified or not can never be known. Significant in this account is that both sides were closely examining the habits of the other. As historian Patricia Seed has noted in her study of many of the "ceremonies of possession," the Europeans had procedures they tended to repeat with little variation in most of these early encounters. More ritualistic in their ordering of things, and possibly more aware of the changes this encounter would portend for the future, the Portuguese followed at Vera Cruz their usual script.

Because the Tupi wore no valuable jewelry or adornments of gold or silver, displayed no precious stones, and apparently lived a subsistence existence, Cabral was not inclined to waylay his ultimate goal of reaching India for an extended stay in Brazil. For whatever reason, he decided not to take any of the indigenous with him on the ship,

15

as Columbus had done on his return voyage to Spain after landing in the Caribbean islands. It was more feasible for several reasons to leave behind members of their party in a settlement as a way of claiming Portuguese dominion. On the one hand, Cabral was going on to India and would not be returning to Portugal for a year or more and, on the other, he had expendable *degredados* (convicts impressed into service) on board whom he would as soon unload. Cabral determined to leave on shore the *degredados*, and they were joined by a few more apprentices who slipped off ship and chose to remain behind on the Brazilian shore. After only nine days in the new land, Cabral sent a supply ship with some samples of the local food and foliage, along with Vaz de Caminha's letter, back to the court in Portugal, and he sailed on to India.

The Brazilwood Trade

The explorers with Cabral, already seasoned in trips to Africa and Asia, were less enthralled with the myths of fantastic beings and the expectation of finding the Garden of Eden or "El Dorado" that motivated the Spaniards. They nonetheless pursued rumors of emerald mines and entered the abundant forests in search of gold. In the forest they found nothing of great interest to them except the wood from a tree that produced a fine dye. It is unclear if the messenger ship that returned to Portugal carried the first sample of a dyewood from a red tree, or if the Portuguese found this wood only on their second expedition to Brazil in 1501.

The dyewood's significance is actually all in its name. The Portuguese called it *pau-brasil,* possibly from the word for glowing coal. As taught to them by the indigenous people, the dye was extracted from the red-orange core of a tree trunk which gave off a reddish violet dye when submerged in water. Since the Portuguese explorers were introduced to this dye in South America at a time of growing interest in textiles and dyes in Europe, harvesting brazilwood proved to be a lucrative enterprise for a small number of merchants who plied the trade. One might think of this second expedition as a "name dropping" trip of sorts. First, the brazilwood trade would eventually lend its name to the new territory, replacing the original "Vera Cruz" with "Brazil." Secondly, the expedition's pilot was Amerigo Vespucci, who plotted the fleet's course according to the meridians demarcated by the Treaty of Tordesillas and wrote up his findings in a number of letters that circulated through Europe. The popularity of these accounts got Amerigo's name attached to the vast, previously unknown continents.

Of the few accounts of the brazilwood trade that were recorded, even fewer remain. It is known that on the second expedition the Portuguese ships explored the southern coastline and visited Guanabara Bay, on whose banks the future capital, Rio de Janeiro, would be built. At Cape Frio on the coast north of Rio the ships were loaded with brazilwood. Chroniclers evinced little interest in recording just how they obtained the wood. Probably the Portuguese relied heavily on the skill and brawn of the Tupi people for their knowledge of the forest, their ability to identify the trees, and their technique in felling them. Portuguese merchants established rudimentary trading houses along the coast from which they bartered with the Indians for the wood. The Tupi relied on European axes or felled the trees by burning the bases. They then stripped the trees of their bark and cut the trunks into shorter sections which they carried on their shoulders from the forest interior to the coast. They welcomed the Portuguese metal saws, axes, and knives, all of which considerably reduced the drudgery of harvesting the dye. Warren Dean reports that the new tools eliminated the tiresome chore of flaking stone and tempering wood, and lessened the time to fell trees and carve canoes by a factor of eight.

In contrast to the Europeans, however, the Tupi did not apply the new skills to the accumulation of goods, and even looked with curiosity and wonder upon the Portuguese, and later the French, who seemed to risk life and limb, and exhaust themselves, in order to accumulate goods to be sent back to a far-off place. If the Portuguese were discouraged by the Tupi's unwillingness to buy products from Europe and to engage in a recognizable trade, they nonetheless interpreted the Tupi's contentment as a sign of their inferiority. The trade was lucrative, and after a few years the Crown established a royal monopoly to prevent the factors, as the Brazilian merchants were called, from developing too much independence and stepping outside the boundaries of the colonial taxing and revenue collection systems.

2

THE PORTUGUESE COLONY (1530-1800)

In 1530, King João III turned his attention to Brazil. He responded to the alarming news of French and other European explorers plying the Brazilian coast and to rumors that gold and precious stones had been discovered. He sent a commander, Martim Afonso de Sousa, with a large expeditionary force to the southern section of the coastline with orders to determine the validity of the precious metals claim. De Sousa sailed into Guanabara Bay, set up a camp, and sent a party to the interior in search of the rumored gold. The expedition eventually reached the Paraguay River to the west, and de Sousa set about looking for the famed Inca Empire, assuming that it stretched as far as the river.

Colonial Settlements

In 1532, the Portuguese established the first colonial town at São Vicente, near the present port of Santos. In 1549 the Crown sent a royal governor to establish the colonial capital in Salvador on the Bahia de Todos os Santos (Bay of All Saints), since known as Bahia, meaning the Bay. The capital signaled the Portuguese intent to keep and to supply the colony, to protect it from rival European interlopers, and to explore the best means to make the territory pay for itself.

During the latter half of the 16th century, Portuguese enterprises in Asia began to suffer reverses. In the face of increased competition from the Dutch in Asia, the Portuguese Crown determined to place greater stock in ensuring that Brazil was a secure area for settlement, trade, and exploitation. Portugal hoped to rely more heavily on Brazil to supply goods that were profitable on the European market. As a means of developing agriculture and other extractive enterprises, the king divided the coastal region into sections that were handed out to *donatarios,* or courtiers. Martim Afonso de Sousa received one and there were nine others. Later the Treaty of Tordesillas divided the coastline into 15 parallel strips extending inward to the vague demarcation line.

Each tract of land was called a captaincy, a system the Portuguese had already established in the Azores and Madeira. The Brazilian captaincies were, however, far larger parcels of land than those in their Atlantic possessions. Some of them were larger than all of Portugal itself. This method of settlement had the advantage of parceling out the land quickly and thus preventing its seizure by a rival power. Conversely, it threatened to create a kind of New World feudal order, with large expanses of land headed by a Portuguese noble who was able to exercise complete control over his dominion far from the watchful eye of the Crown. Ideally the *donatarios* were sufficiently motivated to profit from agriculture, trade, mining, and lumbering enterprises to provide adequate wealth for themselves and revenue to the Crown in the form of taxes and duties. The danger lay in granting to colonists wealth so exorbitant that it would one day equal or outstrip that of the lords in Portugal. As opposed to the brazilwood trade that had been carried out by merchant capitalists granted concessions from the royal monopoly, the captaincies represented a transplanted system of feudal land governance. Because power now rested in land ownership, not simply in trade, and land required laborers, disputes erupted between the church and settlers over who held sovereignty over the indigenous people.

Missionaries

The first Europeans to arrive in Amazonia and in the interior regions of the Atlantic coast encountered a number of indigenous groups with distinct cultures living along rivers and trading with each other. Their diet consisted mainly of fish from the rivers and vegetation from the forests. When the indigenous populations came into contact with Spanish and Portuguese explorers in the early 16th century, they successfully fought off colonizing efforts. However, the Pope's explicit intent in the Treaty of Tordesillas had been the right to "discover and acquire" the lands of the Americas in order to win converts to Christianity. Indeed, when King João III of Portugal sponsored the first expeditions to South America, he proclaimed that the main reason for the exploration was to win converts. For much of the colonial period until the late 18th century, Catholic missionary priests vied with the colonists for control over the native population: the settlers to enslave them, the priests to convert them. For their part, the slavers relied on a law passed in March 1570 stating that it was acceptable to enslave Indians who rejected Christianity and who were thereby captured in a "just war." The priests countered that the Indians had to be allowed time to accept the Christian teachings and had to be protected from slavers so that they could convert. Probably, thousands of Indians worked as coerced laborers for the Portuguese settlers in this gray area of captive from a "just war."

Indian Slavery in the Amazon

Missionary priests accompanied the Spanish and Portuguese explorers in the Amazon region, and some of the first European settlements in Brazil were established by the religious orders. By 1616, the Portuguese missionaries reached the mouth of Pará, where along with other explorers, they established a settlement at Belém. Every year Portuguese slavers forged thousands of miles up the Amazon River and through its tributaries in search of Indians who were brought back at gunpoint and sold in the marketplace of Belém and in smaller trading posts along the way. The demise of the indigenous population was overwhelming. The Indians died by the thousands from disease, overwork, and depression resulting from the complete destruction of their habitations.

The priests sought to protect the Indians from the slavers by launching their own expeditions and luring the natives into missions, called *aldeias*. Large missions, such as the one on Marajó Island at the mouth of the Amazon, incensed the Portuguese slavers. The colonists accused the priests of enslaving the Indians for the prosperity of the religious order. In 1693, the Crown divided the Amazon basin among four missionary orders, the Franciscans, the Mercedarians, the Jesuits, and the Carmelites. By the middle of the 18th century, 50,000 Indians had been moved into the missions controlled by these orders. The largest and most organized *aldeias* in the region were under the control of the Jesuits, who likewise incurred the wrath of the colonists. The Indians of the Amazon region were decimated at the hands of the Portuguese colonists on the one hand, but even the protecting arm of the priests proved detrimental to the native population. Disease, overwork, brutality, destruction of their traditional life, and depression, whether resulting from the control of the priests or the settlers, produced a catastrophic demographic decline in the indigenous population.

The *Bandeirantes*

Although Indian slavery was never practiced everywhere in Brazil, at least on a very large scale, it was widespread in the state of São Paulo in the South and in Maranhão in the North. The colonists originally planned to use the coerced or willing labor of the Indians, following the pattern that was becoming well established in Spanish America. However, by the early years of the 16th century, the Tupi along the Atlantic coast had begun to die out and to retreat from the Portuguese settlers, who were proving less than willing to share the land equally with their hosts. The Portuguese then sought to capture Indians from the interior. Mem de Sá in Bahia in the 1570s initiated a widespread campaign to capture Indian slaves, but ran into opposition from the Jesuit priests who condemned the abusive enslavement of the indigenous people. The virtual war between the missionaries on one side, and the colonial army and settlers on the other, spread throughout the colony.

The most famous slaving efforts were carried out by *bandeiras,* large companies of mixed-race Indian/Portuguese warriors conscripted by colonists to penetrate the interior in search of Indian slaves and gold. The members of these *bandeiras,* called *bandeirantes,* were supplied in São Paulo with guns, gunpowder, chains, collars, bows and arrows, and a crude supply of provisions including manioc and some flour. The Jesuits, who had sequestered the Guaraní Indians in missions on the border with Paraguay, were a particular target of the *bandeirantes* in the early 1600s. Antônio Rapôso Tavares led the most successful attack, in 1628, against a cluster of several Jesuit missions in the interior of São Paulo. Attacking with a force of 3,000 men, Tavares burned the missions to the ground, captured the inhabitants, and marched them back to São Vicente in chains.

In São Paulo, Guaraní Indian slaves worked in agriculture and as porters, and assisted with trade. The Portuguese colonists referred to the slaves as *forros,* or freedmen, although they treated them as captives. When coffee cultivation began to spread through the state of São Paulo in the early 19th century, Indians were replaced with slaves from Africa. In the north, in Maranhão and Pará, Indian slaves worked transporting lumber and other forest products from the interior to the coast.

While the Portuguese Crown remained superficially committed to the protection and Christianization of the Indians, they were willing to exploit the *bandeirantes* for their own ends. In 1647, Tavares led a *bandeira* across South America in an attempt to find another route to Peru. The expedition explored much of the interior of Brazil and effectively extended Portuguese dominion into territory previously claimed by Spain. As a makeshift group of disaffected whites, mixed-race, and Indian recruits, the *bandeirantes* never established political sovereignty over the territories they explored. They did, however, lead the way for subsequent bands of settlers, prospectors, and traders who effectively established Portuguese control over much of the landmass of South America. Despite the *bandeirantes'* expeditions, by the end of the 16th century the loss of Indian life from disease precluded their use as slaves, and even their survival in anywhere but the distant reaches of the Amazon.

Indigenous Resistance

Portuguese military records from the early 1700s note the need to ship cannons and artillery to distant outposts in Pará to guard against Mura attacks. The Mura successfully resisted the Jesuits' missionary efforts, and for more than 30 years beat back slaving parties, entice-ments from the priests, and retaliatory attacks. They were one of the few groups that saw all whites as the same and chose to have no part of any of them. Their mode of attack has intrigued scholars, how-ever. Rarely, if ever, did they burn colonial settlements to the ground and annihilate the encroachers, rather they attacked and drew back in guerrilla warfare tactics. As the historian David Sweet has said, the Portuguese were simply "kept on the defensive, and prevented thereby from ever fulfilling the colonial government's production quotas." (Sweet 1992:59). Cases of successful indigenous resistance to Portuguese military occupation, religious and civilian settlements are few, but one group came to be known as "the abominable Mura" because it resisted for so long and managed through cunning and bravery to maintain autonomy.

Moreover, the Mura were willing to exchange fish and forest prod-ucts with the Portuguese for tools and other items they needed. They were not, however, willing to convert to either the white man's religion or way of life. Their fierce resistance plagued the Portuguese in Pará and other parts of Amazonia until the late 18th century.

Eventually the Mura made peace. Sweet speculates that this came about for several reasons. In the first place, they were exhausted after decades of warfare. Second, many of the warrior men who had carried out the battles (or had been most willing to do so) had died. The dev-astation of the male combatants, leaving a community with a majority of women and children, may have made it difficult to persevere in what increasingly seemed to be a war of diminishing returns for the Mura. Finally, the community of Mura had changed by century's end. Their ranks had expanded to include other native peoples who had had contact with the settlers and were more willing to adapt to the European ways. Coexistence with the Portuguese was not as difficult for the newcomers, and eventually most of the community acceded. (Sweet 1992:49–80)

Imperial Rivalries

From the 16th through the late 18th centuries, Portugal and all the major trading nations of Europe managed their empires according to the principles of mercantilism. The fundamental premise of mercantilism was for the metropolis, sometimes called "mother country," to accumulate gold, or wealth. From the point of view of Portugal or a similar colonial power, wealth from the colony provided the means to engage in world trade in order to fill the coffers of the homeland.

Mercantilism, however, had a price at home and abroad. First, for much of the colonial period the colony was tied to an export-oriented economy. In colonial Brazil this translated into a system of plantation agriculture, dependent on slave labor from Africa. Brazil remained locked into an export economy from early on, despite numerous attempts at encouraging a more diversified domestic economic system. Eventually, however, the colonists tired of enriching distant merchants, bankers, and nobles at their expense. The seeds of colonial independence movements actually were planted just about simultaneously with the flag of possession.

Second, for Brazil, mercantilism led to what has been called a "boom-bust" cycle. If a commodity sold well, the section of Brazil from which it came prospered. When the commodity no longer sold well, because another country out-produced Brazil, had a better and cheaper variety, or when it ran out, as with the gold mines, that area of the country went into decline. Many difficulties have resulted from the boom-bust cycle, not the least of which is a persistent pattern of wide disparities in wealth across various geographical regions.

Finally, imperial expansion engendered imperial rivalry. The European powers were thrown into constant warfare to secure and protect their holdings. In that fierce competition there were winners and losers. The empires that managed their affairs best—which might mean brutally, rapaciously, violently, or efficiently, depending on the circumstances—ended up the victors. In the more than three centuries of colonial expansion and rivalry, power passed back and forth across Europe, armies battled on land and sea, tremendous wealth was gained and much of it lost. From the point of view of history, Portugal did not manage its empire as well as England, for example. From the point of view of the indigenous people of America, or of the slaves working in the cane fields of Jamaica or Pernambuco, or the conscripted soldiers thrust into hopeless wars, or many of the indentured servants and backlands settlers, which empire came out on top might not have made much difference.

Dutch Occupation of the Northeast

For the most part, Portugal did not have to expend extensive effort defending its colony from rival European powers. The initial confrontation with the French was short-lived, and there were frequent border disputes with the Spanish. The Portuguese relied on a close alliance with England, forged in the first century of colonial expansion, for both military and financial protection.

The most serious threat to Portuguese dominion came from Holland and centered on the prosperous sugar-producing zones in Bahia and Pernambuco. The Dutch invaded Brazilian territory and occupied parts of it on and off from 1625 to 1654 and intercepted the slave trade from Angola. The occupation of Brazil was mainly the work of the private Dutch West India Company working in the interest of Holland. Using French, German, and Dutch mercenaries, the company invaded Bahia and captured the colonial capital at Salvador in 1624. They moved north and over the next 10 years occupied Recife and a number of towns in Pernambuco. Portugal sent several armadas to reclaim the territory, but the most valiant resistance came from local Brazilian fighters, especially the governor of Pernambuco, Matias de Albuquerque. Albuquerque's resistance made him a hero for a while, but his subsequent retreat in 1635 proved humiliating and cost him a few years in a Portuguese prison. Eventually the Dutch West India Company began to suffer financial reverses, and it sought an end to the war in 1636. After a series of long truces interrupted by war, the Dutch were driven out in 1654. Credit for the Portuguese victory actually goes more to the colonial resistance than to the Crown, although the latter did provide the military support to defeat the Dutch. Because Portugal needed Dutch help in Europe to fight against Philip IV of Spain in the mid-1640s,

King João IV of Portugal was reluctant to take on the Dutch West India Company in the Brazilian Northeast.

While the Dutch army was made up of mercenaries from several European states, the Portuguese employed Italians, Spaniards, and Portuguese to do their fighting. Before its end, the nearly 30-year-long Dutch-Portuguese war involved many Europeans. Native Brazilians and black slaves fought on both sides, the latter offered freedom in return for service while Indians were paid or promised land grants. Throughout the conflict, any number of Portuguese colonists and Dutch occupiers changed sides, collaborated across enemy lines, and sought to profit from the war. It was a bloody conflict that brought thousands of colonists, Europeans, blacks, and Indians to their death and caused the dislocation of thousands of civilians who literally had to walk for miles to escape burning cities. The loss of property included the sinking of thousands of ships, burning of hundreds of sugar mills and fields, and such widespread personal and public losses that the area never fully recovered.

One of the key features of the Dutch occupation of Pernambuco was the influx of Jews and New Christians (Jewish converts to Christianity) who had left the Iberian Peninsula during the Inquisition at the start of the 17th century and had settled in Holland. Prince Maurice of Nassau, a Calvinist who governed Pernambuco from 1637 to 1644, allowed Catholics and Jews to practice their religions openly. Two synagogues were opened in Recife in the 1640s and many Jews left Holland to settle in Dutch-occupied Brazil. When the Dutch were defeated in 1654, the Jews emigrated to Surinam, Jamaica, or New Amsterdam (later New York).

Rivalries between the Spanish and Portuguese for control of territory sometimes worked in favor of the Jesuit missionaries who sought to protect the Indians from settlers from either country. Especially in the Amazon region, the period spanning the late 16th until the mid-17th century was a time when missionary experiments were able to flourish away from the eyes of the colonial authorities. In addition, because Spain controlled Portugal from 1580 until 1640, disputes over sovereignty on the international level, if not always so clear on the frontier itself, remained in abeyance. Then from 1637 until 1639, on the eve of Portugal's declaration of independence from Spain, Pedro Teixeira, a Portuguese captain with secret orders to win the Amazon for his homeland, led an expedition from the Atlantic side, a tactic that alarmed the missionaries who feared that the Indians under their protection would be impressed into slavery. In 1640 Portugal became independent of

Spain and was able to keep the vast Amazon region under its own control and to extend its claims to the southern areas along the border with Paraguay. Essentially what had evolved since the early 16th century was a three-way dispute over the rights to land and Indian labor that pitted the Spanish and Portuguese colonial states against each other and against the Jesuit missionaries. For their part, the Dutch and French kept a sharp eye on this rivalry in hopes of being able to grab territory for themselves as well.

Settling Disputes

In 1755, the marquês de Pombal outlawed Indian slavery. It resurfaced for a short while in the late 18th century but was never very extensive. Devastated by disease, malnutrition, and overwork, Brazil's indigenous population, which numbered more than 2.4 million in 1500, fell to less than 1 million by the end of the 18th century.

Before slavery was outlawed in 1755 there were a number of attempts to resolve the conflict between the missionaries and the colonial states. In 1750, Spain and Portugal, along with Jesuit missionary representatives from both countries, attempted to reach an agreement over territorial boundaries both in the Amazon region and along the border with the Spanish province of Río de la Plata, and to set down guidelines on who held sovereignty over the Indians. By the terms of the Treaty of Madrid, signed on January 3, 1750, Portugal gave to Spain lands near the Río de la Plata (present-day Argentina and Uruguay) and Portugal's colonial boundaries were set, designating the Guaporé, Mamoré, Paraguay, and Madeira Rivers as the borders. The treaty called for the removal of seven Jesuit missions containing 30,000 Guaraní in the borderlands between Paraguay and Brazil, a move that was sharply protested by the missionaries and subsequently greeted with bloody resistance when the colonial armies tried to evacuate the settlements.

Because of the stringent objections of powerful forces on all sides, the Treaty of Madrid was annulled and superseded by the Treaty of El Pardo in 1761, which restored the Jesuit missions, at least temporarily. The boundary disputes were on their way toward settlement, although they persisted for another century, and a few exist yet today.

During the century after the 1750 Treaty of Madrid, Portugal managed to annex more of the northern and western territories from Spain. Ultimately about 60 percent of the Amazon rain forest came under Portuguese control, with sections of it extending into neighboring areas colonized by the Spanish (Peru, Ecuador, Bolivia, Colombia, and Venezuela), as well as those colonized by the Dutch (Guyana and Suriname) and by the French (French Guiana.)

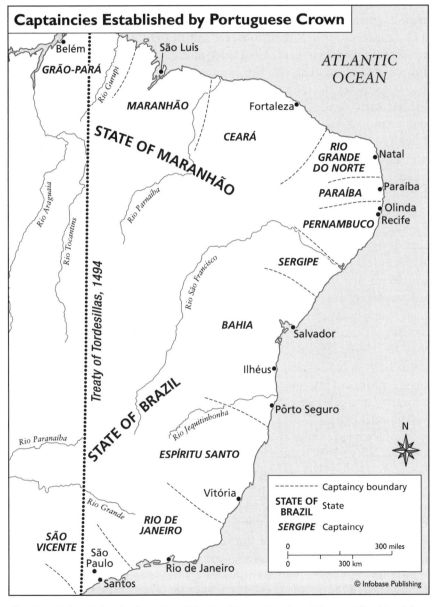

Captaincies Established by Portuguese Crown

(Based on Cathryn L. Lombardi and John V. Lombardi, Latin American History: A Teaching Atlas. © 1983. By permission of the University of Wisconsin Press.)

The Transatlantic Trade

Portugal's trading relationship with its colonies followed a pattern similar to the triangular trade that characterized England's trade between the Americas, Africa, and Europe. An average of 50 ships crossed yearly between Portugal and Salvador da Bahia, carrying European and Asian manufactured goods, wine, flour, dairy products, and salt to Brazil. They returned with sugar, tobacco, cotton, coffee, lumber, medicinal roots, gold, precious stones, balsams, and gums. Ships bound for Brazil from Africa brought slaves, wax, and some minerals, returning to Africa with vegetables, seeds, and tobacco. Ships sailed from Portugal to Africa loaded with alcohol and coarse textiles. This active transatlantic trade was matched by a vital system of trading vessels up and down the Brazilian coast, from the Northeast to Rio de Janeiro in the Southeast and as far as the ports of Argentina.

Intent on the prosperity of the metropolis at all costs, the Portuguese mercantile policy sought to ensure the dependency of its colonies in America on Europe, while holding their African and Asian trading partners in an equally docile relationship. In so doing, the Crown's policy was based on obtaining revenue through tariffs on goods produced in the Americas, tithes, the "royal fifth" or *quinto,* on silver and gold, and duties on any goods such as slaves, merchandise, and animals once they entered any part of Brazil. The collection of duties, levying of taxes, and oversight of trade from Africa, Brazil, or Portugal, as well as within Brazil, required an extensive and loyal bureaucracy. The only way to ensure absolute loyalty to the metropolis that Portugal, or any colonial system, devised was to grant the royal officers a healthy share in the profits. This only further drained resources from the domestic economy and relegated the Brazilian colonists to a lower echelon in the world marketplace.

By the same token, the more the Crown officials profited, the greater the risk of increasing the discontent of the colonists. Protests were frequent, particularly in municipal council meetings. There were often petitions from landowners and merchants, as well as from shopkeepers and small-scale tradesmen, declaiming the burdens of taxes and demanding the recall of particularly corrupt colonial officers. Not only were the latter distrusted for their arrogance and good salaries, but frequently the colonial bureaucrats sought to enrich themselves either by taking advantage of the gray areas of Crown oversight or straight-out corruption. Indeed, many colonial officials considered being assigned to Brazil, with its proximity to great wealth in sugar and gold, as an opportunity to amass a fortune for their retirement in Portugal.

The Trade in African Slaves

The most important leg of the transatlantic trade was the buying and selling of African slaves. It was an enterprise that produced enormous profits for the slave traders and especially for the European merchants and bankers who engaged in it. The Portuguese led in developing the trade in the 15th and 16th centuries, followed by the Dutch in the 17th century and the British and the French in the 18th century. The merchants, as well as the developing economies of Europe, accumulated a good portion of the initial investment capital for expansion into other areas of trade and manufacturing from the profits garnered in the trade of human cargo. In addition, the slave trade was instrumental in opening up new ports and trading routes for Britain in particular. That nation entered the transatlantic trade more than a century after the Portuguese, Spanish, and Dutch, but the slave trade provided Britain with the jump start necessary to eventually triumph in the colonial trade wars.

Beginning in the 16th century, Portugal turned to Africa to meet its labor needs in Brazil, essentially simply extending to America the slave trade that was already well underway between Africa, Portugal, and the Atlantic islands. The slave trade drew on an already established trade network within Africa and between Africa and southern Europe. European agents rarely traveled inland from the African coast, relying instead on the well-established web of dealers who apprehended slaves far to the interior of the continent and traded them through various intermediaries until they reached the vast warehouses of the coast. The slave traders acquired slaves from various parts of the West and West-Central coast of Africa. Most came from the areas now known as Ghana, Angola, Nigeria, and the mouth of the Congo River. A few came from the Portuguese colony of Mozambique in East Africa.

Conditions of the Slave Trade

Long before they were sold in the Americas, slaves had passed through exceedingly harsh conditions in Africa. Enslaved in their native regions, they were sold to merchants who marched them in chains hundreds of miles to the African coast. To keep track of their "merchandise," which is what the African human being became once captured and traded into slavery, the slaves were branded several times, each marking a change in ownership in the trek from the interior to the coast. The forced march took weeks, even months, during which time the captives were held in unsanitary and crowded warehouses, deprived of food and water, and transported onto the slave ships, upon which the

29

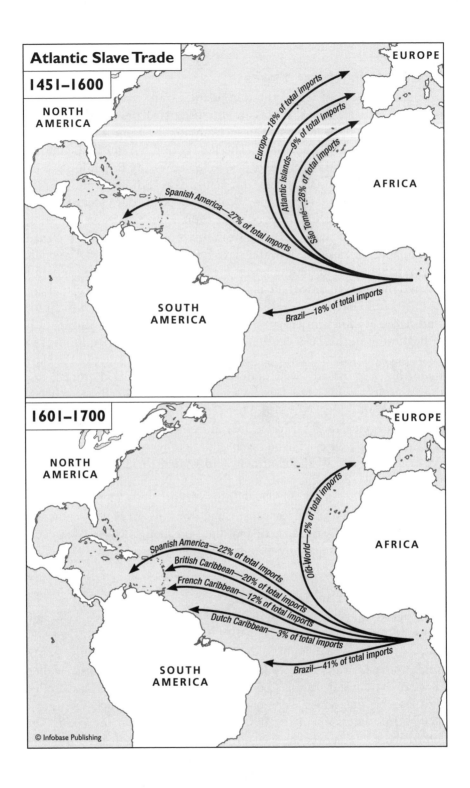

Atlantic Slave Trade

1451–1600

NORTH AMERICA

EUROPE

Europe—18% of total imports

Atlantic Islands—9% of total imports

São Tomé—28% of total imports

AFRICA

Spanish America—27% of total imports

SOUTH AMERICA

Brazil—18% of total imports

1601–1700

NORTH AMERICA

EUROPE

Spanish America—22% of total imports

British Caribbean—20% of total imports

French Caribbean—12% of total imports

Dutch Caribbean—3% of total imports

Old World—2% of total imports

AFRICA

SOUTH AMERICA

Brazil—41% of total imports

© Infobase Publishing

30

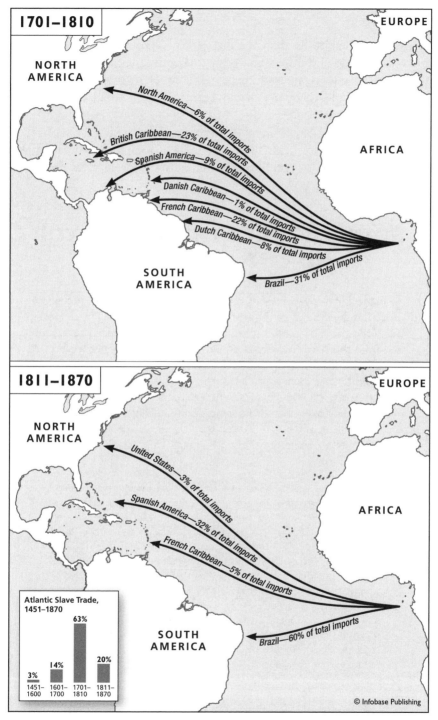

1701–1810

EUROPE

NORTH
AMERICA

North America—6% of total imports

British Caribbean—23% of total imports

Spanish America—9% of total imports

Danish Caribbean—1% of total imports

French Caribbean—22% of total imports

Dutch Caribbean—8% of total imports

AFRICA

SOUTH
AMERICA

Brazil—31% of total imports

1811–1870

EUROPE

NORTH
AMERICA

United States—3% of total imports

Spanish America—32% of total imports

French Caribbean—5% of total imports

AFRICA

Atlantic Slave Trade,
1451–1870

		63%	
	14%		20%
3%			
1451–1600	1601–1700	1701–1810	1811–1870

SOUTH
AMERICA

Brazil—60% of total imports

© Infobase Publishing

(Based on Cathryn L. Lombardi and John V. Lombardi, *Latin American History: A Teaching Atlas.*
© 1983. By permission of The University of Wisconsin Press.)

ordeal began again. By the time the slaves reached the Brazilian coast, many were dead and others nearly so. Generally they were given a short period of time to recuperate in Brazil in order to increase their value before being sold to owners, who again marched them off to distant plantations and mines.

Very few records describing the conditions under which the slaves traveled on the voyage from Africa to the Americas have survived. Historians know of the inhumane conditions from looking at the captives' death rate

PRINCE HENRY THE NAVIGATOR AND THE SLAVE TRADE

In the following passage, Gomes Eannes de Azurara, a Portuguese scribe, reveals the extreme brutality of the slave trade. Prince Henry the Navigator, the famed teacher, explorer, and Renaissance figure, profited from the slave trade because slaves were a part of the "currency" he received from the Crown for his services. As was no doubt typical of the era, Prince Henry divided up the slaves he received and assigned them to work at different tasks. Whereas the scribe is distressed at the misery of the slaves, there is no indication that Prince Henry was bothered. Most likely the prince viewed the Atlantic slave trade as a natural extension of a commerce that was already well established between Africa and Europe.

"Oh powerful destiny, doing and undoing with your turning wheels, arranging the things of this world as you please! Do you even disclose to those miserable people some knowledge of what is to become of them, so that they may receive some consolation in the midst of their tremendous sorrow? And you who labor so hard to divide them up, look with pity upon so much misery, and see how they cling to each other, so that you can hardly separate them! Who could accomplish that division without the greatest toil; because as soon as they had put the children in one place, seeing their parents in another, they rose up energetically and went over to them; mothers clasped their other children in their arms and threw themselves face down upon the ground with them, receiving blows with little regard for their own flesh, if only they might not be parted from them!"

Source: Conrad, Robert E. *Children of God's Fire: A Documentary History of Black Slavery in Brazil.* Princeton, N.J.: Princeton University Press, 1983, p. 10.

SLAVES ON THE MIDDLE PASSAGE

The following is a very rare document, written by an African man, Mahommah Gardo Baquaqua, who was captured in 1840, toward the end of the slave trade, near the Niger River and sold to Brazil. Baquaqua gave this account of the Middle Passage to the writer Samuel Moore in 1854:

"The only food we had during the voyage was corn soaked and boiled. . . . We suffered very much for want of water, but was denied all we needed. A pint a day was all that was allowed, and no more; and a great many slaves died upon the passage. There was one poor fellow so very desperate for want of water, that he attempted to snatch a knife from the white man who brought in the water, when he was taken up on deck and I never knew what became of him. I supposed he was thrown overboard. . . . When any one of us became refractory, his flesh was cut with a knife, and pepper or vinegar was rubbed in to make him peaceable (!) I suffered, and so did the rest of us, very much from sea sickness at first, but that did not cause our brutal owners any trouble. . . . Some were thrown overboard before breath was out of their bodies; when it was thought any would not live, they were got rid of in that way."

Source: Conrad, Robert E. *Children of God's Fire: A Documentary History of Black Slavery in Brazil.* Princeton, N.J.: Princeton University Press, 1983, p. 27

and ship captains' logs. Slavers tolerated a death rate of 25 percent for crossings that averaged 40 to 50 days. According to Joseph Miller, one of the foremost historians of the Middle Passage (as the trip from Africa to the Americas is called), captains, merchants, and crew members devoted considerable effort to packing the human cargo as tightly as possible, some managing between 300 to 400 slaves per vessel.

Brazil was the major importer of slaves from Africa to the Americas. According to Robert Conrad, a historian who has translated some of the key documents on the trade, "During two-thirds of Brazil's recorded history it was an established and nearly unquestioned practice to uproot black people from their native societies and transport them across the Atlantic to Brazil, there to be sold to planters, miners, and town dwellers to do the harsh work of a frontier society." (Conrad 1983:3) Brazil's reliance on slaves until the mid-19th century was nearly total, and the main method of replenishing the slave population was through the slave trade rather than by natural reproduction. As a point of comparison, Brazil began utilizing slaves from Africa to work the plantations as early as 1551 and had imported substantial numbers by the end of the 17th century, when slaves began to be sold in the British colonies of North America. By 1685, *before* the traffic to North America had begun, more slaves had already entered Brazil than would *ever* reach the North American colonies, or its successor, the United States. Estimates have put this number at 4 million to 5 million by 1810, with approximately twice as many men as women. Most were adults, fewer were teens and very few came as children. During the first half of the 19th century alone, more than 1 million slaves were imported to Brazil. By comparison, during the same period of time the slave population in the United States grew by 2 million through internal reproduction. Slaves in Brazil had a low rate of reproduction and a high mortality rate, especially on the sugar plantations and in the mines.

Plantation Agriculture

In the initial period, as reported by Alfred Crosby in his studies of European exploration of the Americas, the settlers devoted a considerable amount of effort to investigating the plants in the new lands. Some of the most important foods in today's cuisine, notably potatoes, corn, tomatoes, beans, and a host of other fruits and vegetables, were brought to Europe by explorers from many different countries. For their part, the Europeans introduced bitter oranges, lemons, rice, bananas, yams, coconuts, ginger, and sugar from Africa and Asia to the North and South American continents and the societies of the Caribbean Sea. They also brought grapes, wheat, barley, and other grains from Europe.

Of all the Old World crops, the one that most transformed life in the Americas was sugarcane. Originating in India and cultivated along the edge of the Mediterranean Sea, as well as in the Canaries and Azores off the coast of Africa, sugarcane took to the Americas and flourished far more than it had anywhere else in the world. Although cultivated on other Portuguese islands with success, in the Americas the sugar crop required no fertilizers and in the wet tropical climate it needed no irrigation. De Sousa ordered the construction of the first sugar grinding mills in São Vicente, staffed by slave labor. For the next 300 years, Brazil's economy, politics, and culture were intimately tied to the production of sugar and to the slave system that provided its labor.

The plantations that developed in the captaincies were of a variety of sizes. The largest estates were modeled on the feudal manors of Europe. There were also smaller farms on the outskirts of the big estates. These small producers raised cassava, vegetables, and other goods for sale to the large plantations, and worked the land with fewer slaves. The holdings even in the heart of the sugar region did not fall into a single pattern of huge estates worked by hundreds of slaves. Instead the countryside was a hierarchy with the largest plantations at the top, followed by estates of smaller size, down to sharecroppers and tenants who often eked out a living on the margins of the plantations.

The planter ruled over his family, his slaves, servants, and even freedmen and other smaller farmers in his domain. The church, government authorities, and commercial agents of the region were in his sphere of influence, if not in his direct employ. The *casa grande,* or big house, was the focal point of the estate's activities and it was from this locale, generally from the front porch, that the planter gave orders to his overseers and staff, heard petitions, dispensed judgments on local disputes, offered his blessing to the newborn, and directed the activities of the church and nearby towns.

The big estates contained their own blacksmiths, carpenters, housekeepers, bakers, seamstresses, tool and barrel makers, a sugar mill, storage bins, and in some cases even a dock from which to send the sugar to a larger point of disembarkation. Plantations could function with little contact from the outside world, except for financing and money. For the latter they were dependent on distant banks, even as far away as Europe. Generally the family of a large planter kept a house in Recife, Salvador, Rio de Janeiro, or another larger town where they resided for part of the year. The female members of the household and the children especially tended to spend much of the year in the town houses.

A plantation with a sugar mill, workers and slaves included, was called an *engenho.* The *engenhos* of the Northeast had the appearance of towns. Not only did they have mills for refining the sugar, but they also provided housing for the 20 or more Portuguese overseers and mechanics who worked there. In addition, on the largest estates there were cabins for 100–150 slaves and barns for animals, including oxen and other animals used to power the mills, cattle and sheep for food and milk, a large garden for vegetables and orchards with fruit trees. *Lavradores* were smaller landowners whose estates did not include mills and complex systems for producing and processing of sugar. These landowners leased land from the *engenho* master, paying with either a share of his crop or payment from the sale of the sugar crop. Such an arrangement kept the *lavradores* in perpetual debt, as well as dependent on the *engenhos* for seed, tools, the expertise of the overseers and mechanics, sometimes as a source for slaves, and always for the use of the mill.

Declining Profits in Sugar

Initially the big planters, or *senhores de engenho,* saw little reason to make the sugar mills and plantations more efficient. They purchased consumer goods from Europe, especially textiles, furniture, and fine crafts, rather than invest in producing those goods domestically. The planters relied on the labor of slaves, whom they worked to death, using up their human capital in much the same way they ravaged the land and lavished their wealth on consumer goods. In a word, from a purely economic point of view their management style was shortsighted. They rejected efficiency and refused to see the need to improve on their operations.

In the late 18th century, the planters found themselves outproduced by more modern plantations in the Caribbean. The Brazilian mills stood in disrepair, the plantation soil was exhausted. Slaves were in short supply and expensive to replace, as the heightened demand for slaves from buyers in North America and the Caribbean islands drove up the price of slaves and placed them out of reach for all but the most wealthy planters. One of the wealthiest areas of agricultural production on the entire planet in the early 17th century was bankrupt less than 100 years later.

Between 1650 and 1715, Brazil's income from sugar declined by two-thirds, mostly as a result of increased competition from the Caribbean, where Europeans were importing sugar from their own islands. The spread of sugar cultivation, combined with some innovations and increased efficiency in production in French and British colonies of Saint-Domingue (Haiti), Jamaica, and other islands of the West Indies, lowered the international market price for sugar. Added to this overall inefficiency, the price of slaves increased to a point difficult for Brazilian planters to meet. Their share of the market declined and the market itself fell off as a number of importing countries in Europe began to utilize beet sugar. Buyers for Brazil's expensive and inferior sugar began to disappear.

For Brazil's Northeast this was a disaster. The plantations were not designed for any other purpose but the cultivation and refinement of sugar. The infrastructure of roads, ports, and shipping lines serviced the sugar regions, while financial and commercial interests funded the towns and cities that existed at the behest of the planters. When the price of sugar fell and the demand for Brazilian sugar diminished, not only the agricultural sector went into a depression, so too did the entire region's economy. The heavy reliance on the prosperity of one crop, located in one region, and sold to buyers abroad, was a disastrous model for economic development.

Not all planters were content to sit by and watch their profitable way of life deteriorate. Peter Eisenberg's study of the sugar estates in Pernambuco showed that a number of planters attempted to introduce more modern techniques. They mechanized their mills and experimented with wage labor and a diversity of crops. Their efforts proved to be too little too late, however. Sugar continued its long decline throughout the 19th century until it accounted for only 6 percent of total exports. It was a no-win situation for the Brazilian sugar planters. The decline had a devastating impact on the entire northeastern region from which it has never really recovered.

Mining

At the start of the 18th century, just as sugar was plummeting in the Northeast and dragging that region down with it, gold was discovered in the province of Minas Gerais (General Mines). The population of the area expanded from a small number of indigenous people in 1695 to 30,000 by 1709. Most of the population growth stemmed from the arrival of Portuguese migrants from other areas of Brazil and the slaves who came in their service. In response to the increased population, the colonial government established two new captaincies, one in São Paulo in 1710 and one in Minas Gerais 10 years later. Drawn by the lust for gold and the same rumors of finding "El Dorado" that had infected the Spanish conquistadores more than a century before, thousands of migrants, overwhelmingly men, poured into mining regions.

The Brazilians had little knowledge of mining technology and lacked even the basic understanding of how one panned for gold, what it looked like, and what to do with it once discovered. For its part, the Crown never sent any experts to teach mining techniques nor even to oversee the operation beyond ensuring that it collected the "royal fifth" (a one-fifth tax) from the mining profits. Small and large companies plied the trade, utilizing slaves to do the hard labor. Many succeeded in circumventing the royal inspectors, smuggling out a considerable profit in gold and later in diamonds. Most of the profits did not even remain in either Portuguese or Brazilian hands. Northern Europeans, especially British technicians and mine operators, provided the tools, chemicals, and expertise to run the mines, bought the diamonds, and paid out a share of the profits to the Brazilian operators.

Mineral production expanded from 1709 until it reached its peak in 1760 and then began a slow and steady decline. During the 18th century, Brazil supplied about 80 percent of the world's gold, approximately 2 million pounds of the precious metal. How much was smuggled out illegally is much harder to estimate, but the amount is thought to have been quite substantial. Similar to sugar production in the Northeast, gold and diamond profits transformed the area of Minas Gerais, and the neighboring captaincies of Mato Grosso and parts of São Paulo, into prosperous regions for a while. When the mines began to dry up, the mining companies retreated into bankruptcy and the itinerant miners lost their jobs.

Whereas a few Brazilian entrepreneurs and mine owners got very rich, most of the profits from mining ended up in the hands of other Europeans. The per capita income was actually higher in sugar than it ever was in mining, even at its peak. The wealth that a few miners obtained, and the prosperity generated in a number of towns, can be seen today. Ouro Prêto, a major city in Minas Gerais, boasts lovely houses, 13 churches, numerous parks, fountains, government buildings, and splendid rococo architecture. Paintings on the walls of the many two-storied mansions display a colonial elite decked out in the latest fashions from Europe. They entertained in style with cutlery and china on their dinner tables, in houses with elaborate furnishings and libraries filled with books in French, English, and Portuguese. It was a moment in Brazilian life that displayed inordinate splendor, but it lasted less than 50 years.

British Preeminence in Brazil

The movement of gold, and later diamond, profits from Minas Gerais to Lisbon and from there to London followed a well-trod money trail. From the beginning of the 18th century, in fact, Portugal served as an intermediary for trade that poured revenue originating in Brazil into the coffers of English banks and merchant houses. In 1703, Portugal signed the Treaty of Methuen with Britain, ensuring a market for Portuguese wines and agricultural products in return for the purchase of British manufactured goods. Such an agreement guaranteed that Portugal would not develop the manufacturing and trading operations

Originally established in the 18th century, the city of Ouro Prêto is today a UNESCO World Heritage Site. The elaborate baroque architecture testifies to the wealth and splendor of the state of Minas Gerais in the era of the mining boom. (Agência Brasil)

to compete with Britain. The balance of trade, and advantages of this arrangement, accrued to Britain's favor. Very quickly the demand for manufactured goods in Brazil outstripped Britain's need for Portuguese products. To fill the deficit, Portugal paid with gold. The industrial revolution thus passed Portugal by, while the ready supply of gold to pay off its debt concealed both the nation's stagnation and its effective colonial dependence on Great Britain.

For Brazil, the situation was even worse. While Portugal exerted political power, Britain was the economic heartland. In essence Brazil was forced to support Portugal's moribund colonial bureaucracy, while providing revenues enough to keep both the Portuguese merchants and the British bankers content. Inflationary pressure was intense, eating up the profits from gold in both Brazil and Portugal. When the gold boom ended by the early 19th century and the diamond mines fell to producing only a handful of gems by the 1830s, the bottom fell out of an entire region's economy.

The profits from gold and the quick wealth from diamond sales did more harm to Portugal than good in the long run. In the first place, the influx of gold drove up prices throughout the Portuguese empire, endangering its holdings in Asia and Africa as well as in the Americas. Second, gold and precious gems, and the immense wealth and profligacy the trade engendered, contributed to 18th century absolutism. Prior to the gold rush the Portuguese king was reliant on the parliament, or Cortes, for sustenance. The Cortes served as a check on the absolute power of the monarch because it controlled the purse strings. This balance of power shifted when gold began to pour in from the Americas. The monarch was able to skim off his share of the revenue in the "royal fifth," or *quinto*, and was thereby no longer reliant on the Cortes for money. The monarchy then spent much of the money on itself. It became bloated with attendants, court officials, dandies, and hangers-on. In the early 19th century when the Portuguese court fled Napoleon's invasion of Lisbon and took refuge in Brazil, these royal parasites came along and were a constant source of aggravation to the colonists.

Pombaline Reforms (1750–1777)

As a result of the sudden appearance of great wealth that mining had generated and fears on the part of the Crown that the newfound wealth would stimulate the colonists to demand more autonomy, the king presided over a number of administrative changes in the colonial relationship. What King José I of Portugal actually had to do with these far-reaching changes is unclear. Most certainly he was consulted, but it was the powerful statesman Sebastião José de Carvalho e Mello, the marquês de Pombal, who designed and administered the reforms.

Pombal initiated a series of measures that sought to promote settlement in the colony, to restrict the power of the church, especially that of the Jesuits, to secularize laws and turn over law enforcement to secular authorities, to consolidate finances in the hands of fewer officials closely aligned with the Crown, and to impose more efficient methods for the collection of taxes. In 1763, he initiated the move of the colonial capital from Salvador to the more dynamic port of Rio de Janeiro. The royal treasury board in Lisbon oversaw fiscal matters in the captaincies and managed the enforcement of financial matters from the seat of colonial power in Rio. Similar to the acts that the British Parliament had imposed on its American colonies in the mid-18th century, and the Bourbon Reforms passed by the Spanish Crown at the same time, the Pombaline reforms were an attempt to reassert control over a vast colony that was in many ways beginning to chafe under royal supervision. By the mid-18th century, the European powers were in need of money to pay for their wars and exploits around the globe, and each turned to their American colonies as a source of revenue.

The marquês de Pombal especially viewed hostilely the actions of the Jesuits in protecting the Indians from the settlers. While not in favor of Indian slavery, Pombal did encourage marriages between Portuguese settlers and the Indians in hopes of advancing the settlement of distant reaches of Brazil. He also saw the Jesuit missions—and the wealth they generated for the order from Indian labor—as a threat to colonial authority. For similar reasons the Spanish court likewise distrusted the Jesuits and sought their removal from their colonies. In 1759, the Jesuits were expelled from Portuguese and Spanish America, their properties seized by the state, and the Indians dispersed into the settlement. Contrary to Pombal's wishes, most did not intermarry with the Portuguese settlers, but either died of disease, overwork, dislocation, or simply escaped to the interior.

Effects of the Gold and Diamond Rush

The Pombaline Reforms may not have been implemented solely to keep the wealth from gold mining in the hands of the Crown. They were broad reforms that addressed a series of perceived weaknesses in Portugal's colonial administration. On the other hand, Brazil's progression from one boom cycle to another produced an unstable pattern of expansion, prompting the Crown to more closely supervise its holdings. The brief moment of wealth generated by the gold and diamond trade helped to bring about the authoritarian monarchy. In addition inflation, bloated royal coffers that supplied the wasteful courtiers, demise in the control of the parliament, stagnation in the Portuguese commercial and manufacturing sector, and increased dependency on British goods and finances stemmed from both this sudden explosion of wealth and the Crown's attempt to keep as much as it could for itself.

Small-Plantation Economies

Although sugar in the Northeast and gold and diamonds in the Southeast were the primary export items of the colonial era, tobacco, cacao, rice, and indigo also were produced for export and for internal consumption. As opposed to the elaborate operations that dominated mining and sugar, however, the cultivation of crops such as tobacco could be carried out on small plantations utilizing fewer slaves. Most of these crops required less acreage, no elaborate technology, and less financial investment. More modest plantations also supplied food for

Port city of Salvador da Bahia, ca. 18th century. At lower right, slaves are carrying a person in a sedan chair. (James Fletcher and D. P. Kidder, Brazil and the Brazilians. Courtesy of Little, Brown and Company.)

the urban and domestic markets, especially a wide range of fruits, vegetables, manioc, corn, wheat, and other grains.

Smaller farms dotted the coastline from Bahia south, and thrived in those areas where they were not overpowered by large estates. Affected by the boom-bust cycle, especially as towns rose and fell in step with the exigencies of the international demand for sugar or minerals, many of these enterprises disappeared in the wake of the export market crisis. On the other hand, there was a constancy to the domestic market, and many of the smaller planters made a substantial living marketing goods within Brazil.

The significance of the domestic producers should not be minimized. Bert Barickman writes of the variety of farms and small producers who flourished in the late 18th and early 19th centuries in the Recôncavo ("bay shore"), a tropical sugar-producing zone extending about 25 miles inland from the Bay of All Saints. Contrary to the image of Brazil as a place based solely on an export economy, Barickman shows that there was a vital domestic market for flour, cassava, and other foodstuffs. These small planters employed a few slaves, very often women and children, and made a living supplying the neighboring *engenhos*. Tobacco planters also operated smaller plantations, and in contrast with the large sugar estates, more readily experimented with scientific production techniques such as crop rotation and fertilizers.

The existence of smaller plantations and the reliance of the big estates on buying food from the small planters does not undermine the overall picture of Brazilian slave plantations. From the point of view of political power, the *engenhos* ruled, controlled the market, and determined eventually the level of prosperity in the region. Domestic producers, no matter how efficient and profitable, never had the political clout to divert economic resources from sugar production to other enterprises. The domestic market never developed to the point where it replaced the region's reliance on exporting sugar. With more farsighted policies, it could have, but that was not a priority of either the Crown or of the planter elite. Rather than encourage and reward the domestic producers and entrepreneurs, the monarchy taxed them, and provided no economic concessions in the form of loan guarantees or tariffs on imported goods. The Crown did not see any benefit in developing a prosperous Brazil, for fear that prosperity would engender independence. Similarly, the richest planters who were tied to the sugar economy jealously guarded their political and economic privileges. It was a pattern not dissimilar from that in the antebellum South of the United States, where, although cotton was king and the big planters called the political shots, many farmers worked smallholdings with a few slaves to supply the local market of towns and plantations with food and other goods.

Cattle Raising

The history of cattle raising best illustrates the colonial authorities' disdain for developing a domestic market. First introduced by Martim Afonso de Sousa in 1531 and replenished by other Portuguese settlers in subsequent years, Brazilian cattle raising began in São Vicente, Bahia, and Pernambuco. Originally the ranches existed in tandem with the sugar plantations, supplying meat, hides, and tallow to the plantations. Oxen were used to turn the grinders in the mills, to clear trees, and to till fields. As sugar prospered in the late 16th century, the Portuguese crown prohibited cattle ranching in the same areas as the plantations. This was a way of devoting the best land to sugar cultivation because the Crown considered it far more profitable than ranching. Relegated to the interior, cattle raising expanded to the hinterlands of São Paulo, Minas Gerais, and Pernambuco, and gradually spread to the southern areas of Paraná, Rio Grande do Sul, and Santa Catarina near Argentina and Uruguay.

It was cattle raising more than any other single enterprise that was responsible for joining northern, southern, eastern, and western Brazil. The ranches filled in the spaces between the centers of sugar production and mining, even connecting to regions near the Amazon basin and eventually pushing Portuguese settlement to the border with Argentina, Uruguay, and Paraguay. In the late 17th century, the sugar-producing Northeast and the mining regions of Minas Gerais were linked by the cattle raising of the São Francisco River valley. The river, 1,500 miles long, served as a main artery for trade between the regions, and cattle ranches along the way served as focal points for trade along the river.

E. Bradford Burns, a noted historian of Brazil, argued "the cattle industry was far more important in the long run than the short. It provided essential support for other economic sectors but contributed only slightly to colonial exports." (Burns 1980:87) During the colonial period, Brazil did not export meat and no more than a few hides. Exports from the cattle sector were insignificant compared to those in sugar, minerals, even cotton and tobacco. The ranches were important, however, as an enterprise that pushed into unexplored territories and drew together the vast distances that separated the settlements.

There was never, in mining, agriculture, cattle raising, or other smaller enterprises, a single size, a single method of production, or even a single workforce. Small plantations interspersed with larger ones, some mills relied on more modern machinery, and wage labor occasionally supplemented slave labor. For the most part, though, slavery dominated the era, while the most powerful planters, miners, and cattle barons held sway over smallholders. Development was never uniform, nor of long duration, in any given region. The boom-bust cycle characterized production during much of the early colonial period, and continues to some extent into the 21st century.

3

SOCIETY IN EARLY BRAZIL: SLAVERY, PATRIARCHY, AND THE CHURCH (1530–1889)

For longer than the first 300 years of Brazil's existence, slaves originally from Africa and, later, those born into slavery locally were the main labor force. Slaves worked as field hands on both sugar and coffee plantations, as well as on ranches in the South and in mines in the Southeast. Those who had been captured along the coastal regions of Africa brought their fishing skills to Brazil. They worked on whaling expeditions as sailors, oarsmen, and in warehouses extracting and processing whale oil. As opposed to the southern United States where most slaves were field hands and urban labor was synonymous with wage labor, slaves filled *all* jobs in Brazil in urban and rural areas throughout the entire country. They worked as skilled laborers, domestic servants, field hands, in the military, and occasionally even in the supervision of other slaves.

Peddler selling women's clothing with a slave carrying the goods on his head, ca. early 1800s. (James C. Fletcher and D. P. Kidder, Brazil and the Brazilians. Courtesy of Little, Brown and Company.)

In the late 16th century, Bahia and Pernambuco imported 30,000 Africans from the Guinea coast. In the 17th century, as the sugar economy grew to dominance in those areas, 500,000 slaves had been imported and sold before 1640. In the 19th century, as slavery was being abolished in other parts of Latin America and the Caribbean, it expanded in the coffee-growing areas of the Southeast. By century's end, and final abolition, most of the slaves were working in producing and shipping coffee. The master class and the entire Brazilian economy relied on the work of slaves. If slaves did everything, many of the white masters did very little in the way of producing for their own livelihood, taking care of their own houses, themselves, their children, or the world they inhabited.

Slavery in Agriculture

Because of the importance of sugar, and, in the 19th century, coffee, as well as other agricultural exports, more than 70 percent of slaves worked as rural laborers in the fields and in the adjacent mills. They worked in the production of tobacco, rice, cotton, and, eventually, coffee. Slaves were the only source of labor on many large plantations, but worked on small farms as well, alongside the owner, who was often a free person of color. Slaves on the small farms cultivated fruit, manioc, corn, beans, and other staple crops.

On the *engenhos*, large sugar plantations with attached mills, slaves worked in all aspects of the production process from planting and harvesting the cane, to processing it in the mills. Maintenance of the mill machinery, repairs and the most dangerous task on the plantation—feeding the stalks into the milling machines to extract the cane syrup—were handled completely by slaves under the watchful eyes of overseers. When production fell behind schedule, the overseers were quick to use the whip, a practice that increased the chance of accidents for slaves charged with loading the cane into the mill and pulling free the stalks.

Especially on the plantations, slaves worked long hours, did not reproduce their own population, and died young, of overwork or disease. Working conditions were terrible, living quarters unhealthy, crowded, and dirty, and diet nutritionally inadequate. Most slaves were engaged in agricultural labor where conditions were always the harshest. Examinations of planters' account books reveal that many owners did not provide any food at all for their slaves. Instead, they "allowed" them one day a week to tend their gardens and grow their own food. Essentially this meant that slaves had no rest from work at all. Typically, on the sugar and tobacco plantations at harvest time, slaves worked around the clock, some to the point of physical exhaustion and even death.

Slave Labor in the City

Most slaves, male and female, worked in the fields. There were, however, many men and women who worked in cities as house servants, drivers, coachmen, laborers, and tradesmen. Male slaves supplied most of the manual labor for the shipping business. A Dr. Thompson of the Royal Navy observed the work of coffee carriers on the dock in Rio de Janeiro in 1848 and reported his findings to a commission of the House of Lords in Britain that was investigating the working conditions of slaves in Brazil. According to Dr. Thompson, the coffee carriers who were hired out by their masters and required to return a share of their wages to their masters and to use the rest for their own subsistence, were the hardest-worked slaves in Brazil. He noted the toll the work took on their lives: they lived for an average of only about eight years from the time they reached Brazil.

In the cities, female slaves worked as cooks and waitresses in bars and restaurants, preparing and serving food and drinks to customers. Usually the same slaves worked in the owner's house cleaning, cooking, washing clothes, and caring for children. Male slaves worked as coachmen, drivers, sedan-chair porters, and stable hands. Hundreds of thousands of slaves worked in homes, shops, and manufactories, as craftsmen, shoemakers, tailors, carpenters, seamstresses, street vendors, in fisheries, even in the military and as personal servants to the Catholic priests and nuns.

Nineteenth-century travelers to Brazil frequently reported that there were few carts or wagons drawn by horses and mules in the cities. Instead, slaves "are the beasts of draught as well as of burden. The loads they drag, and the roads they drag them over, are enough to kill both mules and horses." (Conrad 1983:121) Brazilian elites were carried about on sedan chairs, cargo was moved on the backs of slaves or in parcels and carts dragged along the ground; slaves were chained to heavy trucks and impelled on by overseers generous with the lash. Slaves brought from Africa their skill for moving huge, heavy loads on their heads and could be seen in rural and urban areas transporting cotton, textiles, jars of water, and any other item on their heads.

Curtained sedan chairs, called *cadeiras,* suspended from a single pole that rested on the shoulders of two or more slaves, were the universal form of travel for both men and women in Brazilian cities. "You meet with captains of ships, English and American sailors, fashionable ladies, bishops and fat priests, passengers from emigrant ships, the old and the young, the lame and the blind, all riding about in these cadeiras." (Conrad 1983:129) The *cadeira* and hammock were essential indicators of wealth. The chair might be cooler, covered as it was with cloth to keep out the rays of the sun, and it was convenient, but it was most of all a sign of social station. Only the poor whites walked, and even they were attended by a slave carrying a wide umbrella to guard against the sun's rays.

Platoons of slave children and adults of both sexes scurried through the streets of the cities, carrying on their heads enormous tubs filled with the daily slop and human excrement collected from homes and workplaces and conveyed to dumps along the beach or other places. One observer compared the work of slaves with that of oxen: "A week ago I stood to observe eight oxen drag an ordinary wagon-load of building stone for the Capuchins up the steep Castle hill; it was straining work for them to ascend a few rods at a time; today I noticed similar loads of stone discharged at the foot of the ascent, and borne up on negroes' heads." (Thomas Eubank 1856, in Conrad 1983:122).

Varied Tasks for Female Slaves

In urban areas, masters exploited their female slaves to make money from the sex trade, just as planters used female slaves to cut and plant sugar. The first-named enterprise was quite profitable. The masters and mistresses (the latter being quite prevalent in the sex trade) set up young slave women and even girls in the windows of makeshift brothels along the streets of districts well known for the sex trade in Rio, Bahia, São Paulo, and other cities. Seminude, the slaves gestured and talked to passersby to build their business. An outraged police officer reported to a municipal judge that many of the prostitutes were very ill with syphilis yet still were required to sell their bodies for one milreis a turn and were whipped if they did not bring in 10 milreis a day. The profits to the owners were very high.

In addition, slave women were used as wet nurses, called *amas de leite,* for their mistresses. Lactating female slaves whose mistresses did not require them were hired out. These slaves were usually young women in their late teens and early twenties, both African and Brazilian-born, unmarried and without children. Mistresses who had given birth to a number of children close together might keep a wet nurse in the house, and when she was not needed but had a good supply of milk, they would rent her to another mistress. Little is known of what happened to the newborn children of the wet nurses. Robert Conrad speculates that the infants may have been taken from the slave mothers to orphanages or they may have been sold. The newspapers were filled with advertisements, such as this one, indicating that the slave's own child was removed from her, no doubt to raise her value as a wet nurse: "For rent, a wet nurse with very good milk, from her first pregnancy, gave birth six days ago, in the Rua dos Pescadores, No. 64. Be it advised that she does not have a child." (*Jornal do Comercio,* Rio de Janeiro, December 10, 1827. Quoted in Conrad 1983:133) Writing in a medical journal in Rio de Janeiro in 1843, a French doctor relied on absurd and convoluted logic to recommend black wet nurses to white women: "Let us recognize in the first place that white wet nurses would be preferable in every respect, if in this climate they offered the same advantages as those of the African race. The latter, organically formed to live in hot regions, in which their health prospers more than it does in any other place, acquire in this climate an ability to suckle babies which the same climate generally denies to white women, since the physical organization of the latter does not harmonize as well with the effects of the extreme temperature of these equatorial regions." Quoted in Conrad (1983:135)

Elite slaveholding women maintained a personal retinue of slave women. Secluded in their town houses or isolated on rural plantations, some elite women relied on personal slaves as their only company. It was not unusual for the enslaved wet nurses, nannies, and house servants, male and female, to grow fond of the infants and children they tended and even to develop a loyalty to their mistresses and masters. Such loyalty had its rewards. A valued personal servant, male or female, who had served a family faithfully for many years, could be granted his or her freedom later in life. Some historians have argued that the fairly common practice of freeing particularly devoted house servants, or of allowing slaves to hire themselves out and accumulate money, even enough to buy their freedom, indicates that slavery in Brazil was more benign than in North America or the English colonies. There is no empirical evidence for this assumption. Slavery pervaded Brazilian society and overall was brutal, evidenced by the short life span of slaves. Some masters were undoubtedly kinder than others, but that fact alters little the base inhumanity of the system.

Slavery in the Mines

For the slaves who worked in the pits, mining was sometimes a death sentence. They stood in water, panning for gold or diamonds all day, were given very little to eat, and suffered from constant fevers and lethargy resulting from mercury and other minerals used in the processing of gold and metals. The water was contaminated, the environment polluted, and the life of a slave often quite short. Those slaves lucky enough to find a diamond or hit a gold vein were granted their freedom, but the occasion was rare.

Auguste de Saint-Hilaire, a French traveler to Brazil in the 1820s, visited a number of mines near Diamantina in Minas Gerais and left this account:

> For their nourishment the blacks receive each week one-fourth of an alqueire [about 3¼ pounds] of fubá [corn flour], a certain quantity of beans, and a little salt, and to these provisions they add yet a slice of roll tobacco. When beans are unavailable they substitute meat. The black slaves eat three times a day, in the morning, at noon, and in the afternoon. Since they have very little time at their disposal during the day, they are forced to cook their food at night, and at times they have no fuel other than dried herbs.
>
> Forced to stand constantly in water during the time when they are panning for diamonds and consuming foods of little nutritive value, their intestinal tract is weakened and they become morose and apathetic. Aside from this, they often run the risk of being crushed by rocks which, undermined from the mineral beds by digging, loosen themselves and fall. Their work is constant and agonizing. Ever under the watchful eye of the overseers, they cannot enjoy a moment of rest. (Quoted in Conrad 1983: 141)

Slave Discipline

Discipline was maintained at all times, and there are numerous accounts of sadistic tortures and inhuman punishments used to maintain absolute order and continuous work. By law, masters could inflict "moderate" punishment on slaves, and in cases when slaves were accused of more serious offenses, such as running away, theft, or hitting a superior, the master would bring the slave to the police station and, upon his word only, the slave would be punished for a fee. The ledgers from police stations indicate that masters regularly paid for an average of 200–300 lashes for each slave, including women and youths. Slaves on the plantations would be punished by the masters and the slave drivers, who were themselves often free people of color, sometimes called mulattos. In cases of extreme cruelty, masters could be prosecuted and fined, but it is important to recognize that for every prosecution that appears in the legal record, hundreds, maybe thousands, went unnoticed.

In the court records in the state of Rio de Janeiro there is an account of the beating of two slaves that resulted in their deaths. The driver and the slaves' master were investigated but neither was charged with any crime. Apologists for slavery have often pointed to the number of cases brought to court in which a master was accused of wrongdoing, to the point of killing a slave. It is important to remember, however, that it was rare for masters even to be charged. Almost never were they convicted of a crime.

A drawing from the early 19th century depicting various forms of punishment for slaves. Slaves were chained to heavy logs or fitted with iron collars and masks as punishment for running away or attempting to do so. The mask might have been used to punish slaves who spoke disrespectfully to a master or overseer. (James C. Fletcher and D. P. Kidder, Brazil and the Brazilians. Courtesy of Little, Brown and Company.)

Slavery and the Church

The Catholic Church was involved in the entire history of colonial Brazil from the first moment the Portuguese set foot on land. Whereas some of the priests had attempted to protect the Indians from slavery, there was no general outcry from the church in opposition to the enslavement of Africans. In accordance with Catholic doctrine, the priests did regard all men and women as equals in the sight of God, and therefore carried out their responsibility to convert the Africans to Christianity. The church had the right to require that all owners have their slaves baptized, that the sacraments and weekly mass were made available to the slaves, and that on the Christian "day of rest" the slaves were allowed to refrain from unnecessary labor. These practices

INQUEST FOLLOWING THE DEATH OF SLAVES

The following report is of an inquest that took place on July 27, 1886, two years before abolition, indicating that many masters were not tempering their behavior even as the end of slavery drew near.

> Each slave received three hundred lashes fifty at a time, applied with the usual instrument of five strips of raw leather; and, the punishment having been completed, they were treated in the jail by a professional. While being transferred on the road to their master's plantation, their wrists were tied with thin ropes, and in this way, joined in pairs, they were forced to accompany their guides, who followed on horseback, beating them on the way. [The slaves] Alfredo and Benedicto died on the road, the doctor who examined the bodies declaring they had succumbed to pulmonary apoplexy.

Source: Conrad, Robert E. *Children of God's Fire: A Documentary History of Black Slavery in Brazil*. Princeton, N.J.: Princeton University Press, 1983, pp. 315–316.

were followed in the main, since most of them interfered little with the slaves' work. Brazilian slaves were required to marry in the church and the couple could not be "honorably" separated, although it may have happened. This practice differed from the United States where slaves were not allowed to marry and there was no restriction against separating those who paired off in informal marriages.

Despite occasional interventions to correct the worst abuses of the system, to reprimand particularly sadistic owners, and to encourage manumission, there is no evidence that the Catholic Church took a stand against slavery. Even had it sought to criticize slavery, the church had no power over the slaveholders. Quite the contrary, the planters sometimes built chapels on their plantations and retained priests to attend to the spiritual needs of their households and slaves. Priests and nuns had personal slaves, and the brotherhoods, monasteries, and convents had large numbers of slaves working for the institution. A particularly revealing indication of the church's participation in the slave system is a record of lottery prizes from the Santa Casa de Misericórdia in the city of Ouro Prêto. Slaves as young as one year old, others six, eight, 16, and 32 years old, along with leather couches, an English writing desk, a musket and "horse bridle of fine silver" are offered as prizes in a fund-raiser for this Catholic charity. (Conrad 1983:183)

Finally, unlike some Protestant sects in the United States, especially the Quakers, no part of the Catholic Church ever stood in opposition to the slave system or tried to use its considerable resources and power to end slavery. In one of his most biting comments, Brazil's leading abolitionist, Joaquim Nabuco (1849–1910), remarked: "No priest ever tried to stop a slave auction; none ever denounced the religious regimen of the slave quarters. The Catholic Church, despite its immense power in a country still greatly fanaticized by it, *never* raised its voice in Brazil in favor of emancipation." (Conrad 1983:153)

African Religions in Brazil

The Catholic Church made sure that all slaves brought from Africa were baptized upon their arrival in Brazil, often at the dock. Priests were obligated to administer the sacraments, observe the holidays, and otherwise make available to the slaves the full range of Catholic rituals. The slaves, however, adopted Catholicism loosely and incorporated its outward ritual into their own system of African religion. In some cases, slaves may have adopted Christianity as a facade. As opposed to the United States, where slaves were not allowed to continue African rituals and did so only clandestinely, the slave quarters of Brazil were alive with the languages, religions, and ritual of Africa. In addition, slaves were always running away and establishing maroon (runaway) communities on the edge of the areas controlled by the white settlers. It was within these enclaves, called *quilombos*, that the Africans' religious and cultural practices flourished.

Slaves came from different areas of Africa, although a large number were of the Yoruban ethnic group from Nigeria and Benin, while others were Bantu-speaking people. The language and cultural differences that separated the slaves initially made it difficult for them to communicate with one another when they reached Brazil. Over time, however, the various African customs blended together to form an Afro-Brazilian culture within which the strongest influence was Yoruban ritual and practice. The Yoruban religion held to a belief in a single supreme being, called Olorun or Olodumaré, who was made accessible to the devout through numerous intermediaries known as *orixás*. Because the relationship between Olodumaré and the *orixás* approximated the Catholic system of God surrounded by saints, the slaves' religion evolved into a mixture of Catholicism and Yoruba belief. This practice

53

of superficially worshiping the Christian God and praying to the saints, allowed the slaves to substitute their African deities and develop a syncretic religion known as *candomblé*.

Practitioners of *candomblé* rely on a spiritual force, called *axé*, to facilitate their interaction with the *orixás*, who in turn are the intermediaries with the Oldumaré. A devotee increases his or her *axé* by carrying out various rituals and participating in ceremonies in a *terreiro*, or place of worship. The rituals involve dancing rhythmically, smoking cigars, reenacting religious stories, and, at their peak, entering into a trance which shows that one has submitted to the power of the *orixá*.

Unlike Christianity, however, the African religious practice is womancentered. The priestess is known as *mãe de santo*, "mother of the *orixá*." Similar to the function of the Catholic priest, the *mãe de santo* serves as the communicant with the *orixás*, guides the congregation in the performance of rituals, and individually counsels members in the appropriate practice to solve their personal problems. *Candomblé's* rituals could be seen as more accessible to its followers than much of Christianity, Roman Catholicism in particular. It is based on a belief in natural forces, and the followers call on *exus*, or messengers, who manipulate natural forces and entice or trick the gods into granting favors. The first *candomblé* center outside of the slave quarters was founded by three formerly enslaved women in Salvador in 1830.

Slave Resistance and Rebellion

Throughout the approximately 350 years the slave system existed in Brazil, the number of revolts was high, running away from slavery to the woods and sparsely settled backlands quite frequent, and the establishment of maroon communities of runaways, or *quilombos*, well known. One of the main reasons was that Brazilian slaves remembered Africa and kept the traditions of that far-off land alive within the slave community. In contrast with the United States, where slaves' direct knowledge of Africa was minimal after a generation or two, in Brazil most slaves had contact with new arrivals, and nearly every slave community had members who spoke African languages, practiced African religions, played African musical instruments, cooked food in the style they knew in Africa, and organized their families and their gender relations according to the ways of Africa. For example, the practice of holding women in high esteem as priestesses, healers, and storytellers is apparent in the African-inspired religions of Brazil similar to their practice in Africa.

The cultural closeness of Africa to the Brazilian slaves is thought to have caused an exceptionally high incidence of rebellions and other forms of resistance. In Bahia in 1809, a group of Aja-Fon and Yoruba slaves ran away from sugar plantations and formed a *quilombo* from which they attacked a nearby village to get food. They controlled the village of Nazaré for several months before being defeated by troops sent from the capital. Revolts were frequent throughout the 19th century; probably more than 20 occurred in Bahia alone between 1809 and 1835, mainly composed of groups of African-born slaves who formed into *quilombos* and then attacked neighboring towns and plantations.

Several revolts were inspired by Muslim slaves, the best-known of which was the Malé Revolt in Bahia in 1835. *Malé* is the Yoruban word for Muslim, and the revolt was led by Muslim preachers. Planned to begin on January 25, the day of a Catholic holiday that corresponded with the end of Ramadan, the plot was uncovered by the police before it was scheduled to begin. More than 500 slaves participated anyway, fighting for most of a day before being defeated by the local police and militia. The captured rebels were punished with whippings, death, and, for the freedmen, deportation to Africa. The latter might seem an odd form of "punishment" for ex-slaves, but actually it was used quite often as a way to discipline freedmen. One can only conjecture that if a freed slave was returned to Africa, his/her chances of being re-enslaved were fairly high. Nonetheless, Islam and African animist religious beliefs helped unify the slaves after they reached America, and provided an inspiration for revolt.

Finally, slave revolts were frequent in Brazil because slaves were a majority of the population in many areas, with the rest of the society made up of other people of color. By 1808, out of the total population of about 3 million, slaves made up 38 percent of the total, with the rest spread fairly evenly among whites, mulattos, and free blacks. That meant that in Brazil 63 percent of the population was made up of slaves, former slaves, or the descendants of slaves. By contrast, South Carolina and Mississippi were the only states in the antebellum U.S. South where blacks made up more than half of the population. Because the free black population was so small throughout the South (1 percent or less), runaways had little chance of melting into a community of people of color.

Palmares

The most famous *quilombo* was Palmares (meaning "land of the palm trees") in the southern part of the captaincy of Pernambuco (today in

55

the state of Alagoas) which endured from the end of the 16th century until 1694. Containing 11,000 inhabitants at its height, with several villages spread out over 370 square miles, Palmares survived hundreds of military assaults by the Portuguese and Dutch, who briefly controlled the area in the mid-1600s. The settlements sported blacksmith shops, a church, and irrigated fields that produced corn, cassava, potatoes, and sugarcane. The original residents were men, but through capture and barter, they obtained women to reproduce the population of the settlement. Despite its outlaw status, Palmares traded with the Portuguese settlers in the surrounding region and even grew to rely on them for warnings about encroaching military attacks.

The community used Portuguese as a common language, but many African languages also were spoken since many of the residents were first-generation arrivals in Brazil. The religion likewise was a blend of Christianity and African belief, and it was within this environment, isolated from Catholicism, that the form and ritual of candomblé evolved. As in Africa, polygamy was allowed. A succession of five kings ruled Palmares in its century-long existence. The most famous defender of Palmares was the general Zumbí, who held off six military expeditions. Both the Portuguese army and the Dutch, during their occupation of Pernambuco in the 1640s, attempted to invade Palmares repeatedly. Under Zumbí's leadership, the insurgents were finally defeated in 1694 after defending the quilombo from a single two-year-long sustained attack by the Portuguese army. Down to 500 members, the Palmeiros were no longer able to hold out. Zumbí was captured and beheaded; the surviving resisters were sold into slavery. Palmares, for its heroic history and the strength of its African culture, holds a revered position in Brazil today, somewhere between myth and symbol of national resistance, especially in the songs, tales, and histories of Afro-Brazilians.

Slavery's Long Duration

Slavery lasted longer in Brazil—some 350 years—than in any other American nation. It permeated every aspect of life and left an enduring legacy. Scholars have pointed to the flexibility in the Brazilian slave system as a reason for its incredible longevity. Some slaves negotiated agreements whereby they could live away from their masters, usually practicing a trade and contributing a portion of their earnings to the owner in return for a degree of freedom. Some enterprising slaves were able to purchase their freedom, and many were freed upon the death of their master, especially his illegitimate offspring.

Undoubtedly, the main reason that slavery existed for so long was because it was an unquestioned system in Brazil until the early 19th century. Books were published in Europe and North America calling for the end to the slave trade and to slavery itself, but until 1808 almost none of them ever reached Brazil. The debate over slavery that raged in the capitals of Europe, North America, and in other Latin American nations went largely unheard in Brazil until several decades into the century. Slavery had ended in Argentina, Chile, Uruguay, and Mexico by the mid-19th century as a part of their struggles for independence from Spain, and was followed later by much of Latin America. The U.S. Civil War, ending in 1865 with the defeat of the Confederacy, brought to the fore the debate over slavery throughout the hemisphere, especially in Cuba, where it was abolished in 1873, and Puerto Rico, where it was abolished in 1880.

Because of the peculiar course of its independence struggle, and because of its extreme dependence on slaves to carry out all its productive work, Brazil remained tied to slavery much longer than virtually any other country in the Americas. It would take Brazil a whole century of maneuvering and debating over the nation's political status before the question of slavery appeared on the national agenda.

Social and Cultural Norms

Slavery was above all a part of a broader system that sanctioned the rights and privileges of property owners. Slaves were property. Nonetheless, it would be impossible to consider laws and property rights in early Brazil without considering the ways that male dominance intersected with sexual power. Both the white elite and the free and unfree common people lived in a society with defined and engendered social expectations, hierarchical rules, and legal restrictions.

For its first 400 years, Brazil was organized around large landed estates and was ruled by a white elite of mainly Portuguese background. Landowning families formed dynasties that passed their inheritances down from generation to generation, while investing in a wide range of enterprises, including import-export houses, mines, shipping lines, infrastructure, and eventually, in São Paulo and Rio de Janeiro in particular, in manufacturing. Culturally and politically the *fazendeiros,* the *poderosos do sertão,* meaning ranchers, or literally "powerful men of the backlands," the mine owners, and a small urban elite of government officials and merchants exerted near complete control over the social, political, and economic life of the colony and subsequent empire.

57

Patriarchy

In a manner certainly not isolated to Brazil, the landowners ruled their wives, their families, their estates, and their entire communities in accordance with then-accepted patriarchal norms. Masculinity was valued and viewed as an indicator of strength and power. Men were expected to be worldly, brutal if necessary, quick to defend their honor and their property, while women were expected to remain secluded, chaste, faithful, and devout. These gender characteristics permeated the society and largely determined the social conventions under which the small sector of wealthy whites and mixed-race elites functioned. On the other hand, these social norms did not permeate, and were even reversed, in working-class and slave communities.

As in Spain and Portugal, marriage was the only officially sanctioned means for the expression of sexuality in colonial Latin America. That did not mean that it was the only outcome of courtship, nor the only channel for the expression of sexuality. Asunción Lavrin has written extensively on marriage, courtship, and gender relations in Latin America. Significantly, she points out that "Premarital sexual relations, consensuality, homosexuality, bigamy and polygamy, out-of-wedlock births, and clandestine affairs between religious and lay persons have been a common daily occurrence since the sixteenth century. It is only recently, however, that historians have begun to examine the circumstances, nature, legislation, and social consequences of sexuality in colonial Latin America." (Lavrin 1989:2)

That patriarchy was the only accepted form of gender organization in colonial and imperial Brazil in no way implies that men and women, white, black, and mixed race, always followed the accepted moral order. Certainly men, and white men especially, had greater license to establish unsanctioned relationships with slaves and free women. Many people engaged in affairs, and the full range of alternative sexual practices existed in colonial Brazil, just as it has throughout history. The alternatives were simply rarely, if ever, discussed.

The center of the landed estate was the big house, or *casa grande*. It varied in size, luxury, and accouterments of wealth and fashion according to the region or the prosperity of the planter who owned it. Typically it was a two-story dwelling, but many in the coffee region were rambling one-story houses similar to the haciendas of Mexico. The houses had separate parlors to greet guests, large dining rooms, and sometimes ballrooms. There were many bedrooms, both for the family and to accommodate travelers who came and stayed on for a while as guests of the planter and his family. The ground floor had a pantry, an

Plantation with house, barns, storage sheds, and a row of slave cabins, ca. 1800s. (James C. Fletcher and D. P. Kidder, Brazil and the Brazilians. Courtesy of Little, Brown and Company.)

attached, or sometimes detached, kitchen, and often a chapel where a clergy member resident on the plantation held services for the family, slaves, and other laborers. There were separate or attached small houses or rooms for storing the linens, kitchen supplies, and goods for furnishing and cleaning the house, as well as places to keep food, wine, and the goods produced on the plantation. The house generally had a large porch or veranda from which the planter oversaw his estate, greeted his guests, and meted out punishments and rewards to the slaves. Indeed, much of the business of the estate was conducted from the veranda. Standing amidst other buildings that serviced the plantation, the *casa grande* was the pinnacle of power in Brazil's patriarchal society, and for the patriarch who ruled from it.

The patriarch's importance in plantation society was reinforced by his dominance over his family, especially his wife and children. The principle of patriarchal authority granted the father control over his children, although legitimacy was determined through the mother's line. Since the father's wealth determined the social status of the children, it was his privilege and responsibility to make basic decisions about the children's lives, including education, marriage partners, occupations they followed, whether they joined one of the religious orders or entered the military. There were, in fact, some fairly standard criteria for what happened to the children in the family. The first son usually went into the family business (mining, plantation agriculture, trade). A second son might enter the military or one of the professions (law, medicine) and another son would join one of the religious orders. Daughters were betrothed at young ages to suitable partners selected from among the family's business and social acquaintances. When suitable marriage partners were not available, a fact that occurred more to men than women since the latter were more often in short supply, a marriage might be contracted with a family in Portugal. Whereas marriages for both sons and daughters were arranged, a young girl usually had the least say in the choice of her partner. Not infrequently she could find herself betrothed, often to a much older man, by the time she reached her 15th birthday.

Marriage Choices for Men and Women

Except for those entering the religious orders, marriage was expected, and only on rare occasions would a member of an elite family remain single. For men this did not pose as much of a problem as it did for women. Since marriage, while expected, did not mandate fidelity to one's wife, men might find an arranged marriage to a woman for whom he held little affection nothing more than a bother. Social convention allowed for him to take a mistress and to have a slave concubine, who might even live in the family home. His illegitimate children were accorded a favored place among the retinue of slaves on a plantation and, if necessary, he would expect his wife to attend to the needs of his children by other women. They were considered his children, even if not sanctioned by a Christian marriage and even if they remained slaves. Finally, he was free to show his preference for his mistress over his wife.

For a white woman from the elite class, on the other hand, an undesirable marriage or distasteful marriage partner was more troubling. She could not take any other lovers (overtly anyway), and she was required to be available to her husband if and when he desired her for any reason. She was, however, a privileged member of society. Indeed, on the plantation, the planter's wife played a strong role in directing the day-to-day activities of the large household and probably derived satisfaction from performing her function well. When her husband was absent from the estate for business or pleasure she made decisions regarding the management of slaves and production. Nonetheless, a female from an elite family was subservient to her father and elder brothers, and then to her husband once she married. As the mistress of the estate she was required to manage the affairs of a house that often included her husband's illegitimate offspring, as well as her own children.

Marriage and the Dowry

Despite the limited options available to elite women in Brazil, the Catholic Church had some guidelines that determined the marriage process. Whereas arranged marriages were sanctioned by the church, no girl or young woman could be forced to marry against her firmly stated will. If she refused, and refusal was not easy in the patriarchal and authoritarian climate of early Brazilian society, she was not to be forced. The church held as sacrosanct the doctrine of "free will," dictating that decisions such as marriage had to be entered into freely. If a daughter refused a partner, and was offered no other, her usual option was to enter a convent and become a nun. If she chose a religious life, the wealth set aside for her dowry was turned over to the convent. This allowed these female-headed institutions to become some of the wealthiest in Latin America. Convents invested their considerable resources derived from dowries in real estate, banking, and trading goods in the market, including slaves.

In the 18th century, the Crown became concerned that many women were refusing to accept the marriage partners offered them and were choosing instead to return to Portugal to enter convents. In an attempt to prevent women from leaving, the colonial administration passed laws making it illegal for a young woman to travel without a member of her family on a ship to Portugal, and even then families were to provide considerable evidence that the daughter truly was "called to a religious vocation," and not using it as a means of avoiding marriage. How the parents and religious or administrative authorities determined whether the girls had legitimate vocations or not, is unclear. In addition, there is no record of any effort on the part of the colonial government to suggest that so many women might not join the convent if men were more devoted to their wives and families. Such a proposal would have been outside the thinking of either the church or the government in a society where patriarchy was unquestioned.

In Brazil, as in the rest of Latin America among the elite families, the marriage contract could be an elaborate document detailing the financial resources and obligations of both partners. For the bride, her worth was measured in the size of the dowry she brought to the marriage. Her parents as a means of support provided the dowry for their daughter in her marriage or in a convent if she chose to be a nun and not to marry. Occasionally other institutions, such as charities, contributed to the dowry when an otherwise distinguished family could not afford one adequate to secure an honorable marriage. As Muriel Nazzari has explained in her work on the Brazilian dowry, the practice derived from

61

medieval Portugal and came to Brazil with the first settlers. It was an important feature of the marriage contract from the 16th through the 18th centuries and remained for longer among some elite families.

The sum of the dowry was an advance on the daughter's inheritance, and thus represented a percentage of the known wealth of the family. In the case of very elite families the dowry could be extensive, including imported linens and silks, furniture, silver and cutlery, china, slaves, land, houses, mines, precious metals, and a sum of money. Unlike in North America, however, women retained rights to their names and to their property through the dowry system. In Spanish America, the practice was for a wife's dowry to revert to her in the event of her husband's death, and her dowry was retained in her own account throughout her married life. In Brazil, however, the bride's dowry was not maintained separately after her marriage and immediately became a part of the couple's common property, no matter whether her share of the initial contribution had been greater than the groom's or less. As a result, if a husband squandered his wife's wealth or the couple suffered considerable losses, she might find that her dowry was no assurance against poverty in the event of his death. Nevertheless, elite families had an interest in managing the properties and assuring that a daughter was not impoverished in a marriage. Fathers and brothers took an interest in the disposal of their sibling and daughter's dowry and noted if it had not been well cared for.

The dowry was not a concern for poor girls when they married at any time in Brazil's history. Marriage in the church or as a recognized civil institution was actually less common among poor, working-class whites, or among free and slave blacks and people of color, than among the white elite. Legal marriages were inhibited because the church and the state charged exorbitant fees for the civil and the ecclesiastical licenses and ceremonies. Thus, the issue of the dowry and the legal matters of inheritance laws were solely the concern of property owners with considerable resources. Most members of society entered into common-law marriages and many still do.

Even in elite society, the dowry lessened in importance as Brazil entered a more modern society. Whereas in the 16th and early 17th centuries brides often gave more to the marriage in the form of a dowry than did their husbands, in the late 18th and early 19th centuries husbands gave more. According to Muriel Nazzari, in the 19th century dowries in São Paulo began getting smaller and were less often offered. When a dowry was provided, the amount in proportion to the size of the parents' estate lessened as well. Not only was the marriage of a daughter or a son no longer such a substantial investment for the family as in the earlier centuries, but the items offered were more often consumer goods rather than property and production assets. Finally, toward the end of the 19th century marriages were held increasingly without dowries having been offered at all.

Intersections of Gender, Race, and Class

A description of a fine lady traveling through the streets of Rio de Janeiro in the 18th century provides a picture of the differences that separated elite and slave women:

> *The gentry here are usually carried in a kind of chair, orna-mented in a very grand manner; but instead of two poles, as in Europe, they use but one, to which the chair is suspended, and this is carried upon negroes' shoulders. This vehicle is always followed by at least one or two negro servants, dressed in a fine livery, but bare-footed. A lady is usually attended by four or five negro girls, who, besides a decent clothing, are ornamented with several rows of necklaces, and large gold earrings. (Conrad 1983:128)*

The description reveals the paradox of the master-slave relationship. The slaves who attended the lady were dressed well, even elaborately, as the use of the jewelry for the slave girls indicates, to show off their master's wealth, but they were always required to be barefoot, to show that they were slaves.

Male dominance characterized all of the society, but gender expectations functioned in diverse ways depending on race and social class. White females were expected to be secluded as well as chaste. It was said that a woman from the elite class left her house three times: when she was baptized, when she married, and for her funeral after she died. Quite likely white women left more often than that, but a free hand in the street was not theirs. Slave women performed all of the needed tasks in the public sphere, and slave and working-class women were free to meet and converse with each other in the street. Because slave, mulatto, and poor white women were expected (even required) to be sexually available to men, they were stereotyped as having lower moral standards.

For the most part, both elite and laboring men were able to lead lives independent of their familial responsibilities. There was no shame against profligacy, nor were men sanctioned for sexual promiscuity, for

These engravings from the 1800s show a sedan chair with curtains. The first shows an elite woman peeking out from the curtains of her sedan chair. She is carried by two slaves, with her other attendants walking behind. Regardless of their formal attire, all the slaves are barefoot, as an indication of their enslavement. (Thomas Ewbank, Life in Brazil)

taking a concubine, or for engaging in extramarital affairs, often with much younger women. Impregnating women, be they indigenous, enslaved, or lower-class whites and women of color, was considered a sign of masculinity and potency that contributed to a man's honor. Pregnancy was thought to prove the virility of men, and virility was key to the concept of male honor and prestige.

Women who enjoyed the greatest equality with men were those who managed farms and small businesses with their husbands, since wives were often responsible for the commercial side of the business and for the marketing of goods. Among free whites and mulattos, women headed families when men had died or deserted the family, often assuming the full management of businesses, farms, and mines. In Brazil, as in all of Latin America, marriage placed limitations on a woman's status and power, although gender, per se, was actually a less confining restriction. A few women, such as widows, never-married women, nuns in convents, and women whose husbands had abandoned them or the family, frequently acquired the means to support themselves and their children when necessary. Some even prospered. Other women who were abandoned fell into prostitution.

Money, or the social class it accorded, was a key determinant of status within the patriarchal order. If possessing a concubine conferred honor, only wealthy men could afford to support one, at least with any public status. Social convention did not prevent laboring men from

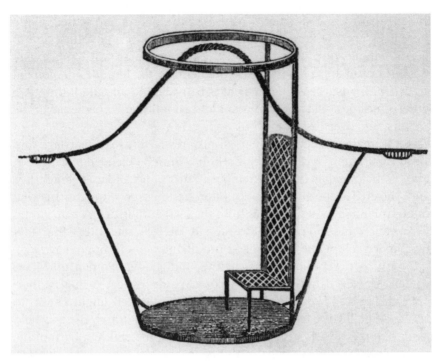

The drawing shows the construction of the sedan chair without the curtains. (Thomas Ewbank, *Life in Brazil*)

having extramarital affairs or even taking slave mistresses, but their financial resources might have limited the amount of money they had to spend on these matters.

Church and the Patriarchal Order

White men assumed for themselves all formal positions of authority in society, creating laws and enforcing social conventions that protected the patriarchal order. In all of this, the church both approved and complied, although it attempted, usually feebly, to restrain the most blatant violations. The state and the Catholic Church both accepted (or did not oppose) unsanctioned unions between Portuguese men and Indian or African women as a part of the customary right of men to dominate women sexually and physically. Based on their own particular reasons, however, these two powerful institutions did attempt to draw a line between acceptable and unacceptable practices. The state's position on mixed-race marriages varied over the centuries. Some colonial officials argued against the practice because such unions threatened white supremacy and the Portuguese colonial order, especially with regard to the inheritance of property. Under the empire, these restrictions were thought not to apply. In the mid-18th century the Marquês de Pombal encouraged, unsuccessfully, marriages between Indians and Portuguese settlers in hopes of bringing Christianity, stability, and obedience to the Crown's rule over the indigenous population.

In the main, the enforcement of any restrictions on marriage and consensual unions was lax. The Catholic Church defended marriage, at least publicly, and attempted to impose European standards of morality. Since the civil authorities were not interested in preventing extramarital unions, planters took their cues from the civil authorities. A man would take a concubine and use slave women for his own pleasure, while staying married to a white woman and producing heirs through her.

Except in exceptional cases, neither indigenous women nor slave women, nor even free women of color, could expect to marry their white masters and/or lovers. Then again, the women might expect to extract some favors: less work or transfer from the rough life as a field hand to domestic service, possible freedom for the children born of the master and the concubine, the ability to bargain for special liberties,

Salvador da Bahia boasted 350 churches, including many with gold-plated altars. (Photograph by Erich Goode)

or a grant of freedom for herself in the master's will. Since the church fathers looked the other way in the case of widespread sexual relations between masters and their slaves, they assuaged their conscience by calling on the master to manumit (free) his offspring upon his death. This, interestingly, was the practice of the priests as well, who were known to keep concubines and to father illegitimate children by their own slave women.

In conclusion, a hierarchical economic and social order influenced, and sometimes dictated, the way people in colonial and imperial Brazil lived, interacted with each other, and made choices regarding their own future and the futures of their children. Because gender, race, class, and social position came together to provide the field upon which all economic and political matters were trans-

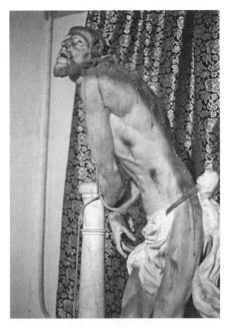

A particularly skilled black artisan, Francisco Xavier Chagas, crafted statues that graphically displayed the body of the persecuted and bloodied Christ in a series on the Passion of the Cross. The sculptor's work is thought to be a thinly veiled allusion to the suffering slaves endured under the master's whip. (Meade-Skotnes photo)

acted, social norms and expectations varied among individuals, within regions, and over time. This variation left Brazilian society twisting within a paradox. It sought to demarcate family lines, property holdings, racial lineage, and community ties through a complex set of rulings that restricted the social movement of individuals outside prescribed boundaries. Even so, the freedom that patriarchy granted to men to populate the country with illegitimate children blurred racial and gender categories. So long as the power of the slaveholders remained uncontested, the patriarchal order held firm. It was reinforced in a myriad of institutions of elite power, including kinship, godparenthood, nepotism, and clientelism, along with dowries, arranged marriages, and the subservience of women to men.

4

FROM COLONY TO REPUBLIC (1800–1889)

In the last decades of the 18th century, news of the independence of the North American colonies from Britain and of the revolution against the monarchy in France stirred intellectuals in Brazil and in all Latin American cities. Men of property and standing in the major cities met to voice their disgust with the monarchy and the privileges granted to Portuguese merchants and Crown officials. Well-to-do men hatched conspiracies to overthrow the government, but never sought to involve the poor, free or unfree persons, in their plans. If women were involved, their participation was seldom, if ever, recorded. For the most part, the revolutionaries hoped to decapitate the social order while leaving the structure intact. In this scenario, the wealthy Portuguese would simply leave, and the wealthy Brazilians would take their place.

Anticolonial Conspiracies

One of the best-known plots, the Inconfidência, involved a dentist named Joaquim José da Silva Xavier, who went by the nickname Tiradentes (meaning "tooth-puller"). With the exception of Tiradentes, the Inconfidência conspirators were oligarchs in Ouro Prêto, then the prosperous capital of the mining area of Minas Gerais. They planned to assassinate the governor and declare the province independent, apparently presuming that such a bold initiative would inspire similar actions throughout the colony. Their plan was discovered, and all the conspirators were tried and sentenced to banishment in Angola, with the exception of the nonaristocrat, Tiradentes. The royal authorities seized this opportunity to demonstrate to the public what would happen (at least to the hapless commoners) if they organized an independence movement. Tiradentes was hanged on April 21, 1792. The corpse was decapitated and the head displayed on a post in the center of Ouro

Prêto. The remainder of his body was chopped into quarters with the pieces left on display in locales around the town.

Despite its failure, the Inconfidência is remembered as an early sign of revolutionary thinking among the elite. Although never reaching the levels of intensity or organization that marked the revolutionary groups in Buenos Aires, Caracas, Lima, Mexico City, and elsewhere, clusters of men came together in the last decades of the century to voice their discontent with colonial rule. Brazil's separation from Portugal, however, followed a quite different road.

Independence from Portugal

Independence began in 1808 when the Portuguese court of the House of Braganza fled Napoleon's invading army for the colony in Brazil. The court sailed under the protection of its British allies, who were fighting Napoleon's forces, from Lisbon to Salvador da Bahia. The monarch and the 10,000 courtiers in his party found the old colonial city too cramped to accommodate them, so they moved a month later to Rio de Janeiro. When the court arrived in Rio de Janeiro, it elevated the colonial capital to the capital of the empire. Even when the Portuguese military managed to drive the French out of Portugal, the Prince Regent, João VI, remained in Brazil, possibly reluctant to trade the tropical splendor of Rio de Janeiro for Lisbon. Finally on December 16, 1815, after 13 years in Brazil, the Prince Regent declared Brazil on equal status with the homeland in a united kingdom. In 1821, under threat from the Cortes of losing his imperial throne entirely, João VI returned to Portugal, leaving behind his son, Pedro, as the Prince Regent of Brazil. A little less than half of the court and military that had accompanied the king to Brazil a decade earlier returned with him.

In 1822, the Portuguese Cortes sought to end the dual kingdom status and restore Lisbon as the sole center of the empire. It demanded that Dom Pedro give up his throne in Rio and return to Portugal, and that Brazil once again assume a subordinate status. Acting with the support of the Brazilian aristocracy, who were anxious to preserve their considerable landholdings from which they exported sugar, coffee, and cotton, and with the backing of the British, who were eager to monopolize the trade with Brazil, the monarch moved to secure Brazil's autonomy from Portugal. While on a trip near the Ipiranga River on September 7, 1822, Dom Pedro declared Brazil's independence with what came to be known as the Cry of Ipiranga: "Independence or Death!" On December 1, the 24-year-old monarch had himself crowned Emperor Pedro I, a title more in keeping with the French conqueror Napoleon Bonaparte than anything in Portugal's monarchical tradition. Two years later he promulgated the first constitution.

Brazil did not fight a long and bloody war to separate from Portugal, as did its neighbors in their fight for independence from Spain. There were small uprisings among Portuguese military units in the Northeast who remained loyal to the seat of government in Lisbon, but no prolonged war. What Brazil had instead was a smoldering discontent among native-born Brazilian merchants, planters, and lower-level bureaucrats against the privileged and arrogant Portuguese who had elbowed their way to the top of the former colony's economic and political life. This hatred of the Portuguese courtiers and their many allies, especially in the urban areas, along with class and regional tensions, did eventually lead to many uprisings.

Ending the External Slave Trade

The power to hold Brazil autonomous and to secure markets for its valuable exports, as well as to insure a steady supply of manufactured goods, rested in London more than in Rio de Janeiro. In 1825 Portugal demanded £2,000,000 (equal to about $7,000,000) as compensation for the loss of its colony. Unable to raise the money itself, Brazil borrowed from banks in London, thereby sealing the new nation's fate to the dictates of Great Britain. The next year, Britain required Brazil to end the international slave trade in return for a favorable trade agreement and full recognition of the latter's independence. The slave trade was the most abhorrent aspect of the slave system to the growing body of abolitionists making their case before the British parliament, in street rallies, and in a barrage of newspaper articles and pamphlets. Although the slave trade continued with the full knowledge of the Brazilian government, the bombardment of the ports and seizure of slave ships on the high seas pushed up the price of slaves on the Brazilian market and contributed to the eventual demise of the system. After several years of negotiating, Brazil finally outlawed the international slave trade on March 13, 1830. In an attempt to stem the continued trade in contraband slaves, the following year the government passed a law freeing any slave who entered Brazil.

Signs of discontent began to emerge from the sugar planters in the Northeast who were losing their share in the international market to the more efficiently produced sugar from Cuba and the Caribbean. Combined with the inability to obtain slaves and the high price for those they could get, men of property grew disgruntled with the political order. By 1830, Dom Pedro I's popularity had begun to wane. Brazil had suffered a humiliating defeat in a territorial war with Argentina (1825–28). In addition, the monarch's costly lifestyle and the favor he showed to Portuguese merchants and courtiers angered the domestic merchants and entrepreneurial classes. Finally his autocratic rule threw him out of favor with Brazil's political elite, many of whom were seeking to build their careers as Brazilian nationals free from the influence of the monarch who showered favors on Portuguese sycophants. In 1831 Dom Pedro I abdicated his throne and returned to Portugal. As his father had done with him, Dom Pedro left behind his son, then five years old, under the protection of a three-man council. The council, or Regency, which was reduced to a single regent three years later, governed in the name of the emperor until the youth's 14th birthday in 1840, when he assumed the throne as Pedro II.

The Regency and Growing Discontent

The decade of the Regency, from 1831 to 40, was not a peaceful time in Brazil's history, although it is unclear whether the fault lay with the regents. Quite likely an adult emperor would have had difficulty maintaining peace during the early years of the century. While in the main uprisings were regionally based, and met with brutal repression from the central authority, they frequently bore the stamp of class, racial, and ethnic antagonisms. Some pitted monarchists against nascent republicans, others favored one monarchical system or monarch (Pedro I of Portugal versus the Regency) over another, and some were protests in which Indians, slaves, freed people of color, and poor whites, in one combination or another, battled the elite. The combination of uprisings and the repression meted out by the central government during this period more than disprove the tiresome and oft repeated notion that Brazil's has been a peaceful historical development.

A bloody uprising occurred from 1835 to 1840 in Belém, the port of Pará. Known as the War of Cabanagem, the working poor, many of them Indians, rose in protest against the autocratic rule of mainly Portuguese-born merchants and political administrators. After raging on and off for five years, the revolt, which stretched from the city of Belém to the interior of the region, was eventually quashed by the imperial army. More than 30,000 insurgents were massacred in a province with a population of only 150,000.

A more famous disturbance broke out in Maranhão in the Northeast. Its fame derived from the role of one of the empire's most illustrious political and military leaders who rose to prominence combating regional revolts. Brigadier Luís Alves da Lima e Silva, who would go on to fame as the Duke of Caxias, led the army against an uprising that joined more than 3,000 backlands bandits and slaves. The rebels were turned back eventually, their leaders apprehended and hung, but not before they captured and held the town of Caxias for an extended period.

A separatist revolt broke out in the southernmost province of Rio Grande do Sul in 1835. Fueled by hostility toward the central authority and the desire to pocket the profits locally that derived from a healthy trade in hides and meat with neighboring Argentina and Uruguay, the gaucho (or southern cowboy) tradesmen and ranchers declared independence from Brazil in 1838. It was this military and political campaign that earned the Duke of Caxias his high honor. He defeated the rebels militarily while politically outsmarting them with several concessions to their economic demands in the name of the empire.

Politics under the Empire

The revolts in Brazil bore a close similarity to the types of regional, *caudillo* (local boss), separatist, and proletarian uprisings that broke out in many cities and rural areas of postcolonial Spanish America. Rather than splinter into dozens of independent republics and autocratic fiefdoms as happened in Spanish America, however, Brazil managed to remain in one piece. A more unified system of slavery and reliance on the export market in a few commodities might have played a role in preventing the break-up. In addition, regions were allowed to maintain relative autonomy under the rule of planters and local strongmen called *caudilhos* in Portuguese, while adhering to a central authority. Although the imperial army was able to defeat insurgents and preserve the empire, many regions remained under the rule of landowners who used their own local police and paramilitary armies to maintain order.

In its broad outlines, the imperial administration of Pedro I, the interim regencies, and the long reign of Pedro II functioned according to a defined hierarchical formula. The imperial center shared power with advisers handpicked from among the large landowners and the merchants who serviced the export market. Dom Pedro I dictated the terms of the 1824 Constitution, appointed the senators who served for a lifetime at his behest, and retained the right to appoint all ministers and to dissolve the parliament. The Chamber of Deputies served as the "repository of democracy" for Brazil, but the members had to meet income and property requirements. The franchise remained in the hands of men of at least some means, while slavery was unquestioned. Internal disputes raged between emergent republican forces and the old-line conservative elites who had the ear of the emperor. Pedro II did not alter this basic top-down chain of command. He had, however, an advantage over his father in that he was born and reared in Brazil. Despite the accusation that Pedro II favored the Portuguese business and political elite much as his father had, he

Portrait of Emperor Pedro II, ca. 19th century. (Hoffenberg Collection)

did preside over a period in which a national bourgeoisie that identified solely with Brazil began to emerge.

Economics under the Empire

In the main, the planters of the Northeast presided over a declining sugar market, worn-out soil, outdated machinery, and reliance on slave labor that had become far too costly to purchase and maintain. Despite attempts to use paid laborers and slaves, some stimulation to the domestic economy, and experimentation with more modern mills, the Northeast could not match the growing efficiency of its Cuban competitors. Mining, cattle raising, and the beginnings of coffee cultivation in the state of Rio de Janeiro served to diversify and stimulate the economy in other regions.

Despite these gains, the country's independent development was marred by its dependence on Great Britain for financial and military backing. From the time the Royal Navy had escorted Prince Regent João VI to Brazil, Britain was able to extract a considerable price from the imperial government for the protection it provided. In 1810, the regent granted British merchants a series of concessions, including a steep reduction of tariffs on British goods sold in Brazil. In so doing,

Britain forced foreclosure on domestic cotton manufacturers who were just beginning to command a market for textiles. By century's end Great Britain had the largest share of clothing goods sold on the Brazilian market and was processing most of Brazil's agricultural products and selling them on the international market. Brazilian economic historian Eulalia Maria Lahmeyer Lobo argues that the brief emergence in 1808 of a traditional commercial bourgeoisie, representing Brazil's domestic trading interests, was derailed later in the century during the push to develop transportation and public works that were financed and overseen by the British. Britain's resultant monopoly on key financial and technical aspects of Brazilian growth effectively undermined the latter's autonomous commercial and financial firms.

According to Bill Albert, at the turn of the century foreign merchants, mainly British, controlled about 60 percent of the coffee sales abroad. The foreign merchant, operating through a few dozen tightly controlled firms, assumed a powerful position linking the rural planters, who supplied the country's chief exports, with the world of trade abroad. Albert explains that Britain's contacts on the world market, control of credit, and increasing interest in processing and warehousing agricultural products allowed Britain to achieve uncontested authority over Brazil's foreign trade.

Brazil's economic dependence on both the export market and foreign investors influenced the autonomy of the industrial elite. By relying on foreign investors, Brazil's own entrepreneurs did not have to take risks with their profits. Likewise the government did not have to have credit reserves adequate enough to bail out failing investors in the early, and precarious, stage of capitalist expansion. In short, Brazilian planters and merchants could get very rich very fast by tying themselves firmly to the coattails of powerful British trading houses, investors, and middlemen. Rather than developing on their own, Brazil's industrial and financial elite tended to serve as intermediaries for foreign investors. They were hampered in competing in the world market on their own terms, buying and selling what they wanted at the best price. This reliance on Britain was a long-term liability that undercut Brazil's ability to emerge as a world power. More important, dependence meant that the interests of the Brazilian people, especially the poor and working class, seldom figured into the political priorities of the national government.

The Rise of Coffee

Beginning in the 1840s, coffee became the most important export item. The story of Brazil's preeminence as a coffee producer and exporter

largely unfolded after independence from Portugal. Today, coffee cultivation bears some of the characteristics of the old plantation system but
also shows the signs of modern agricultural methods. First introduced
into the far northern state of Pará with some seeds from French Guiana
in 1727, coffee was grown in the 18th century in Amazonas and the far
north. It reached Rio de Janeiro by 1770 but moved west as the fertil-
ity on the coastal hills became depleted. By the mid-19th century, the
coffee tree found its home in the states of São Paulo, Minas Gerais, and
eventually in Paraná to the west.

The effect of coffee cultivation on the nation's economy, especially
in shifting the vital center from the Northeast to the Southeast, was
tremendous. Coffee production attracted foreign capital, as well as
generated domestic profits that were poured into manufacturing and
commercial ventures in São Paulo. It facilitated the introduction of
new technologies, encouraged railroad construction, opened up a new
part of Brazil to the west and south of São Paulo state. Coffee planters
in some ways more resembled tobacco planters in the Recôncavo than
the vast sugar estates. Some operators managed vast estates, but others
relied on a few slaves or a combination of wage and slave laborers and
cultivated a modest amount of land.

Slave men and women sorting and transporting coffee beans, ca. early 19th century.
(Hoffenberg Collection)

Coffee production stimulated the large-scale use of immigrant labor on the plantations. Immigrants came mostly from Italy and later from Japan. Like northeastern sugar planters, coffee growers relied heavily on slave labor, but also utilized a combination of slave and free labor. Planters were more interested in boosting technology and experimenting with crop rotation, fertilizers, and innovative agronomy methods to increase production, rather than simply relying on more slaves working longer hours, as had been the practice of some of the sugar producers. Coffee planters adapted to changing international conditions and were receptive to foreign influence. In a host of ways, coffee introduced far-reaching political, economic, and social changes in Brazil, including industrial development, as the planters invested their profits into domestic manufacturing in the state of São Paulo.

On the other hand, coffee production in many ways did not break with the past and reproduced the outdated features associated with sugar: production on large plantations, dependence on a single crop, reliance largely on slave labor, a plantation system governed by a patriarch whose influence over the family, community, and workforce was unquestioned. Some of the coffee estates had more than 200 slaves working on them, far more than most sugar *engenhos* of the Northeast. In fact, on the eve of abolition in the late 1800s, northeastern planters were still selling slaves to the Southeast, indicating that the system was still vital right up until abolition in 1888.

Because coffee trees have a life span of 20 years but take four to six years to mature, a single plantation has trees growing at various stages of maturity. As a result, coffee is not an enterprise in which small or medium-sized farm operators can get very rich. The investment in labor, trees, and extensive acreage makes large-scale production for export an expensive enterprise. Nonetheless, the coffee regions have always supported a number of smaller operators who produce cheaper coffee for the local market along with cassava, manioc, and vegetables. The small-scale coffee farm is most common in the Caribbean islands, but can still be found in Brazil, Colombia, and other major coffee-producing countries.

Changes in Social and Cultural Norms

After the arrival of the Court to Rio de Janeiro in 1808, the cultural life of the city improved remarkably. It changed from a sleepy town of few entertainments to one offering a semblance of what was already available in Lima, Mexico City, Havana, and the other metropolises of Latin

America. João VI opened Rio de Janeiro and all of Brazil to such innovations as printing presses, institutions of higher education, factories to produce gunpowder and process iron ore, botanical gardens, and new technologies. Most significantly, the lifting of trade restrictions exposed Brazil to new ideas. Modern fashions, as well as the most recent scientific and cultural trends making their way through other cities of the world, now became available to Brazil's urban elites and tiny middle class. For the first time they began to appreciate the literature, art, and music that was stirring their counterparts in North America and Europe. With this awakening came talk of republicanism, even the abolition of slavery, discussion of women's rights, and other new intellectual and political trends. Printing presses allowed for the reproduction and distribution of writings that had previously been unknown.

Under the empire, Rio de Janeiro underwent many changes, including renovation of streets and buildings, creation of parks and plazas, and founding of universities, law schools, *colegios* (secondary schools), and other institutions of higher learning. Movement from colonial backwater to kingdom, on a par with other European monarchies, Brazil transformed into a more modern society, as was happening in other parts of the Americas.

The arrival of the monarchy had brought with it a window out to the world and access to innovations that were stirring abroad. By the second half of the 19th century, the fissures that had always cut through society were increasingly apparent. Place of birth, civil status, wealth, legal status as free or slave, religious orthodoxy, and occupation continued to matter, as they had always mattered in Brazil, but the influx of immigrants from Portugal and a smattering from other places such as the Middle East, Italy, and the rest of Europe, diluted the black-white, slave-master polarity. In addition, as the sugar economy of the Northeast declined and the coffee economy of the Southeast increased in importance, the most archaic and traditional values of the planter aristocracy began to erode.

The Emergence of Urban Culture

In the countryside, the planters still dominated social life, but in the principal cities—Recife, Rio de Janeiro, Salvador da Bahia, and later São Paulo—an increased cosmopolitanism began to emerge. An urban culture developed in which libraries, bookstores, cafés, and the accouterments of European society supplanted the narrow entertainments typical of the empire.

The capital and most important city of the country, Rio de Janeiro, led the way as a center of urban life and diversity in the 19th century. With a population of more than 250,000, Rio had emerged as the largest city of South America by the end of Pedro II's reign. Nestled between the sea, the wide Guanabara Bay, and mountains (called *morros*) that jutted up perpendicular to the flat lowlands, the city was at once a splendid geographical sight and a nightmare of urban planning. Much of the commercial area was crowded next to the bay, and streets simply dead-ended into a haphazard set of docks and wharves. On the docks, merchandise was unloaded that provisioned the empire, from manufactured tools and machinery, crude textiles and fine linens, the elegant furnishings for the finest houses of the country, to vehicles, guns, grains, and more. Loaded onto Brazilian ships by the slave laborers who worked the ports under the steady eye and ready whip of the overseers was coffee, cotton, fruits, hides, lumber, minerals, gold, and other agricultural and extractive goods. Initially slaves entered the port in Rio and from there were sold to planters throughout the county. After 1830, when the external slave trade came to a halt, and with the assistance of considerable British pressure, the slave-auction block was not as busy as decades earlier. Nonetheless, beginning in the late 18th century, the sugar planters sold a steady supply of slaves south, making slave auctions a persistent feature of the docks.

New Currents in Intellectual Life

By the 1820s, Rio de Janeiro sported a National Library, National Museum, Academy of Fine Arts, imposing buildings for the National Assembly, Senate, Municipal Government, naval and military academies. A number of impressive churches in the downtown and on the hills overlooking Botofogo near the sea were visible, as were three- and four-story mansions for the merchant elite and planters. By mid-century, a large number of the prosperous coffee planters kept houses in São Paulo and Rio de Janeiro because they found the salons, busy streets, entertainment, and social connections of the urban setting far more enticing than the dull life of a distant plantation. Even if they had no house there, the elite came to Rio in increasing numbers to handle business matters, to pay homage to the court, and to establish connections with the courtiers. Sons who left the plantations for law and engineering schools often chose to remain, opting for the excitement of urban life over returning to their homes in isolated rural areas.

Into this invigorated urban environment came new political and economic philosophies, fiction, poetry, and music, some of which promised to upset the stability of the authoritarian slave regime. Brazil's first novel, *The Fisherman's Son*, by Antônio Gonçalves Teixeira e Sousa, appeared in 1843, followed by a number of others from various writers. Most were in the romantic 19th-century genre. A witty, satirical theater produced more telling comments on Brazilian society, while poetry, long a favorite, flourished. Translations of popular French essays and other writings appeared in the newspapers, and controversial works advocating popular sovereignty, an end to slavery, and occasionally even calling for social equality, also began to circulate in avant-garde salons and to find their way into the discussions among liberals in academic and political circles. Eventually the new ideas being passed around in the cafés and salons of Rio and São Paulo spread to cities in distant regions of the empire.

Although the court held unquestioned power under the authoritarian constitution written by Dom Pedro I, Brazilian nationals held the majority of positions in municipal councils, in the assemblies and judicial courts, and by 1840, on the throne itself. By the second half of the 19th century, more native-born Brazilians began to resent the privileges the imperial order accorded to Portuguese nationals. Although Brazil was a monarchy, many of its citizens began to see themselves as a nation of America and no longer an appendage culturally or politically of Portugal. Critics of slavery and of the empire hastened to point out at every opportunity that the slave system and the monarchy placed Brazil out of step with its American neighbors.

The Debate over Slavery

A combination of factors brought about abolition in 1888, which had origins in a decree to end the slave trade under pressure from Great Britain in 1831. In 1850, British ships began entering Brazilian territorial waters to seize and destroy ships carrying contraband slaves. The fate of slavery was tied to the monarchy, not only in the minds of a modernizing elite based in the Southeast, but also among planters in other parts of the country. Moreover, slavery was increasingly unpopular in the Northeast where planters faced declining profits. The sugar planters had been selling off slaves for years to the more prosperous coffee plantations of the Southeast. In the Northeast, there had been a gradual transition to sharecropping and debt peonage, which worked better for many planters because it freed them from providing food and subsistence to their workforce.

Ultimately, the victory of the North in the U.S. Civil War was a powerful sign that slavery's days were numbered. The United States had served as a major example for the Brazilian slaveholders in their ideological defense. That the planters of the U.S. South who had exerted such enormous influence on their federal government had gone down in defeat, their Brazilian counterparts took as an ominous sign. More and more, the argument surfaced among the political and economic elite that slavery had to end so that a wage-labor economy could expand. The sugar planters who had mechanized their mills and introduced a combination of wage and free labor feared the type of civil conflict that had ripped apart the United States and ultimately defeated and humiliated the Confederacy. Many of them saw abolition with a payment of compensation from the government for the losses they sustained when their slave property was freed as an attractive way out. They would be disappointed.

A significant factor in ending slavery was the growing strength of the international abolitionist movement. The abolitionist movement, especially in England and the United States, had been distributing broadsides and pamphlets, publishing newspapers and books, and holding meetings. Speakers on the lecture circuit hammered home the horrors of slavery to audiences throughout the country. The English groups had been successful in targeting and eventually ending the practice of slavery in the West Indian colonies, as well as demanding that the British navy police the seas, blockade ports, and apprehend slaving ships on the high seas.

Joaquim Nabuco's Opposition to Slavery

Brazil's abolitionist movement was only a faint reflection of the level of political pressure that abolitionists brought to bear in Britain, the United States, and European countries. The leading Brazilian antislavery advocate was Joaquim Nabuco. In 1883, a mere five years before emancipation, he published the most important abolitionist tract, *O Abolicionismo*. In this document, Nabuco, using his standing as a member of the Chamber of Deputies, denounced slavery as an obstacle to progress and, notably, the health of the empire. A forceful and articulate spokesman, member of an important Northeastern family, and a gifted and fearless writer, Nabuco led the opposition to slavery and opposed compensation payments to the planters. His brash and often arrogant demeanor earned him few friends and many enemies, but he can be credited with bringing the vision of a Brazil without slavery into day-today politics. *O Abolicionismo (Abolitionism)* was a passionate indictment of slavery. In Nabuco's view, Brazilians had to take up the abolitionist cause not only for the sake of the nation, but for their own sake as human beings:

> Let every true Brazilian become the instrument of that cause. Let the young people, from the moment when they accept the responsibilities of citizenship, swear to abstain from the purchase of human flesh. Let them prefer an obscure career of honest labor to amassing wealth by means of the inexpressible suffering of other human beings. Let them educate their children—indeed, let them educate themselves—to enjoy the freedom of others without which their own liberty will be a chance gift of destiny. Let them acquire the knowledge that freedom is worth possessing, and let them attain the courage to defend it. *(Nabuco, quoted in Conrad 1983:457).*

Whereas many abolitionists condemned slavery as a backward system of labor and an impediment to capitalist development, Nabuco denounced it primarily on moral grounds. Moreover, he actively distrusted the republicans who linked slavery with the empire and hoped to end both. By contrast, he argued that the abolition of slavery would allow the empire to flourish. Such monarchist sympathies set Nabuco apart from the well-known figures of the international abolitionist movement, many of whom he admired and copied, such as the British statesman William Wilberforce, or Americans Frederick Douglass, William Lloyd Garrison, and Harriet Beecher Stowe.

War of the Triple Alliance

The rise of social groups with no direct ties, or tenuous ones, to the plantation system contributed to undermining the slave system. In the late 19th century the military gained prominence as a new force. In addition to domestic commercial and manufacturing sectors that were distancing themselves from slavery along with intellectuals such as Nabuco, the military arose as the sector most separate, and even alien, from the planter aristocracy. A distinctive military constituency emerged as a result of Brazil's war against Paraguay which began in 1864. This prolonged conflict is known as the Paraguayan War or the War of the Triple Alliance.

The war broke out after Brazil invaded Uruguay in 1864 with the intent of destabilizing the existing government and putting in place a political party Brazil saw as friendlier to its interests. In response to this blatant interference in the affairs of a neighboring and very small country, Paraguay seized a Brazilian steamer, invaded the southernmost province of Rio Grande do Sul, crossing a part of Argentina to do so. The exact series of events that led to an alliance of Argentina, Brazil, and Uruguay (then under a government friendly to Brazil) against Paraguay is less important than the results. The war lasted for six years in which Paraguayans fought to maintain their right to existence. By the time a peace treaty was finally signed in March 1870, Paraguay had been all but destroyed. The tiny country lost 10 to 20 percent of its population and nearly 40 percent of its prewar industry. More importantly, the war ended in the consolidation of Uruguay and Paraguay as buffer states separating the two major South American powers: Argentina and Brazil. The lesson of the war, even for Uruguay which fought on the side of Brazil and Argentina, was that no small state could survive all-out confrontation with one of its larger and more powerful neighbors.

The Creation of a Professional Military

A side effect of Brazil's military victory in the War of the Triple Alliance was the formation of a professional military. For most of its life as an independent country, Brazil had relied on mercenaries to fight, as in its battle to secure its border with Argentina in 1825. A protracted military struggle for more than five years, such as the Paraguayan War, required more than mercenaries. The army filled its ranks with Brazilians, mostly from the non-elite class. The military emerged as a force apart from the landholding elite, drew much of its strength from middle sectors not tied to the plutocracy, and gained respect from the civilian population by winning the long, difficult war against Paraguay. By the 1870s, the military was a professional fighting force. Moreover, when not in battle, the military began to exert its influence as an interest group within society.

In addition, the members of the military represented a new social force. Added to the other recruits drawn from middle-class, working-class, and urban sectors, the military constituted a distinctive force whose interests were not linked to the traditional ruling sectors. Receptive to emergent ideologies calling for the end of slavery and criticism of the empire, they eventually formed a key group in overthrowing the empire in 1889.

Emancipation of the Slaves

After years of vociferous debate, the General Assembly passed the first reform law in 1871. It was called the Rio Branco, or Free Birth, Law;

Emperor Pedro II appointed the Viscount Rio Branco (José Maria da Silva Paranhos), a prominent Conservative Party minister, to win support in the parliament for a bill that freed the newborn children of slave women. After one of the most heated debates in Brazilian history, Rio Branco succeeded in getting the reluctant legislators to agree. The law, signed on September 28, 1871, meant no person born of a slave mother could be enslaved. In the eyes of many Brazilians, the Rio Branco Law laid the groundwork for the gradual abolition of slavery. In the 1880s, a stronger abolitionist movement began, centered on the planters' demand for compensation for their lost "property" when the slaves were freed.

Encouraged by abolitionists, slaves began to abandon some plantations in São Paulo, as well as in Santa Catarina and neighboring regions. By 1888, the system was near collapse. The Brazilian Assembly passed the Golden Law outlawing slavery on May 13, 1888. It was signed by the imperial regent Princess Isabel in the name of the Emperor Dom Pedro II, who was out of the country. The following year, the empire itself ended, its fate having been sealed by the momentous events that surrounded Brazil's emergence out of the backward system of slavery.

Race in Postabolition Society

The major questions that arose in Brazil and in other societies wresting free of slavery before and after abolition concerned the competition between systems of slave versus free labor on the one hand, and the place of race in determining social status on the other. Thomas Skidmore argues that the widespread view among whites that blacks constituted a biologically separate and inferior race, which permeated the debate over slavery in the North America, was largely absent in Brazil. The reason for this had to do with the large number of free people of color who lived in every part of Brazil by the time abolition occurred. In the United States, for the most part, defined racial barriers divided free people of color from whites in most areas regardless of whether a particular state was slave or free.

In Brazil, free people of color, who in many cases were born into families that had been emancipated for generations, owned property (including slaves), participated in local governments, served in the military, and held positions of influence in the commercial world. For example, Senator Salles Torres-Homen, whose 1871 speech in the Senate appears earlier in this chapter, was the son of a black woman and a white man. As the descendant of slaves on his mother's side, he was in a particularly unique position to demonstrate that blacks were

TWO SIDES IN THE PARLIAMENTARY DEBATES OVER THE FREE BIRTH LAW, 1871

(1) Senator José Inácio Barros Cobra (Minas Gerais) Argues Slaves Are Property:

> The servile institution unfortunately appeared as a main element of our social organization, and for three long centuries it sank deep roots into our laws and soil; it represents immense and important capital investments, and almost the only instrument of agricultural labor. Agriculture is practically our only industry, and so almost the only source of our wealth and public revenue, of our prosperity and credit; as a result the interests associated with slavery are extensive and complex; they are the interests of the entire society that relies upon them . . .
>
> Almost all the other [slaveholding] nations found themselves in quite different circumstances; slavery was localized in the colonies, at great distances, and therefore its abolition could have no effect upon the metropolises. Even in the United States the difference was great, because also there slavery was localized in the southern states, which made up a small part of the republic; so that the solution to the problem there, if fatal to the South, did not damage the greatness and general prosperity of the republic . . . I must point out that the [Free Birth] bill, as now conceived, is unconstitutional: 1st, because it disrespects the right to property; 2nd, because it grants political rights to a class which, according to the Constitution, cannot possess them. However unjust, inhuman, and absurd the domination of one man by another, that is, slavery, may be, it is certain that this condition was legally established by civil law, which created and regulated the master's property right over the slave. Therefore, for good or for evil, slavery became a legal institution among us more than three centuries ago, authorized and protected by law and strengthened by its antiquity, and therefore slave property is as sacred as any other, though illegitimate in principle . . . However, the government's bill attacks and disregards this right, proclaiming the freedom of children of slave women born from the date of the law, and thereby expropriating from the citizen that, which is legally in his possession, without prior compensation in compliance with the Constitution.

Source: Conrad, Robert E. *Children of God's Fire: A Documentary History of Black Slavery in Brazil.* Princeton, N.J.: Princeton University Press, 1983, p. 438–446.

TWO SIDES IN THE PARLIAMENTARY DEBATES OVER THE FREE BIRTH LAW, 1871

(2) Senator Francisco Salles Torres-Homen (Rio Grande do Norte) Defends the Free Birth Law. [The senator was a mulatto. In contrast to the debate over slavery that occurred in the U.S. Congress, in Brazil there were descendants of slaves who participated in the parliamentary debate, although they were very few.]

If [the slaveholders] are asked why the legislator who can reform and amend the laws cannot amend laws that deal with property, they will doubtless reply that property is inviolable because it is based upon natural law that existed before civil law, and is derived from an immutable principle of justice, which sanctifies and affirms for each man the fruit of his own labor, a principle without which society could not exist. We are thus transported to the realm of law and justice, where the rational basis for the inviolability of property in general is indeed to be found.

But, gentlemen, if it is proved that ownership of a human being, far from being founded upon natural law, is on the contrary its most monstrous violation, if instead of being supported by justice it is sustained only by the evil of coercion and force, then the alleged basis of the inviolability of that special property disintegrates and disappears; and the law that supported it is seen as nothing more than an error, or a social crime, and is subject to amendment like any other law that does violence to the nation's interests.

Now, Mr. President, I should not have to demonstrate before this august assembly that intelligent creatures, endowed like us with noble qualities, facing the same destiny, should not be compared, from the point of view of property, to the colt, the calf, the fruit of the trees, and to the living objects of nature that are subject to human domination. An absurd, detestable doctrine! . . .

[Referring to Senator Barros' argument that slavery was intrinsic to Brazil's wealth.]

I might reply that the production of wealth is not the single and paramount aim of society, which is not made up only of creatures who are born, consume, die and are buried in the furrows of the earth which nourishes them, that their destinies are higher, their circumstances, needs, intrinsic makeup, and civilization more complex.

Source: Conrad, Robert E. *Children of God's Fire: A Documentary History of Black Slavery in Brazil.* Princeton, N.J.: Princeton University Press, 1983, p. 448–450.

fully capable of being educated and rising to positions of respect within society. Because of the high status of many mixed-race people in Brazil before abolition, the form of discrimination in the postabolition society differed markedly from the intense white supremacy that characterized southern U.S. life after the defeat of the Confederacy in the Civil War.

Racist notions entered Brazil during the Republic, and the idea of the biological inferiority of blacks gained a following. There were, however, important differences from the United States, and those differences continue as a part of the racial dynamic today. First, there is no history of a color bar or Jim Crow laws, as in the United States. Secondly, race follows a continuum from black to white, with many shades in between, all of which combined with class status, position, and education to determine race. Some social scientists have argued that Brazilians tend to have an ad hoc definition of race, one that can move an individual from white to black based on a wide variety of physical, as well as social and cultural, characteristics. Because race was seen as a continuum even among slaves and free persons of color, it did not become a fixed concept after emancipation.

Nevertheless, the absence of a color bar in Brazil did not mean that after emancipation former slaves moved easily into the free labor market. Nor, by any means, did it mean that racism was absent from postabolition society. In Brazil, as in the southern United States during Reconstruction, the transition to unfettered free labor did not occur easily; in some places it occurred not at all. Long before abolition in 1888, a number of plantations had been utilizing a variety of forms of indebted labor combined with wage labor, in addition to slaves. In the Northeast slaves were too expensive for the cash-strapped sugar planters to buy and maintain, thus they began to turn increasingly toward allowing squatters who were already occupying parts of the land to sharecrop. These sharecroppers were drawn from the ranks of free persons, some of whom were black and many of whom were mulattos. Freed persons who moved from the plantations to the city found themselves passed over for employment, even in jobs slaves had previously held, discriminated against in housing, and barred from many cultural institutions.

Racial Categories and Immigration

Coffee planters desired European immigrants, and actually imported a colony of Swiss and German farmers, but the planters were unwilling to accord the immigrants equality and the wages that they demanded. For the most part the Europeans abandoned the plantations as soon as they could and either established their own farms or obtained employment for wages in the cities. A few colonization projects with German immigrants did take root in Rio Grande do Sul, Espirito Santo, and Santa Catarina, giving rise to a Germanic presence in those states that remains today. Notably, these European immigrants did not become sharecroppers, at least for long, and they refused to accept the servile conditions the planters chose to offer ex-slaves. There is, therefore, a clear indication that despite the racial continuum from black through various levels of mulatto to white that had operated in Brazil from the early years of the colony, racial prejudice functioned in the labor market. A black former slave found far fewer options available to him or her than did a recent German or Swiss immigrant.

By the time slavery was abolished in 1888, Italian immigrants were already taking jobs as laborers in the coffee fields of the state of São Paulo. Their numbers increased in subsequent decades, as did those of Japanese and some other immigrant workers. Although many slaves remained tied to the plantations as debt peons, many left after abolition to try their hand at urban employment. What remained in the countryside was therefore a workforce made up of coerced and indebted freed persons and low-wage immigrant laborers. Even at the end of the 19th century when Brazil stood poised to enter the modern world of free labor as a republic, the legacy of centuries of slavery, along with authoritarian and patriarchal rule, proved hard to shake free. Progressive Republicans, anxious to bring the country into the modern limelight, were few. As part of the legacy that had been in power from colonial days and whose class had set the social conventions of Brazilian life, most white men were unwilling to allow women, former slaves, the rural and urban poor, and the tiny middle class a genuine share in the workings of society. Few women from the elite families objected to their inferior position. Signs of discontent were more apparent among freed persons and the new immigrant sectors, especially in Brazil's expanding urban areas.

Ending the Empire and Founding the Republic

The Brazilian empire was abolished on November 15, 1889, in a military revolt headed by Marshal Floriano Peixoto. Dom Pedro II left for exile in France, and a military officer, Marshal Deodoro da Fonseca, was appointed provisional military chief, a position reached after power-brokering with Peixoto. Notably it was the military that moved to assert its control over the reins of government. Having arrived only recently on the political stage, the military had grown to prominence rapidly in the wake of the patriotic fervor that followed Brazil's victory in the war against Paraguay. Although declared a republic, the new government had little more interest in pacifying the rural peons, freed slaves, backlands peasants, and urban workers than had the empire before it. Real power remained firmly in the hands of the planter elite, concentrated in the coffee regions of São Paulo, and with the commercial and banking interests of the southeastern cities of Rio de Janeiro, São Paulo, and Minas Gerais, in alliance with the emerging strata of professional military. The old families of the Northeast, poorer but entitled, clung to the spoils of the system. A literacy test replaced the property requirement, but since the literate were property holders, and the illiterate rarely owned property, it was not a measure that significantly changed the electorate. Civil marriage was established and the power of the church diminished. A few reformers headed by the liberal spokesman Rui Barbosa prodded the government to improve education, raise the standard of living for urban workers, and carry out a modest land reform, but most of these measures were not even considered for several decades into the next century.

5

CONSTRUCTING A NATION OF FREE LABORERS IN THE NINETEENTH AND EARLY TWENTIETH CENTURIES

C oming a year after abolition in 1888, the founding of the republic on November 15, 1889 could not be seen as unrelated to the end of slavery, a system of labor that had endured for more than three centuries and had isolated Brazil from the modern nations of the Western Hemisphere. Indeed with the abolition and demise of the monarchy, many of Brazil's modernizing elite felt that the time had come for the "sleeping giant" to assume its rightful place as one of the most important nations of the world.

The Rubber Boom

The extraordinary importance of rubber exports from the mid-19th century until the collapse of the market in 1910 gave Brazilians every reason to believe that their country was indeed destined for greatness. The enormous profits to be made in the rubber trade had begun to attract merchants and laborers from all over the world in the 1870s to the rubber-producing regions deep in the Amazon. The rubber boom opened the Amazon area to foreigners more than had any previous exploration.

Although the rubber trade reached its height in the latter part of the 19th century, the process of producing rubber traces back to before the arrival of the Portuguese explorers in the 16th century. Natural rubber comes from a milky white fluid called latex, which is contained in many

The Theater and Opera House in Manaus was constructed and furnished with the finest materials imported from Europe, including electric lights. (Shutterstock/Rafael Martin-Gaitero)

plants. The most important of these is *Hevea brasiliensis*, a tree that grows abundantly in the current Brazilian state of Pará in the Amazon tropical rain forest. The indigenous people had known and made use of latex long before the arrival of the Europeans. They smoked it over a fire until it coagulated and then formed it into various objects. Intrigued by the substance, the colonial government by the late 18th century was ordering latex army boots from the Amazon Indians. Until the 1830s, buying and selling latex was a minor enterprise, involving a scattering of Portuguese merchants who bought the substance from local rubber tappers who "tapped" or bored a small hole in the outer bark of the trees to drain out the sap.

About 1839, British and North American scientists discovered how to stabilize the raw rubber sap by mixing it with sulfur and heating it. Through this process, called vulcanization, rubber began to be used in the industrializing countries for gaskets, as insulation and protection for electricity, and for tires on bicycles and eventually automobiles. The skyrocketing demand for rubber brought huge numbers of migrants to the Amazon, the region with the largest number of latex-producing trees. While it lasted, the rubber tappers extracted the liquid from the trees, molded it into huge balls of rubber, and sold the balls at local trading posts, buying in return their food and supplies, generally at exorbitant prices. Steamboats financed in London transported the rubber to the ports at Manaus and eventually Belém on the coast, from where it was shipped abroad. The rubber boom created instant millionaires or "rubber barons." The Amazonian port city of Manaus burst forth as an emblem of the boomtown phenomenon. Its population soared from a scattering of settlers to nearly 100,000 people in 1910. It boasted a magnificent opera house constructed with imported materials, in addition to the first electric street lighting of any Brazilian city, piped water and gas, and an elaborate system of floating docks. Foreign capital poured into the region to form trading houses and companies, foremost of which was the Madeira-Mamoré Railway, completed in 1912, which linked Brazil and Bolivia.

Nevertheless, by 1910, the heyday of the Amazon rubber boom was over. Several decades earlier the British Royal Botanic Gardens at Kew had planted some rubber seeds it had smuggled out of Brazil and begun to produce the trees in London hothouses in limited quantities. Seeds were sent to British colonies in Ceylon (Sri Lanka) and Malaya (Malaysia) where they were planted in vast, highly organized plantations. Whereas the Amazon trees were always plagued with fungus and other leaf diseases, the Asian variety proved resistant and capable of producing a much higher yield. Seeking a cheap rubber source for the growing auto industry the Ford Motor Company tried to reproduce in Brazil the successful British colonial plantations in Asia. It built its own plantations where domesticated plants were cultivated in near hothouse conditions at a place named Fordlandia in Santarém. However, the South American trees were never resistant to disease and the production never as lucrative as the Asian variety. With the exception of the years during World War II when the Allied forces were cut off from sources in Asia and forced to draw on rubber from Brazil, the cultivated Amazon latex was not able to compete with the high-yield latex of Southeast Asia. Moreover a synthetic substitute for natural rubber had been developed during World War I, and while a market for natural rubber continued and exists yet today, the prosperous days of the rubber boom ended by the first decades of the 20th century.

Conflicting Views of the Republic

The empire's end was not a major event for much of the citizenry. Few shots were fired, some die-hard monarchists denounced the military coup and invaded Rio's municipal chamber, but not much else passed within the notice of the Brazilian masses. Isolated in rural areas, continuing to labor on the plantations in forms of semislavery, toiling in the sweatshops in Rio de Janeiro, São Paulo, Recife, and other cities, most Brazilians doubted that the republic would mean fundamental changes in their lives.

The change, however, should not be ignored. Even distant political movements influence a society in hundreds of ways. Brazilian historian José Murilo de Carvalho has shown that the masses were most likely more cynical than apathetic. Through church brotherhoods, community groups, and mutual aid societies many ordinary people voiced their demands. They may have been unclear on what the republic itself meant, but they were vocal in their opposition to the elitist and distant rule that had characterized the monarchy. A number of organizations and individuals sought a government that paid attention to the good of the entire society, not simply the desires of a small elite. In the end it is apparent through the demonstrations, petitions, and open revolts that marked the First Republic that rich and poor, workers and factory owners, urban and rural residents had different, and often opposing, notions of what the new government should be.

The Constitution of 1891

The Constitution of 1891 was a compromise document that represented the conflicting views of liberal and conservative elites. It restricted the electorate to literate males over the age of 21, thereby excluding 83 percent of the population. Women, the clergy, soldiers, minors, and the mass of uneducated Brazilians were given few avenues through which to voice their concerns. Indeed, in the first election for president in 1894, only 2 percent of the population voted. The Constitution stipulated several progressive restrictions on the power of the church, including a ban on forming new monastic orders and teaching religion in public schools, and granting special privileges to the clergy. On the other hand, it rescinded a provision that had existed under the empire of requiring the state to provide for public education. In that light, whether religion was taught in public schools or not became something of a moot point. There were almost no schools apart from exclusive, often religious, academies frequented by the children of the wealthy.

The new government was divided into three branches: a judiciary, an executive, and a legislature composed of the Chamber of Deputies and the Senate. The imprint of the United States as a political model was clear in other ways, as well. The Constitution provided for freedom of assembly, separation of church and state, rights to the protection of property, all within a federal system that left considerable power in the hands of the states. Until the end of the First Republic in 1930, Minas Gerais and São Paulo held the reins of power, in close collaboration with the states of Rio de Janeiro, Pernambuco, and Rio Grande do Sul.

An admirer of U.S. politics, Barbosa wrote much of the Constitution of 1891, including in it a federalist design, separation of church and state, and three branches of government. He clashed with the United States, however, at the Second International Peace Conference at The Hague in 1907. Barbosa advocated a system of international justice that accorded smaller and poorer nations equal representation with the powerful and rich nations of Europe and North America. Although the proposal did not pass, having been effectively scuttled by the United

States, Barbosa gained an international reputation for the eloquence of his arguments.

An advocate of progressive reforms, including more power to urban industrial and commercial interests, better working and living conditions for factory workers, and greater restraints on the power of the oligarchy and military, Barbosa ran for president in 1910 and 1919. In the latter campaign he took his platform to the masses throughout the country and gained a considerable following among urban middle-class voters, but he lost nonetheless. A dynamic speaker and tireless writer of political tracts, Barbosa filled 150 volumes with writings on education, civil rights, finance, and law.

The abolitionist campaign and the process of creating the new republic involved many individuals working for decades. Historians are generally anxious to show that no single person can change the course of history on his or her own. Nonetheless, one must acknowledge that occasionally a single individual leaves an indelible imprint on history. Rui Barbosa de Oliveira (1840–1923), one of the foremost proponents of abolition and the republic, was such a person.

Economic Policy

Conflicts between the interests of planters and emerging urban commercial and industrial forces surfaced in the first few years of the republic. Planters whose crop was either no longer in demand, or whose operation had fallen victim to poor soil, mismanagement, bad weather, or an inability to make the transition from slave to free labor turned to the government as they had in the past for assistance. As the republic's first finance minister, Rui Barbosa attempted to generate money to meet these demands, and the many expenses the new government was incurring, by printing money, offering credit to new urban enterprises, and attempting to foster economic recovery in nonagricultural sectors. The plan, called the *encilhamento*, which in Portuguese means "saddling up," did stimulate some domestic production that might have replaced the reliance on imported manufactured goods had it been able to last longer. However, the immediate effect was an inflationary spiral that drove consumer prices high, and a rash of bankruptcies as new unstable enterprises went under or lost out to shady speculators and corruption. With urban sectors angry over high prices, unemployment, and unstable currency, power reverted to the traditional coffee interests.

The vitality of the coffee region and the substantial earnings from exports served to bolster the São Paulo economy. Immigrants were a

Rio de Janeiro street market and fair during the Old Republic. (Hoffenberg Collection)

ready source of cheap labor, while good soil and plentiful land allowed coffee fields to expand westward. The income generated from coffee revenues was transferred through banks to help fuel industrial growth in São Paulo. On the other hand, the federal government did not attempt to actively develop other parts of the country, to enact taxation measures that would have distributed the wealth over a broader section of the populace. It did little to provide basic health and education services that would have benefited the mass of recently emancipated slaves. The early years of the republic were marked by wide disparity between social classes while different sectors expressed a range of perspectives on the success or failure of the new government.

French Influence

For prosperous urban dwellers, the early 20th century was a time for adopting modern ideas. Just as Brazil looked to Europe for markets, investment capital, and technology, the modernizing elite began to mimic European culture. Despite their heavy reliance on British investment, it was to France, not to England, that the elite looked for inspiration in matters of style and culture. They adopted French naturalism more fervently than did their counterparts in other countries of Latin America. Ironically, French culture had been introduced to Brazil by the Portuguese court that fled the Napoleonic invasion. Prince Regent João VI had imported French artists, teachers, artisans, and engineers to build and design botanical gardens, the National Library, secondary and professional schools, and to promote the arts, literature, and science according to the French standard. Indeed the Crown, and the courtiers who surrounded it, never let their political disagreements with France interfere with their general admiration for nearly every aspect of French high culture. After the fall of the monarchy, on through the republic, and to some extent up to the 21st century, French culture has permeated the schools, universities, theater, entertainment world, salons, clubs, and cafés of Brazil's intellectual and elite society.

Regional Challenges

On the other hand, the distant backlands remained largely untouched by the changes affecting the coastal cities. To some extent Brazil could be seen as two separate nations—one of modernizing cities on or near the coast, and one of isolated hamlets in the interior mired in the ways of two centuries earlier. This wide geographical and class disparity was often a cause for political and social upheaval. Revolts had always marked Brazil's history, sometimes involving young military officers, at other times the rural masses, members of the disenfranchised and forgotten urban working class. The 19th century had seen the outbreak of widespread social protest. Three social upheavals had rocked the North, Northeast and remote areas in the 1830s and early 1840s: the War of the Cabanos in Pernambuco and Alagoas (1832–36), the Cabanagem rebellion in Pará (1835–40) and the Balaiada rebellion in Maranhão (1838–41). In each case the participants were poor whites, mestizos, mulattos, slaves, and Indians who were protesting high food prices, poor or nonexistent housing, the brutality of the master class, and the general inattention of government officials to the needs of the poor. Consolidating the hold of the republican government brought about even greater disruption in the traditional methods of assuring order.

There were several reasons for the constancy of discontent among many sections of the population. First, the country was large, poorly serviced, weakly administered, and unprofessionally policed. Railways and roads connected plantations and mines to the ports in order to facilitate the movement of agricultural products and metals out of the country and to bring in machinery and other manufactured goods. Products and services, especially medicine, education, or even any form of diversion, bypassed small towns or humble communities where the majority of Brazilians lived.

Second, even if the government had tried to distribute goods and services to the outlying regions, the system of patriarchal authority inhibited any interference in poor communities considered the personal fiefdom of the planters. Finally, whenever a revolt occurred, the planters, usually through their personally appointed administrators, settled disputes themselves, especially when disagreements involved land ownership, taxes, high prices, wages, and working conditions. They relied on their personal armies to maintain order, on judges who were often their relatives or personal friends to mete out sentences for crimes. Rules and regulations were drawn up by the vast array of appointed officials whose loyalty was to the local planter elite and not to a distant state or federal authority. Protesters, no matter how reasonable their grievances, were written off as "bandits" and "criminals" in the legal reports and even in the histories of the backlands.

During the republic a number of highly significant uprisings and rural movements convulsed the countryside. They were so intense and widespread that the government could not simply dismiss them as the work of a few "outlaws" or "criminals." Several military revolts broke out in the southern state of Rio Grande do Sul where rebellious officers chafed under the centralizing authority of the Rio de Janeiro government. The national army intervened on more than one occasion in the southern state to maintain order.

Padre Cícero and the "Miracle" of Juàzeiro do Norte

In the Northeast, two movements in particular grabbed the attention of the government and of the urban wealthy accustomed to ignoring the goings-on of the backlanders. Both movements seemed to pose a major rejection of republican authority. The first was in the far northern state of Ceará, where Padre (Father) Cícero Romão Batista, a priest known for his exceptional piety, began a campaign in 1889 to have a local holy woman, Maria de Araujo, declared the recipient of a miracle. According to witnesses, the Eucharist had turned to blood in her mouth, moments after the priest administered her communion. Fueled by the backlanders' resentment of new taxes, as well as by their suspicion of the governmental and ecclesiastical central authority, the "miracle" catapulted the tiny town of Juàzeiro do Norte onto the national stage and established it as a site for religious pilgrimages to this day.

The so-called miracle assumed a political importance in Brazilian life beyond its religious roots. With the politically ambitious and astute Padre Cícero at its helm, the campaign grew over the next few decades beyond a holy crusade to have Maria de Araujo canonized a saint into a full-scale challenge to central authority. The campaign haunted the local and national governments for years. For its part the church disavowed the miracle and moved to curtail Padre Cícero's promotional activities, stopping short of removing him from his post. Since the local peasants soon came to consider the priest a saint, attempting to recall him may well have inflamed passions yet further.

Whether Padre Cícero truly believed in the miracle or not was irrelevant to his political aspirations. He clashed with both ecclesiastical and political authorities but used his position in an attempt to improve the disastrous economic plight of the *sertanejos,* or backlanders. He led a group of protesters on a long march to the state capital in Fortaleza in protest over high taxes and low wages, and even managed to overturn, for a while, the state government. Although the movement stayed alive into the 1930s, with Padre Cícero assuming a more political and less religious role until his death in 1934, there were no long-term improvements in the lives of the protesters. Today, Padre Cícero is still considered a saint by many in the Northeast, and thousands of pilgrims gather yearly at his grave in Juàzeiro do Norte to pay him homage.

Antônio Conselheiro

The most significant outbreak of the era, and the most direct challenge to the republican government, was the Canudos rebellion in the 1890s. This religious movement was led by an austere backlands preacher named Antônio Conselheiro (*conselheiro* means the counselor in Portuguese). Conselheiro was born Antônio Vicente Mendes Maciel in the interior of Ceará in 1830. His family was not wealthy, but not poor either, and Antônio received the education of a prosperous youth. He studied mathematics, geography, Latin, French, and Portuguese at a local religious school. Although his father had wanted Antônio to enter the priesthood, those prospects diminished when the young man had to step in to help run his family's failing business.

The turning point in Antônio's otherwise rather ordinary life seemed to come around 1860 when his young wife, a cousin he had married

THE COUNJELOR ACCORDING TO MARIO VARGAJ LLOJA

In his novel *The War of the End of the World*, Peruvian writer Mario Vargas Llosa draws on the historical record for his fictionalized portrayal of the Canudos rebellion. He depicts Antônio Conselheiro's messianic appeal to the backlanders.

> *The man was tall and so thin he seemed to be always in profile. He was darkskinned and rawboned, and his eyes burned with perpetual fire.*
>
> *(. . .) The cowherds and peons of the backlands listened to him in silence, intrigued, terrified, moved and he was listened to in the same way by the slaves and the freemen of the sugarcane plantations on the seacoast and the wives and the mothers and fathers and the children of one and all. Occasionally someone interrupted him—though this occurred rarely, since his gravity, his cavernous voice, or his wisdom intimidated them—in order to dispel a doubt. Was the world about to end? Would it last til 1900? He would answer immediately, with no need to reflect, with quiet assurance, and very often with enigmatic prophesies. In 1900 the sources of light would be extinguished and stars would rain down. But before that, extraordinary things would happen. . . . In 1896 countless flocks would flee inland from the seacoast and the sea would turn into the backlands and the backlands turn into the sea. In 1897 the desert would be covered with grass, shepherds and flocks would intermingle, and from that date on there would be but a single flock and a single shepherd. In 1898 hats would increase in size and heads grow smaller, and in 1899 the rivers would turn red and a new planet world circle through space.*
>
> *It was necessary, therefore, to be prepared. . .*

Source: Vargas Llosa, Mario. *The War of the End of the World*. Translated by Helen R. Lane. New York: Farrar, Straus and Giroux, 1996, pp. 1, 5.

when she was 15 and he 27, left him for a soldier. After that Antônio began to wander the backlands towns, dressed in a long tunic of rough cloth, tied at the waist with a wire. He fasted, spent weeks on the road, slept on the floors of barns and sheds offered by the poor *sertanejos*, and began to counsel the poor. He became known as a *conselheiro*, and began to attract groups of people who followed him from town to town, listening to his preachings. Hardly a prophet of the "hellfire and brimstone" variety, Conselheiro had a soft voice and mostly called on the impoverished *nordestinos* (people of the Northeast) to renounce luxuries, live simply, and await the impending Judgment Day, which was predicted to arrive at century's end. In 1893 he and his followers settled into a town in the state of Bahia that they named Canudos. There Conselheiro sought to develop a religious community.

Conselheiro would seem to have posed little threat to the local government and certainly none at all to the distant state capital in Salvador or to the federal capital in Rio de Janeiro. Calling on impoverished backlands peasants to live simply and await salvation at the Last Judgment could hardly be interpreted as a radical or threatening doctrine. The rural planters, however, were alarmed at the convergence of so many followers on Canudos, transforming it into the second largest city of Bahia after Salvador.

Although Conselheiro never directed his followers to overthrow the government, personally he did reject the monarchy, held the former emperor Dom Pedro II in high esteem, and rejected the Republican Constitution of 1891. A secular, positivist document, the constitution separated church and state, established civil marriages, and imposed an order of taxation requiring every citizen to support the federal government. Conselheiro opposed the republic, and even called on his followers to abstain from paying taxes, though the impoverished masses who camped out in Canudos probably paid very little in taxes anyway. In a widely publicized incident, Conselheiro, rebuffing an emissary from the Catholic Church sent to convince him to submit to proper political and ecclesiastical powers, explained: "In the days of the monarchy, I let myself be taken, for I recognized the government; but today I will not, because I do not recognize the Republic." (da Cunha 1944:167)

Conselheiro probably earned the enmity of the landowners because he interfered with the traditional order and chain of authority that served as the government in the backlands. More important, the Canudos rebellion not only undermined the landowners' authority, but attracted a large number of pilgrims who otherwise would presumably have been lining up docilely, begging for work on the large estates. Conselheiro, in the words of Euclides da Cunha, a São Paulo journalist who wrote about the movement, never displayed "the faintest trace of a political intuition." (da Cunha 1944:160) He actually only became a threat because the Brazilian army, under the command of a series of incompetent and overconfident officers, was unable to defeat the peasants in Canudos. In 1897 the army launched four attacks and finally succeeded in destroying the settlement. During one particularly bloody confrontation on July 14, the soldiers tried to take the town, but were forced back and then ended up slitting the throats of more than 2,000 prisoners. The effects of the debacle reverberated in the distant national capital. When news of the failure of the third assault against Canudos reached Rio de Janeiro, Jacobin crowds, including printers, shopkeepers, and other "persons of property," marched on the seat of government at Catete Palace, attacked monarchist meeting halls en route, and stoned the offices of promonarchist newspapers.

Canudos Defeated

Finally, on October 1, the last assault against Canudos began. The army surrounded the village and began firing 15 cannons into it at point-blank range from a place called Favela Hill that overlooked the town. On October 4, they exploded dynamite and kerosene bombs to eliminate the last resisters, mostly women, children, and the elderly. Conselheiro had died, probably of dysentery, some days before the final defeat and had been buried by the pious villagers. When the army overran the village, soldiers disinterred his body, decapitated it, and posted the head on a pike. The victorious army brandished the bloody trophy at the head of their march from the interior to the state capital in Salvador, on the coast. Upon arrival in the capital, the jubilant soldiers paraded the head through the streets in front of cheering crowds. The victory celebrations continued in Salvador and other coastal cities for the next few weeks, always with the decomposing head of Conselheiro as the central attraction. The spectacle comes to us in the words of Euclides da Cunha. "That horrible face, sticky with scars and pus, once more appeared before the victors' gaze. After that they took it to the seaboard, where it was greeted by delirious multitudes with carnival joy." (da Cunha 1944:476)

Conselheiro and his ragtag followers in Canudos had churned up an emotional response. Brazilians had seen their inept national army repeatedly go down in defeat against a few thousand backlanders. Its importance was in more than the fact that the federal government had to send an army of 10,000 troops, losing half of them to thirst, starvation, and the battle itself, to arrest a religious prophet and his poorly armed peasant followers. Rather, it was important because it showed the lengths to which the landowners would go to maintain the appearance of authority. Antônio Conselheiro posed no direct military or political threat to the republic. He was simply a sign of discontent.

The Canudos affair forced the urban and coastal elite to focus on the immense and boundless interior of the country. To Euclides da Cunha,

100

whose brilliant account, *Rebellion in the Backlands,* is still the main primary source on the revolt, Canudos exemplified the contradictory forces within a society torn between its quest for modernity, on the one hand, and the seeming backwardness that gripped the countryside, on the other. Sent as a journalist from a São Paulo newspaper to cover the army's expeditions against the backlanders, da Cunha for the first time traveled to the interior and there observed a people whose customs, language, and appearance were totally different from those on or near the coast: "What we had to face here was the unlooked-for resurrection, under arms, of an old society, a dead society, galvanized into life by a madman." (da Cunha 1944:161)

Whereas da Cunha admitted an enormous difference between the people of the coast and the interior, he did not denigrate them, but instead he observed that the peasants' humility, oneness with nature, and customs represented the "bedrock of our race." Da Cunha's adventure in the interior led him to criticize the urban, coastal society he had long taken for granted. He asked how "civilized" an army is that marches around with the decomposing head of the defeated Antônio Conselheiro mounted on a pike.

Euclides da Cunha stands somewhat apart from the elite of the era because his experience in the backlands forced him to face the disparities in Brazil. Referring to Brazilians' penchant for aping everything European, he surmised that they had all been "deluded by a civilization which came to us second hand," turning the urban elite, himself included, into "blind copyists," adopting a mode of life completely detached from "our rude native sons, who were more alien to us in this land of ours than were the immigrants who came from Europe." Most of the educated, urban, and coastal Brazilians viewed the inhabitants of the agricultural interior more one-dimensionally: as a barbarous drag on the rest of the country. They pointed to the backlanders' superstition, ignorance, poverty, and absence of cultural and political sophistication as indicative of the problems Brazil had to overcome in order to take its place among the modern nations of the world.

Positivism and Eugenics

Similar to other places of Latin America in the early 20th century, the Brazilian elite drew on popular racist theories contained in positivism, a philosophy similar to Social Darwinism, to condemn the poverty and traditions of the poor. Euclides da Cunha, for example, saw the *sertanejos* as suffering from the effects of the intermingling of Indians,

Vista of Rio de Janeiro, ca. 1890. Guanabara Bay is on the right, the old, center city is in the upper left. Castelo Hill (Morro de Castello) rises up alongside the bay. It was leveled in 1921. (Hoffenberg Collection)

Africans, and Europeans, resulting in a mixed race that supposedly stood at a stage lower than that of whites in the evolutionary hierarchy (a hierarchy that placed white, usually northern Europeans at the top and black Africans at the bottom, with southern Europeans, Native Americans, and Asians at various stages in between). As E. Bradford Burns observes, most of the Latin American intellectuals, as well as almost all the governments in the 19th century, aspired to the same goal under a variety of names: "progress, civilization, development, and, retrospectively, modernization." No matter what the name, "the idea was as constant as it was simple: to copy those aspects of Northern European—and, later, United States—culture which most struck the fancy of the elites, thus creating an imperfect and selective process of remolding their nations after foreign models." (Burns 1979:28–29)

It bears remembering that Latin American elites were not alone in their obsession with promoting European culture or in their preoccupation with issues of race. The 19th century was awash with racialist theories. Notions of racial superiority, encased in theories of biological development, moved from Europe to the rest of the world through the active promotion of eugenics societies. European eugenists divided the world among greater/whiter and lesser/darker races, arguing that the poor were poor because they were biologically unfit. This so-called scientific racism provided a nice cover for European colonialists and imperialists, especially in Africa and Asia. It diverted attention from widening class divisions and tensions in societies at home, while promoting the mythology that progress accompanied European expansion and capitalist development.

Likewise, in those countries such as Brazil, where the elites were frantically copying European culture, a rationale surfaced that blamed apparent human inequalities on "natural" or "biological" factors rather than on the absence of equal opportunity or social justice. Both the Europeans and their emulators in the developing world thereby shifted the blame for the misery of the poor away from Europe, as well as away from the institutions of class and imperial domination the Europeans were promoting, and toward biology, about which they could supposedly do nothing.

"Whitening"

A desire to "whiten" the indigenous and African-descendant population became a preoccupation of social engineers throughout Latin America in the late 19th and early 20th centuries. Already a program was under way in Argentina to eliminate people of African descent from urban areas, and eventually from much of the population. With the assistance of the army, the government forcibly relocated blacks from the cities and dispersed them through the countryside, where they eventually disappeared into the indigenous and white rural population. If the white elite of Brazil found this idea attractive, they never implemented it. Given the overwhelming majority of people of African heritage, such a plan was thought to be unworkable in Brazil. Some social planners did argue that a "whitened" population would emerge naturally after generations of racial mixture between white European immigrants and black, or darker-skinned, Brazilians. One of the best ideological representations of this miscegenationist conception is Modesto Broco's late 19th-century painting with the revealing title *The Redemption of Ham*. It approvingly depicts a family that has moved from black to mulatto to white in three generations through the intermarriage of the daughter of a former slave and an Italian immigrant. The practical implementation of whitening rested with an ambitious immigration policy.

Immigration

The policy of whitening rested on an active plan to foster European immigration. From as early as 1850, nearly four decades before abolition, many in government, planter, and commercial circles had been raising the issue of enticing emigrants from Europe to Brazil. As the century progressed and it became increasingly clear that slavery would not exist long into the future, the call for immigrants had intensified.

The crowded, bustling Rua do Ouvidor (Ouvidor Street) ca. 1885. This was a street in Rio de Janeiro where many immigrants from the Middle East, Italy, and Portugal set up small businesses and artisan shops during the Old Republic. Photo by Marc Ferrez. (Hoffenberg Collection)

There had always been a strong correlation between immigration policy and social change. Planters planned to replace slaves with low-paid immigrant laborers, while abolitionists and antimonarchists had seen the momentous changes at the end of the century as a way of freeing Brazil from its backward image. Immigrants were considered key to transforming that image. Even before the end of slavery in 1888, immigrants had been arriving from Europe. Beginning in the 1880s, organizations such as the Society for the Promotion of Immigration in São Paulo and the Rio de Janeiro Central Immigration Society, in cooperation with the Brazilian government, distributed brochures in Europe advertising steady work at good wages. The organization even offered free ship and train fares guaranteed by the Department of Agriculture for anyone willing to immigrate to Brazil's coffee fields.

From 1889 to 1934, 4.1 million immigrants entered Brazil; 56 percent of them settled in the coffee fields of São Paulo, 58 percent of whom were directly subsidized by the Brazilian state. By the time immigration tapered off in 1949, 4.55 million had arrived, mostly Italians, Spaniards, Portuguese, Germans, Russian and Polish Jews, along with Syrians, Lebanese and other Arabs from the Middle East, and a sizable community of Japanese. More than a million of the immigrants came from Italy, more than all other nationalities combined.

Italian Immigration

Italians assimilated most readily into the dominant Iberian culture of Brazil. They spoke a language that was not so dissimilar from Portuguese, they carried with them the same Catholic Mediterranean culture, and physically Italians were imperceptible from Portuguese and Spaniards, the other major nationalities represented in the wave of immigration. Recruited to the coffee plantations, large numbers of Italians migrated to the cities after fulfilling their labor contracts. They formed the backbone of the industrial working class of São Paulo and Santos.

Whereas southern European immigrants, and Italians in particular, were seen as assimilating easily into the urban society, they were also credited with bringing labor militancy, anarchist, anarcho-syndicalist, and socialist ideas to the labor movement. From the 1890s until the 1920s, immigrants and their Brazilian-born children made up the majority of the working class of São Paulo and Santos, as well as the majority of the labor union leadership. At the height of the labor movement, from the teens until the early 1920s, more than 80 percent of the labor union leadership was foreign-born, and 61 percent came from

Italy alone. In Rio de Janeiro, Portuguese immigrants predominated, and shared the leadership and rank-and-file positions in trade unions with native black and mulatto Brazilians.

Many immigrants to Brazil, as to other countries in the Americas, may have planned to accumulate a "nest egg" and return to their homeland. Statistics from the 1920 census show that of the 444,374 foreigners in São Paulo and Rio de Janeiro only 6,441 had become citizens. It is impossible to say by simply looking at a census table if the foreign-born Brazilians refused citizenship because they planned to return to Europe, or if they were merely reluctant to give up their nationality. They stayed, nonetheless. Italian, Portuguese, and Spanish immigrants were an important section of small businesses, shopkeepers, landlords, and city workers. Many remained in rural areas, laboring on the plantations, or after a number of years became planters themselves. Italian names are highly visible on the list of leading industrialists by the 1920s, indicating that a number of immigrants prospered.

Finally, immigrants who organized for greater rights for working people, a share in the national wealth, for better wages and working conditions helped to bring the language of democracy into Brazil's political discourse. Although the anarchist and socialist movements of the early decades of the 20th century were not successful in winning many demands, the constant agitation in factories and in urban areas changed the political climate. Autocratic rural and urban elites who had paid little attention to the needs of the poor, who were accustomed to being waited on by slaves, and who had ruled Brazil for centuries with little opposition from the lower classes found that the world was changing. Immigrants introduced into Brazilian political culture new demands for equality and rights. This added to the culture of resistance already in existence among the descendants of slaves.

Brazil's Changing Identity

In Brazil, as in North America, immigrants brought with them the culture and traditions of their homelands, creating pockets of the old country in the midst of the new one. As historian of immigration Jeffrey Lesser has shown, the more than 4 million immigrants who arrived between 1872 and 1949 brought with them many characteristics of their homelands and created new ethnic identities. He notes, however, that the nearly 400,000 Asians, Arabs, and Jews were seen as both nonwhite and nonblack. As a result, they posed the greatest challenge to the Brazilian elite's ideas of national identity. Although fewer in number than the Christian Europeans, these immigrants who did not fit with the dominant Catholic, white European culture had a considerable impact on Brazilian life.

Catholic Brazil's racial and religious barriers had always prevented the entrance of free, nonwhite non-Christians. From the 17th century through at least 1942, immigration policies were explicitly and unapologetically discriminatory. In the colonial period, heretics (the code word for Jews and Muslims) were banned from entering the country. New Christians (recent converts to Christianity) and *marranos* (the derogatory term used to describe New Christians who secretly practiced Judaism) were actually fairly numerous despite the ban. They had either entered the colony clandestinely or came legally to the Northeast in the 17th century when it was under Dutch control and stayed on after the Dutch were expelled. Throughout Brazil, after separation from Portugal in 1822, non-Christian religions were allowed, but they were subject to constant harassment.

Asian Immigration

The first non-European immigrants came from China in the 19th century. Concerned that European wage laborers were neither economically cheap nor socially servile, entrepreneurs and planters looked to China as a source from which to recruit new workers. The first Chinese were brought in 1854 when the imperial government contracted with a British firm to bring 6,000 Chinese laborers. The total number of Chinese who came to Brazil during the 19th and 20th centuries never totaled more than a few thousand. Some came legally and some were smuggled in by traders anxious to sell "coolie" labor to ready buyers in the far North and in the Northeast.

Despite the low number of Chinese, the argument over allowing Asians into the country polarized Brazilian society. One faction felt that Chinese were willing workers, that they would provide a needed middle ground between the white/black poles inherited from the days of slavery, and that they were a more compliant workforce than the white Europeans. Others argued strenuously to prohibit the entrance of any Asians because they were not white and not Christian. This faction argued that Brazil should only admit white Christians because they would "improve" the race. According to this racist theory, the Chinese would further degenerate Brazil's population, which supposedly was already suffering from the prevalence of indigenous and African people. Few Chinese came to Brazil, but the controversy their entrance engendered was important. It served as the precursor to an intense debate over whiteness, national identity, and the racial make-up of post-slavery Brazil.

The much larger group of non-Europeans came from the Middle East, North Africa, and Japan. Since many immigrants from Syria, Lebanon, and North Africa were Christian, groups in Brazil who might have protested the entrance of non-Europeans were less concerned. Their supporters argued that the members of these communities hailed from lands that had sided with the Iberians in the Crusades and should as a result be considered white. The logic of this position revealed the extent to which racial categories and prejudices continually readjust over time from religion to skin color to other features, and then sometimes back again. Since fewer than 200,000 Middle Eastern and Arab immigrants came to Brazil, and those that did dispersed in many different cities, the intense debate that engulfed the issue of Asian immigrants did not as closely affect Arabs.

Japanese Immigrants

From the time of their first arrival in 1908, the Japanese formed the largest single national group of non-European immigrants. In 1890 the government prohibited Asian and black immigration unless specifically authorized by an act of Congress. Under pressure from powerful planters who saw Asian immigrants as a way of cheaply filling their labor shortage, the Brazilian government lifted the restriction in 1907. On June 18, 1908, the Japanese vessel *Kasato Maru* docked in Santos, the port for the city and state of São Paulo. The ship carried 165 families, a total of 786 people, who had come from Japan to work as "colonists" in the coffee fields of Brazil. Over the next six years, approximately 14,200 immigrants, referred to by the Japanese word *nikkei* (Japanese-American) were brought under similar contracts. Most left the plantations after fulfilling their labor contracts and moved to the city and suburbs of São Paulo.

The flow of immigrants from Japan was interrupted at different points because of wars (especially during the 10 years surrounding World War II) and other restrictions, but continued until 1961. The estimated more than 250,000 *nikkei* settled in São Paulo (73 percent) and Paraná (20 percent), with a scattering to other states: Mato Grosso (2.5 percent) and Pará (1.2 percent). Originally concentrated in agriculture, especially in truck farming, the community spread to many social niches, in particular commerce and, since the influx of Japanese

São Paulo's "Little Tokyo" today. The Tori gate designates the entrance to a Shinto shrine. (New York Public Library Photo Collection)

investment beginning in the 1960s, into industry. Although there have been two state ministers in the government of Japanese background, most of the *nikkei* have concentrated in business and in the intellectual and artistic strata. They have had little impact on Brazilian political life. Through natural increase the Japanese Brazilian community is estimated at approximately 800,000 and is now in its fourth generation. It is the largest concentration of Japanese outside of Japan.

The Continuing Debate over Race and Racism

The entrance of people of Asian and Middle Eastern background was important because of their influence on the debate over whiteness and what constituted the Brazilian national identity. According to Lesser, Syrian, Lebanese, and Japanese immigrants and their descendants not only helped to transform the Brazilian national identity, but also widened the cultural understanding of race. They opened up the so-called triangle theory, which held that Brazilian society was created from the "collision of three races": Africans (blacks), Europeans (whites), and indigenous people. After disease and genocidal policies from the colonial period onward decimated the indigenous population, some social scientists argued that the society was on an African (black)/European (white) continuum. According to that paradigm, if a person is not African or indigenous in origin, he/she must be white. With immigration, however, the cultural make-up has become more complex.

Whereas Brazil may have avoided the intensely racially segregated history the United States has experienced, it has had a history of racism and racially exclusive policies. On January 6, 1921, the Brazilian Congress passed Article 5 of Federal Decree No. 4247, prohibiting black immigrants from entering Brazil. In the next decade, the government imposed these prohibitions on anyone it judged "African" or "Asian," including those who had never even been to Africa or Asia. However, in a twist from blatant racial exclusion policies promulgated in the early decades of the 20th century in the United States, Brazil has attempted to conceal its racist policies. For example, in the 1920s and 1930s the government kept its "whites only" policy quiet and was extremely reluctant to admit that it did not accept black immigrants. When blacks sought to enter Brazil, as a number did, they were simply denied visas. The government's secrecy was based in a kind of "out of sight, out of mind" notion. If racist policies were kept quiet, they reasoned, then protest could be avoided. To some extent this has actually been successful as far as quelling protest is concerned, but it has not done much to alleviate the causes of racial prejudice.

The Political Consequences of Immigration

Political views on immigration were often contradictory, pitting diverse sectors of ruling groups against one another. Some politicians and planters simply wanted to bring in immigrants to fill a labor shortage on the plantations so as to keep the price of labor low. With competition between former slaves and immigrants, those planters argued, they would be able to keep their labor costs down and continue earning the same profits as they had with slave labor. Others saw the influx of immigrant labor quite differently. This group, many of them from the progressive sector of the republican government, argued that European immigrants would bring the virtues of hard work, thrift, and decency to Brazil and that these virtues would eventually replace the traditions of the planter aristocracy as the backbone of Brazilian agriculture. These sentiments were more popular among urban liberals than rural planters.

In reality, neither planter nor urban liberal was able to reconfigure Brazil's culture based on immigration alone. In the first place, most of the immigrants, whether from Europe, Asia, or the Middle East were escaping debt servitude and semifeudal conditions in their homeland not dissimilar from those in the countryside of Brazil. In addition, recent arrivals to the countryside from Europe or Asia were given little incentive to stay and work the land. The planters who exerted strong influence over government policy resisted sharing the wealth of the countryside with the new arrivals. The immigrants found themselves working long hours under brutal conditions for low wages, again not so dissimilar from the conditions they left behind. No part of the immigration program stipulated that the new arrivals to Brazil would be given land and the resources to work it. Contrary to the desires of the planters who wanted cheap labor, or the urban liberals who wanted to populate the countryside with industrious small farmers, immigrants had no choice but to abandon the countryside. They left the rural areas as soon as they could and took jobs in rapidly growing cities.

The republic did not challenge the political control of the coffee barons or landowners. Living and working conditions remained deplorable for most urban and rural workers, even little changed from the days of slavery. In addition, the new republic's leaders were unwilling to allow the political participation of either the rural peasantry or the urban proletariat in the national political process. In many ways the Brazilian countryside resembled the South of the United States after the era of Reconstruction. By the 1890s, southern cotton planters had overturned the reform measures imposed after the Civil War, and the former slaves were tied to the land as sharecroppers in conditions much like those of the antebellum years. A traveler to rural Mississippi or Alabama in the late 19th century, and on into the 20th, might have thought that the Confederacy had won the war and not the Union. That same traveler would have found similar conditions in the Brazilian coffee regions of the Center-South, the old sugar-producing zones of the Northeast, and the extensive backlands.

Despite the move from monarchy to republic and slave to wage labor, many aspects of Brazilian society and culture stayed mired in the past. Whereas the planters wholeheartedly embraced a modern economic system that granted them healthy profits from their coffee exports, and sought to bring in immigrants to work the plantations, they clung to the traditional cultural values of the plutocracy. As for the former slaves, many remained tied to the land even after abolition. They were forced to work as debt peons or sharecroppers on the properties of their previous owners. Decades after the May 13, 1888, decree that freed them, many former slaves worked on plantations, in debt, unable to leave, and with no possibility of ever owning land or rising above their miserable conditions. Jorge Amado, one of Brazil's foremost novelists, relayed a fictional account in *The Violent Land* that stood very close to reality. In his graphic portrayal of the life of the backlands workers on a northeastern cacao plantation, an old man notes, "I was a lad in the days of slavery. My father was a slave, my mother also. But it wasn't any worse then than it is today. Things don't change; it's all talk." (Amado 1945: 85).

In the end, the republic may not have transformed Brazilian society with one fell swoop, but it did begin the process of introducing changes in the political and social scene. Immigrants arrived from Europe, Asia, and the Middle East, transforming the racial and cultural identity of the population. Whereas the power of the rural planters remained entrenched, the republic opened up the possibility that new commercial and industrial forces would become important players in future economic and political policies. Despite warnings from Euclides da Cunha that Brazil was dividing into two incompatible lands—one in the cities along the coast and one in the interior—the republican leaders enacted few policies to improve life for the masses of people isolated in the countryside. More than geographic, the divisions were between the haves and the have-nots in urban as well as rural areas.

6

SOCIETY AND POLITICS
IN THE FIRST REPUBLIC
(1890–1930)

The years from 1890 to 1930 were noted for widespread demographic changes. Many emigrants from Europe abandoned the harsh labor and servile working conditions in the coffee fields and moved to the cities. Industrial development in São Paulo and Minas Gerais, and commercial expansion in Rio de Janeiro and Santos (the port for São Paulo state) saw the increase in urban population and an accompanying shift in power from rural to urban areas. The cities grew, along with urban culture and importance, beginning a trend toward urbanization that stands as one of the key features of today's Brazil.

Brazil in the European Mind

Prior to the late 19th century little had been written about Brazil apart from scientific tracts describing the ecological riches of the Amazon basin. What most Europeans knew of Brazil centered on the country's geography and plant and animal life. Beginning in the 18th century Amazonia became a favorite exploratory site for European scientists. In 1736, a French mathematician, Charles-Marie de La Condamine, explored the region, and through his writings he informed the European public of the abundance of plant resources, notably latex sap from rubber plants, quinine, and curare. In addition he measured the river's depth, its falls, and speed. The Prussian Alexander von Humboldt visited the area at the turn of the 18th century, followed by several expeditions of Austrians, Swiss naturalists, and scientists during the following 50 years.

Despite the forays of European explorers, adventurers, and scientists, and despite their writings that both informed and titillated the reading public with references to exotic civilizations, the vast South American jungle was little explored until the 19th century. As for the rest of Brazil, until the late 19th century, apart from travelers' accounts detailing the abusive treatment of slaves and descrying the horrors of the plantation system, Brazil's potential as a vast, rich country was unknown outside its borders.

Europe was slow to recognize Brazil's contribution to letters and sciences, but even Portugal acknowledged that its former colony contributed one of the most important novelists of the 19th century: Joaquim Maria Machado de Assis (1839–1908). The son of a black father and a Portuguese mother, he received little formal education before entering the printer's trade and becoming a journalist. He founded and was the first president of the Brazilian Academy of Letters. Along with José de Alencar (1829–77), Machado de Assis was one of the first major Brazilian writers to experiment with language and structure, drawing on the views of the common person.

Machado de Assis's masterpiece was the novel *Dom Casmurro* in which he depicted the life of the common man in Rio de Janeiro under the empire. The popularity of *Dom Casmurro* and other of Machado de Assis's books brought to the reading public of Brazil and Portugal the twists of phrase found only in Brazilian Portuguese. Brazil, and most particularly the urban culture of Rio de Janeiro, was beginning to have a place in literary circles outside the parochial confines of the old empire.

Uruguayan author Eduardo Galeano has pointed to the irony of Machado de Assis's popularity in an urban world obsessed with copying everything European. "He is the great Latin American novelist of this century. His books lovingly and humorously unmask the high society of drones that he, son of a mulatto father, has conquered and knows better than anyone. Machado de Assis tears off the fancy wrapping, false frames of false windows with a European view, and winks at the reader as he strips the mud wall." (Galeano 1987:257).

Rio de Janeiro

As the new century unfolded, the republican government wanted to communicate to the rest of the world that Brazil was now a country with enormous economic potential They placed their hope in attracting investments in and trade with the lovely and impressive capital of Rio de Janeiro. Rio was geographically well situated to service ships passing from the Brazilian Northeast to Buenos Aires farther south; the harbor was wide, deep, and sheltered from the ocean on a large bay. Rio de Janeiro was then, and is still, breathtakingly beautiful, with the blue sea rimming high rocky mountains and lower hills covered with tropical vegetation. As the capital of the newly formed republic, Rio de Janeiro hosted foreign dignitaries and travelers from Europe and North America. It was one of the first cities that independent commercial agents and merchants from established European firms encountered in their search for stronger trade relations with Latin America. Despite the fact that the state of Rio de Janeiro no longer produced much coffee, the majority of the São Paulo crop still passed through Rio's port. The word on Brazil was getting out. A small but nonetheless promising literature extolling the country's virtues, chronicling the beauty of Rio de Janeiro, and discussing Brazil's geography and natural resources began to appear in libraries and bookstores in England, France, and Germany.

Poor Sanitation and Epidemics

The main problem that stood in the way of the elite's pretensions to greatness was the poor state of public health in the capital city, as well as in the other coastal cities of Recife, Salvador, and Santos. Rio de Janeiro was especially unhealthy not just because it was in the tropics but because it rested on a few strips of land wedged between sharply rising hills, the ocean, and the bay. The land flooded during the rainy season, when water from the bay rose above the ineffective retaining walls and poured into the streets. Because the drainage system was so inadequate, it remained marshy even after the water receded. Worse, this battle between land and sea meant that for much of the year pools of stagnant water stood in the downtown areas, providing an ideal breeding ground for mosquitoes carrying yellow fever and malaria. A British traveler described Rio in the late 19th century as a "labyrinth of narrow streets, some not more than seven yards wide. West and north of the busy and squalid port area the city is built around marsh and swamps. Here where the poorer inhabitants congregate, is a happy hunting-ground for the yellow fever scourge." (Bell 1914:20)

Epidemics periodically ravaged the capital, particularly the poor districts. In 1850, a massive epidemic of yellow fever left 90,000 ill and 4,160 dead. Between 1850 and 1908, the disease returned to claim another 60,000 victims, 15,179 of them in major epidemics between 1890 and 1898. In 1891, a year in which thousands of new immigrants entered the capital, four terrible epidemics struck—yellow fever, malaria, smallpox, and influenza—leaving 4,454 dead from yellow fever alone. In addition, typhoid, malaria, dysentery, and tuberculosis continued to devastate the populace in the years when the most destructive epidemics stayed away. Although wealthy residents were able to escape the city during epidemics, they were distressed at the severity of the yellow fever outbreaks and the damage that the presence of disease was doing to the reputation of Brazil's coastal cities among foreign business circles. Since ships usually stopped in Rio and Santos before traveling on to Montevideo, Uruguay, and Buenos Aires, Argentina, captains risked carrying disease to other ports and infecting personnel over a wide stretch of the continent. During the epidemic seasons, officials at the ports of neighboring countries refused entry to any ship whose last stop was Rio, which was enough to keep most shipping companies from docking in the city during the hot summer months of December through March.

On the one hand, the epidemics and abysmal health and sanitation threatened commerce and foreign trade. On the other, the decrepit state of sanitation seemed to epitomize the ineptness of the republic and to call into question what, if anything, had been gained under the new government. The many failed military expeditions against Canudos had shaken the public's confidence in the government. There was known to be widespread discontent among the military forces over morale and low pay, and rumors of impending coups, all of which the population found unsettling. One Carioca, as the residents of Rio de Janeiro are called, commented: "From a practical and utilitarian point of view, the population of the city of Rio de Janeiro has not gained any advantage from the Republic; on the contrary, life here has become much more difficult." (*Jornal do Brasil* 1891:2)

Crime and Disorder

A further outcry involved an increase in crime, including prostitution and other signs of urban vice in the most central areas of the capital city. Observers complained that visiting dignitaries and businessmen, along with foreign travelers, were being accosted as soon as they left the ship's dock. A key complaint involved the abysmal state of law enforcement and the near absence of an official police force.

Organized gangs made up of practitioners of *capoeira*, a deadly martial art perfected by runaway slaves, fought for territory in the gambling, crime, and prostitution rings that proliferated in Rio de Janeiro and other cities at the turn of the 20th century.

Capoeira is an extremely rapid type of combat that relies on kicks, sometimes delivered by leaping through the air and attacking an opponent. Slaves developed this technique to compensate for having their hands bound. With fast and tricky movements, rebellious slaves and runaways were able to inflict considerable damage on their opponents. Variants of *capoeira* developed that involved use of the hands armed with machetes *(maculele)* or with sticks *(maracatu)*.

Capoeira reached its pinnacle as a form of fighting during the Old Republic when law and order stood on fragile footing in most of the cities, unemployment and casual employment were widespread, and ruthless street gangs existed as the arbiters of law. Politicians and the wealthy hired *capoeiristas* as their own personal bodyguards. Local gang bosses arranged for these bodyguards to serve as private security forces protecting the mansions and businesses of prosperous urban residents. In an attempt to replace the gangs with a civilian police force, the federal government passed a law that created a special police force designated solely to wiping out the *capoeiristas*. The law imposed rigid penalties on anyone caught practicing the deadly martial art, including expatriation or exile to the distant region of Acre. Despite the efforts of a series of police captains, many of them skilled *capoeiristas* themselves, the practice did not die out.

One method of getting around the law against *capoeira*, which was on the books until 1920, was to transform its practice into a "folk dance" and form of traditional Afro-Brazilian art. Today *capoeira* can

Contemporary capoeira performance. This martial art was at one time practiced widely by gangs of young men who fought on the streets of Brazil's cities. (AP Photo/Silviol Izquierdo)

117

be seen in street festivals and arenas, with the practitioners engaging in combat to the beat of drums and the one-stringed instrument, the *berimbau*. Outside the law, however, gangs engaging in drug trafficking and other illegal activities continue to use the traditional martial arts in combat.

Urban Renewal

On December 18, 1889, the new republican government passed a public health and sanitation bill calling for a series of improvements in the health of Brazil's cities. The 1889 law was only partially implemented, but it did signal a change in the earlier haphazardly enforced public health and disease prevention laws. It centralized plans to change sanitation codes and establish prophylactic and medical care, and it set in motion a beautification and renovation campaign in the capital that would later prove controversial. Under the terms of the law, a London-based firm, the Rio de Janeiro City Improvements Company, began widening and paving streets, excavating for a dump, and developing a system for the collection and incineration of garbage.

In 1902, Francisco de Paula Rodrigues Alves was elected president of the republic. Under his authority and at his direction the renovation of the Brazilian capital became a top priority. Rodrigues Alves came to federal office with a well-established reputation for overseeing urban renewal plans. While governor of the state of São Paulo, he had successfully renovated the state capital, including the installation of a lighting system and network of electric streetcars by the São Paulo Tramway, Light, and Power Company and a widespread sanitation and public health program under the auspices of the municipal government. Rodrigues Alves, a native of Brazil's coffee-producing region, understood the pivotal role of Rio de Janeiro in promoting the import/export market and furthering Brazil's reputation abroad as an attractive center of commerce and capital expansion. Because he came to the presidency from a regional background as a conservative politician under both the empire and the republic, and because he was a member of a prominent Paulista (resident of São Paulo) family, Rodrigues Alves was in the enviable position of being a man with support from all major political sectors. He was, however, personally motivated for pushing the reforms: He had lost a child in one of Rio's yellow fever epidemics. As a reforming president, Rodrigues Alves was is said to have been the ideal instrument for enacting change and bringing together old and new forces.

Soon after his inauguration, the president authorized the beginning of the massive public works project, paid for by loans from English banks, new taxes, and bonds. He convened a team of experts, headed by the city's elderly mayor, Francisco Pereira Passos, to draw up a renovation plan. The commission studied the then well-known urban renewals that had transpired in Buenos Aires, Paris, and London during the late 19th century. In addition to the mayor, other members of the team included the engineer Lauro Müller and the ministers of transportation and of public works, Paulo de Frontin and Francisco de Bicalho, respectively. The planners and construction crews worked at an astonishing pace. Between 1903 and early 1905, they demolished 590 buildings in the center of Rio de Janeiro, including the crowded tenements (called *cortiços,* meaning "beehives") that housed most of the city's poor and working-class residents. The tenements were notorious for their poor ventilation, cramped quarters, and lack of plumbing, and the epidemics always registered the highest death toll among those who crammed into the narrow dark rooms. Nevertheless, they were the only places available to most poor people. As a result, in the name of public health, the city removed the only housing the poor could afford and moved thousands out into the streets.

The showcase for the renovations was the transformed Avenida Central (later renamed Avenida Rio Branco). The stately artery was lined with institutions of cultural refinement in their best Parisian beaux arts facades: the Municipal Theater, the Monroe Palace, the National Library, the Academy of Fine Arts, the Grunle Hotel, the military and naval clubs, and the new offices of the city's main daily newspapers, the *Jornal do Commercio, Jornal do Brasil,* and *O Paiz.* Considered the personal triumph of Paulo de Frontin, the Avenida Central was modeled after the main streets of Paris and displayed the Brazilian variant of French civilization down to the choice of institutions it showcased (fine arts, academia, journalism, the state, commerce, and tourism) and the precision of the facades. Frontin had worked from a central plan and had drawn on the design pioneered in the Parisian Great Works made famous by Georges Eugene Haussmann. The style was uniform to the extent that the architect for every building had to build according to specified height and width requirements as determined by a jury that oversaw the process.

A British traveler, Alured Grey Bell, echoed the sentiments of many European observers of the day. He declared the renovation "a comprehensive project boldly conceived and brilliantly executed," and raved that "ugly specimens of architecture without art and habitations without hygiene" were torn down and replaced with "many elegant shops, several 'picture palaces,' and scores of business buildings, banks, shipping offices, import houses and others." (Bell 1914:23) The greatest compliment was the declaration at the opening ceremonies for the Avenida Central that the renovation had even surpassed the recent reforms in Rio's archrival, Buenos Aires.

The project in a little more than six years filled marshland, channeled water run-offs into a series of pipes and canals, constructed a boulevard and seaside promenade, widened and opened streets so that the sea breezes could transverse the city, modernized the port facilities, and connected the docks by rail with the surrounding countryside. The Beira-Mar, a retaining wall against the sea topped by a promenade that started at the south end of the Avenida Rio Branco, just behind the Monroe Palace, and stretched to Praia Vermelha (Red Beach) at the northern edge of Copacabana, was one of the most heralded of the improvements. Although the majority of the city's population made little use of the several-mile-long promenade, it was quite popular with British visitors and businessmen as a place to stroll, be seen, and greet friends. No matter that it was essentially off limits to the majority of Rio's poor, a local paper proclaimed it a sign of "the Rio of the future." Curiously, it was a future in which the poor were quite literally held in the dark. By 1905 downtown Rio de Janeiro was electrically lighted, while most of the areas where the poor and working class lived had yet to be connected even to the existing system of gas illumination.

From 1903 to 1911, new docks, with an expanded system of warehouses, wider and deeper berths for ships, British-style cranes for unloading, and new piers and landfills, replaced the outdated waterfront. The importance of the harbor and dock renovations should not be underestimated. Though surpassed by Santos in later years as the leading port for the export of coffee, Rio de Janeiro as late as 1906 still handled 41 percent of Brazil's imports. Because many foreign visitors, businessmen and diplomats disembarked in Rio, it was essential that the city leave a positive impression in the minds of travelers and potential investors. The modern port enhanced the already breathtaking entrance to the city through the mouth of Guanabara Bay.

Eradicating Disease

In March 1903, President Rodrigues Alves appointed Oswaldo Gonçalves Cruz the director general of public health. This appointment signaled the beginning of new aspect of the urban renewal plans: the offensive

The European influence was apparent on the newly renovated Avenida Central (later Rio Branco), ca. 1908. (Hoffenberg Collection)

against disease and the periodic epidemics that ravaged the city. Cruz had received his medical degree from the Faculty of Medicine in Rio de Janeiro in 1892 at the remarkably young age of 20. He had studied at the Pasteur Institute in Paris, the foremost center of microbiological research in the world at that time. Scientists from all over the world came to the Pasteur Institute to learn of the latest research on eradicating tropical disease in the French colonies in Africa and Southeast Asia. When Oswaldo Cruz returned to Brazil in 1899, he oversaw a campaign to stop the spread of bubonic plague in the port city of Santos and was subsequently given full authority to carry out the sanitation of Rio.

In addition to the sanitation of Havana, New Orleans, and other tropical and semitropical cities, the full-scale assault on yellow fever in Rio de Janeiro stands as a landmark in the history of disease prevention and control. Oswaldo Cruz based his plan for Rio on the findings of Cuban physician Carlos Finlay (1833–1915) and the successful eradication of yellow fever carried out under the direction of the

U.S. military physician Walter Reed (1851–1902) in Havana in 1900. The campaign against yellow fever involved destroying the breeding grounds for the *Aedes aegypti* mosquito and its larvae and ordering the drainage of pools of stagnant water. Plague was to be eliminated by killing rats and using vaccines and serums against the disease in victims. Smallpox could be wiped out with vaccinations, now common in much of the world but then available only to a few in Brazil. Dr. Cruz's public health crews, who earned the name "mosquito inspectors," moved throughout the city, spraying, killing rats, ordering the demolition of all unsanitary housing, and systematically implementing the various aspects of the code.

Opposition to Urban Renewal

Many of the city's poor and working-class residents were hostile to the public health plan. They argued that the renovations only made the downtown pretty for the city's elite and foreign visitors. The tenements where the poor were forced to live, were earmarked for removal to make way for the beautifications, and no housing was built in their place. Fearful of vaccination and poorly informed of its benefits, people resisted getting smallpox immunizations. Vaccination, it seemed, was merely the most tangible aspect of a sanitation drive from a health department that meted out different treatment for rich and poor. To many, the public health measures did not seem to improve the health of the poor; rather, they appeared to make matters worse. The city exploded in riot on November 11, 1904, the day the mandatory vaccinations were to begin. The disturbances ended four days later, leaving much of central Rio in shambles.

No matter how angry were the protests of the city's poor, once the dust settled, and the protest's leaders jailed, exiled, or killed, the urban renewal proceeded on schedule. In the end, the city's poor were moved from the downtown to the distant suburbs and company-style towns rimming the outskirts. In subsequent years they took up residence in the shantytowns, called *favelas,* that began to dot the urban landscape of Rio and all Brazilian cities. The origin of the word *favela* is a telling reminder of the governmental inattention to the country's least empowered. *Favela* is the name of a plant, and it was from Favela Hill that the Brazilian army launched its last assault on Canudos in 1897. When the soldiers got back home to Rio they demanded pay for their service but received none from the inept and bankrupt government. They therefore camped out on a hill above the war ministry that they christened Favela

Hill, after the one in Bahia. As more and more shantytowns formed in Rio beginning in the first years of the 20th century, they came to be called *favelas,* and their residents *favelados,* as they are called today. The term is used interchangeably with *slum* or *shantytown,* but a *favela* is technically a residential area that stands outside the municipal system of taxes, distribution of city services, postal delivery, and even law enforcement.

Over the years, Rio de Janeiro has been nicknamed a *cidade marvilhosa* (marvelous city) because of its natural beauty and vivacious culture. Unfortunately the city has not provided all its residents with the access to beaches, lighting, sanitation, and health so often extolled in tourist literature. In addition, the repression that greeted the November 1904 riot became a common feature of political administration during the republic, as the republican liberals further retreated from any earlier democratic-reformist impulses and opted for authoritarian solutions to the problems of urban society. As is evident today, the problems have remained and even intensified. Government inattention to food and housing shortages, poor transportation service, and deplorable sanitary conditions have provoked discontent and rioting, in Rio's working-class neighborhoods and in the shantytowns of other cities of Brazil to this day.

The Alliance of "Coffee and Cream"

The other major urban development in the early years of the 20th century occurred in the coffee-growing region of São Paulo. Whereas Rio de Janeiro was attracting the attention of the federal government in its plans to showcase a beautiful capital city, São Paulo was beginning its ascent toward becoming the foremost industrial city and region of the country. São Paulo had grown to importance in the later days of the empire, having become the center of the abolitionist movement. The crucial transformation in the Republican Party occurred because the planters of São Paulo, key members of the slaveholding elite, declared themselves in favor of abolition. When slavery ended in 1888 and the republic was declared in 1889, the Paulista (as the residents of São Paulo are called) elite saw their chance to assume control of the nation's political structure.

In 1890, the Paulistas formed what came to be known as the "coffee with cream" (*café com leite*) alliance with their powerful counterparts in bordering Minas Gerais. The name derived from São Paulo's importance in producing coffee and Minas Gerais's importance in dairy products.

The São Paulo/Minas Gerais bloc controlled politics, in cooperation with key members of the Rio de Janeiro government, until 1930. Just as Rio was growing, so too was São Paulo, probably at a faster rate. Between 1890 and 1920, with the arrival of emigrants from Portugal, Italy, Spain, the Middle East, and Japan, São Paulo's population grew from 65,000 to 600,000.

The industrialists of São Paulo became highly successful because of the importance of coffee as Brazil's leading export commodity. Coffee magnates invested in other aspects of basic industry while revenues from the coffee exports poured in to enrich the Paulista banking establishments. Although during the republic São Paulo was not a pivotal cultural center as was Rio de Janeiro, it was beginning to show signs of becoming the country's major city. When in the 1960s the federal capital was moved from Rio to Brasilia, the old capital began to lose some of its importance to the dynamic cultural and economic center in São Paulo.

Unlike Rio de Janeiro, where the population was employed primarily in dockworks, small manufacturing, and commercial enterprises, São Paulo saw the rise of a major industrial working class. As industry grew from 1890 to 1920, so, too, did the working class and labor union militancy. During the republic there were frequent street demonstrations against inadequate housing and high prices in Rio de Janeiro. By contrast, in São Paulo the protesters were more often trade unionists.

Working-class Militancy: The 1917 General Strike

From 1917 to 1921, Paulista anarchist- and communist-inspired trade unions led a series of general strikes for higher wages, better working conditions, an eight-hour workday, and union recognition. The largest strike occurred in 1917. It began when women workers at the Rudolfo Crespi textile mill walked out after their demand for a 25 percent wage increase was refused. The women were joined by the men in the mill, and the strike spread from textiles to other industries. Under the coordination of the São Paulo Committee in Defense of the Proletariat, a city-wide confederation of labor leaders, a general strike closed down nearly the entire city during the months of June and July. The city's leading newspaper, *O Estado de São Paulo*, estimated that 20,000 workers were on strike by July 12. Effectively shut down were all the workshops, mills, factories, gas and light companies, and most transportation. On July 14, the leading industrialists of the city met with the committee's

Child laboring in a factory, ca. 1910. This was a common feature of factory life during the early years of the century. (Hoffenberg Collection)

representatives and offered a 20 percent wage increase, union recognition, no reprisals against those who had been on strike, and a promise to "improve the moral, material and economic conditions of the São Paulo working force." (Dulles 1973:53).

Social peace was short-lived, and labor militancy accompanied the growth in industries over the next decades. The city of São Paulo grew from a population of 239,820 in 1900 to 1,033,202 in 1934. In his study of the Paulista working class, Joel Wolfe points to the confluence of many problems affecting working people that contributed to their increased militancy. The city was dangerous, epidemics were frequent, living conditions unsanitary, cramped, unsafe, and frequently menacing. Workers responded with walkouts, an attempted general strike in 1919, the formation of factory commissions throughout the 1920s to voice unified demands to the industrialists, and, finally, organizing into left-wing parties. The Brazilian Communist Party formed in 1920. Although the party was never large, it drew to it some of the foremost factory organizers and early anarchist trade unionists and played a strong role in raising worker consciousness during the 1920s.

Workers' demands for higher wages and better working conditions fell on deaf ears. Even in the face of widespread walkouts, industrialists relied on repression, backed by the army, to crush strikes and break up picket lines. The militancy of the São Paulo workers, however, was established during the republic.

Cities of the Northeast: Salvador and Recife

During the republic, as the Southeast grew, the Northeast continued its precipitous decline. Nonetheless, two of Brazil's major cities have long been Recife and Salvador da Bahia (which is often called Bahia) in the Northeast. Founded in 1549, Salvador was the most important city in Brazil's early years. It was the capital until 1763, when the court moved to Rio de Janeiro, but it remained one of the wealthiest and largest cities until the late 19th century. The wealth that poured out of the sugar economy is most apparent in Salvador, a city of ornate churches, luxurious houses, and some of the finest representations of colonial architecture in the Americas. As the center of the slave trade in the Northeast, Salvador was, and remains, a city with a majority black and mulatto population. When Brazil's political and economic center shifted to the south, Salvador's centrality to Brazilian culture endured. Not only was it the center of African culture, with a dispro-portionately high number of major black artists, musicians, and lite-rati hailing from Bahia, it was also a center of slave resistance. Today Salvador da Bahia is the city most associated with Afro-Brazilian music and culture, and it shares with Rio de Janeiro a zestful, ener-getic popular culture, and street life.

In contrast, Recife, the capital of Pernambuco, was the key north-eastern city most associated with commerce and early manufacturing. During the 19th century, it served as a center of opposition to the growing power of the federal government in Rio de Janeiro. Recife had grown up in the 16th century as the commercial center of the sugar trade and was during that time the largest city in Brazil. By the late 19th century, it had a population of 100,000, but its growth was mostly due to migrants who poured in from the increasingly impoverished coun-tryside. Different from Salvador which, despite the decline in sugar production and the loss of political power, retained its importance as a cultural center, Recife in the early 20th century came to be seen more and more as the capital of a declining region.

Republican Politics

The big agricultural interests of São Paulo and Minas Gerais dominated national politics throughout the republic. When the republic came to an end in 1930, it did so largely because the alliance between the two powerful states had broken down and because the interests of the urban sector, both entrepreneurs and workers, assumed greater prominence in Brazilian national life. From 1889 to 1930, the urban sectors experimented with flexing their muscles, to greater or lesser degrees of success. In the midst of periodic upheavals involving military cadets and rebellions from backlands peasants, the government in Rio proved increasingly less viable, and the task of running the society fell to the urban middle and upper classes. Increasingly, the urban sectors were not content to leave the management of the government in the hands of the rural oligarchy. The latter usually passed measures that supported their own narrow agenda of selling agricultural products abroad, and not a whole lot else.

For most of the First Republic, the presidency passed back and forth between the handpicked successors of either the Minas or São Paulo factions, neither one paying much attention to the demands of the urban working class and poor for higher wages and tolerable working and living conditions. In 1920, the average worker in Brazil earned about 60¢ a day for 10–12 hours of work, six days a week. Women earned only 60 percent of what men were paid for the same job and suffered harassment and even physical beatings when they protested their conditions. Whereas life on the countryside was known to be wretched, the urban elite were proud of the beautification of Brazil's large cities and claimed that a better quality of life for urban residents had resulted from the 1904 public health campaign. Nonetheless, an average worker (rural or urban) in 1920 had a life expectancy of 28 years, indicating that all the highly touted public health measures were not serving the majority of the public. Sixty-four percent of Brazilians over the age of 15 were illiterate, which prohibited them from voting. Poor urban as well as rural families worked together (parents and children) on the agricultural estates and in the factories, cut off from the prosperity being felt among the industrialists and coffee growers.

Signs of Unrest

In the cities, there were more signs of unrest. In July 1922 a group of junior officers, called *tenentes*, took over the garrison in the Copacabana area of Rio de Janeiro, in an attempt to prevent Artur da Silva Bernardes, the latest president elected in the agreement between Minas Gerais and São Paulo, from assuming office. The *tenentes* denounced the rule of the planter oligarchy and called for an end to electoral corruption. Although the young officers fought valiantly, earning themselves a place in the romantic heroes hall of fame in Brazilian history, they were easily crushed. The Rio *tenentes* did inspire similar movements among junior officers in other cities, giving rise to another revolt in São Paulo in 1924. The rebel officers held the city from July 5 through 28 and were joined by angry workers who raided food warehouses and targeted the holdings of some of the city's leading industrialists. Joel Wolfe quotes the U.S. consul report on the uprising which noted that the workers overran the warehouses of those industrialists considered most responsible for keeping food and consumer prices high.

After a concerted army attack on the rebel worker and soldier barricades, the government reclaimed control of the city. More than 1,000 residents died, 4,000 were wounded, and an estimated 300,000 temporarily evacuated the city. Despite its militancy, the uprising was a complete failure that probably brought more suffering to the city's poor in the form of destroyed property, food shortages, and increased police repression.

Hearing of the Paulista revolt, a young officer, Luís Carlos Prestes (1898–1990), from Rio Grande do Sul in the far South, and a small group of insurgents began to march north in a dramatic move to join their comrades in São Paulo. The march, called Prestes Column, eventually traveled 14,000 miles through the interior of Brazil from the Argentine border in the South to Bolivia in the North, before they dispersed. Their travels placed them in contact with the rural peasantry and made the soldiers aware for the first time of the wretched conditions that prevailed on the countryside. Increasingly drawn to more radical doctrines, Prestes and his followers extended their program to include a full range of demands for land reform along with improved working and living conditions for the urban workers. Prestes did not, however, succeed in drawing together a movement that included rural and urban workers alongside the junior officers, that was powerful enough to threaten the dominance of the coffee oligarchy.

With the exception of the well-known messianic movements in Canudos, Juàzeiro do Norte, and, in 1912–16, in Santa Catarina, the landowners' power went uncontested. One of the largest millenarian movements broke out in the border areas between the southern states of Santa Catarina and Paraná in 1912. Similar to the Canudos rebellion in Pernambuco a decade earlier, the Contestado (which took its

*Front page of a socialist working-class newspaper announcing a May Day rally in 1913. The drawing depicts a worker who has broken free of his chains and stands atop a pile of skulls labeled "bourgeoisie, capitalism, clergy, militarism, and aristocracy." (*Voz do Trabalhador, ca. May 1, 1913)

name from the "contested" frontier region that lay between the two states) was led by a prophet, José Maria. He brought the peasants and small farmers together in a religious, political, and economic campaign against corrupt local and federal government authorities, greedy landowners, and the Brazil Railway Company, all of whom were conspiring to profit from the sale of land that had been granted to the railroad through a series of government concessions.

Similar to Antônio Conselheiro in the Northeast, José Maria tapped into the discontent of thousands of landless peasants, built on rural distrust of a distant and uncaring republican government, and called for his followers to organize themselves into "holy cities" to await their salvation. Actually, José Maria called on peasants and landowners to live together in holy cities as a way of resolving the tensions over land and wages that divided the social classes. More than 25,000 rebels joined the movement in various cities in the years beginning in 1912. A federal army eventually crushed the rebellion, losing more than 7,000 soldiers in the process. Todd Diacon, who has written the major work on the Contestado rebellion, notes that this was one of the largest uprisings in Brazilian history.

Emerging Movements of Writers and Artists

Whereas the 1920s was a time of considerable upheaval, it did not witness any fundamental transformation in the political landscape. Nonetheless, it was a period in which previously silent urban workers, women, Afro-descendants, and members of the artistic and intellectual sectors emerged as members of the active citizenry.

Brazilian modernism burst on the scene in the 1922 Week of Modern Art. Led by novelist, poet, literary and art critic, musicologist, and teacher Mario de Morais Andrade (1893–1945), a group of avant-garde artists and writers held an exposition in São Paulo in mid-February 1922. Andrade, hailed as the "Pope of Modernism," was the key organizer of the Modern Art week. Known as a tireless advocate of the true Brazilian identity, Andrade researched and promoted indigenous cultural forms, called on Brazilians to recognize their "Tupi Indian soul," as well as sought to understand the syncretism of European with indigenous and African cultures that has produced the Brazilian national identity. He reproduced and analyzed particular words and patterns of speech, especially rough and everyday colloquialisms, in order to grasp the essence of Brazilian psychology as manifested in speech.

Andrade's major work was the dense and mystical story *Macunaima*. Although considered by critics as a masterpiece that defines the soul of the Brazilian people, both the book and the movie made from it rely on a logic and aesthetic that has generally been very hard for foreigners to understand. Its bawdiness and sexuality indicate that Brazil was not caught in the repressed throes of Victorian sensibilities at work in England and North America at the time, but was carving out a more earthy and realistic cultural expression.

Initially the public viewed the exposition with extreme hostility and ridicule, even damaging some of the paintings and loudly jeering at public readings. The writers and artists performed and exhibited work designed to build on Brazilian themes, to celebrate aspects of Brazil's indigenous and African cultures, and to break with the restrictive and mechanical styles then in acceptance. Despite the movement's initial rejection, modernism flourished for the next 20 years in Brazil as an aesthetic and political movement. Eventually, it was embraced by the foremost artists and writers of the century. Modernism as an art movement is credited with not only bringing Brazilian arts and literature into the modern age, but showcasing Brazilian talent to the world, especially Europe.

Rising Discontent with the Republic

Eventually, the ongoing unrest expressed by the *tenentes* and other groups came to a head in the late 1920s. An economic downturn began to destabilize the previously undisputed "coffee and cream" oligarchy. Under the presidency of Washington Luís de Sousa Pereira (1926–30) the urban industrialists grew increasingly dissatisfied with the practice of the federal government subsidizing the profits of coffee planters during years when the world price fell off. This practice, called valorization, allowed planters to produce year after year without concerns for rotating crops, improving methods of planting, preventing soil erosion, and preserving the soil. When world coffee prices fell in the 1920s, and then demand for coffee collapsed in the worldwide economic crisis of 1929, the urban middle classes voiced their displeasure with the rule of the corrupt and inept coffee oligarchs.

Political peace dissolved in 1930 when Washington Luís chose another Paulista, Júlio Prestes (no relation to Luís Carlos Prestes), as his successor rather than following the standard practice of turning power over to the Minas Gerais oligarchs. A dispute broke out that pitted the newly formed Liberal Alliance, made up of urban sectors and disaffected politicians who were not from São Paulo and included the Minas Gerais group, against the powerful Paulista planters, the Conservatives. The Liberal Alliance candidate was Getúlio Vargas from Rio Grande do Sul. Júlio Prestes, representing the Conservatives, narrowly defeated Vargas in the election, carrying a few of the key districts in what was considered a fraud-packed election. Refusing to accept the results, Vargas and his supporters from his home state of Rio Grande do Sul in the far South, along with many of the *tenentes* from the failed military uprisings of the 1920s, toppled the republic and installed a new one.

The military coup that placed Vargas at the helm of the government ended the First, or Old, Republic and introduced a new phase in Brazilian politics. The rule of the "coffee and cream" oligarchy had come to an end. The Paulista planters, joined for most of the time by their allies in Minas Gerais, who had ruled from the mid-1890s until 1930, no longer controlled the government directly. Given the importance of coffee as a key export, the planters would continue to exert enormous influence, but the 1930 revolution marked the decisive entrance of new groups into the political equation.

In summary, the success of the First Republic had been in its ability to set the stage for a new and different Brazil from the monarchy and slavocracy that had dominated since the first days of the colonial era. The republic, regardless of its faults, had been a significant break from the monarchy of the past. Yet the large estates were intact, and much of Brazilian life, especially in the distant reaches of the rural backlands, had changed little over the four decades of republican government.

7

FROM GETÚLIO VARGAS
TO THE MILITARY COUP
(1930-1964)

G etúlio Vargas moved to centralize power in the hands of the federal
government, and in so doing angered many governors and local
power brokers in the states. He intervened to establish new "presidents"
in the states, bypassing the elected officials everywhere but Minas
Gerais, where the elected governor was allowed to continue. Vargas
wrapped his authoritarian measures in national and often nationalistic
terms, reflecting the impact of the world economic depression and the
rise of fascism abroad. The Great Depression cut deeply into Brazil's
revenues from coffee exports and showed clearly that the nation was
highly dependent on foreign sources for industrial goods. Eventually,
Vargas nationalized rail and sea transportation and established a number of state-owned firms including Petrobrás, the national oil industry,
Chembras, the national chemical industry and others. Borrowing a page
out of Franklin Roosevelt's New Deal, Vargas increased the scope, size,
and importance of the federal bureaucracy.

Class Stratification in Modern Society
Vargas gained considerable support from organized labor after he had
made sure anyone who opposed him had been eliminated. The government initiated construction on some of the long-promised workers'
housing in Rio de Janeiro and São Paulo. The housing was opened
with much publicity and fanfare, and Vargas took credit for finally
completing a promise that had been held out to the urban masses
since the urban renewal of the early 20th century. In all the official
propaganda, little mention was made of the fact that the housing was
far from adequate to meet the needs of the growing urban population,

LUÍS CARLOS PRESTES AND THE BRAZILIAN COMMUNIST PARTY

L uís Carlos Prestes (1898–1990) was secretary-general of the Brazilian Communist Party (PCB) from 1943 until 1990. He had become well-known throughout Brazil as the leader of the 1925 *tenentes* uprising and the Long March, or "Column," of several thousand young army recruits and their supporters that marched through the backlands.

Prestes traveled to the Soviet Union in the early 1930s and became a devout follower of the Comintern, leading the Brazilian left through the various twists and turns of the interwar international communist program. He helped plan the uprising of 1935, an event staged from the Northeast rather than from the industrial Southeast, and which was an abysmal failure. He was arrested in 1936 and sentenced to more than 16 years in prison for his part in the abortive uprising. From prison, Prestes supported Getúlio Vargas's policy in 1945 and then openly campaigned on a moderate platform after he was freed that year. During a brief period of democratic opening from 1945 to 1964, the PCB was very active, and Prestes ran for the Senate in the mid-1940s, but lost.

In the 1960s, Prestes led the PCB in support of various presidential candidates. Because of the PCB's following among progressives, leftists, and trade unions, communist support was considered influential in

was a showcase for Vargas's favored unions, and was not extended to the poorest areas of the country. Most reforms focused chiefly on the urban sector, including national electrification, a national steel industry, expansion in public health services, more schools, and better education. The labor movement was supportive of Vargas's minimum wage law and the passage of labor legislation that had the effect of bringing the urban working class into the national political arena.

Vargas's own ideological convictions are hard to pin down. He may have operated in ways that promoted Brazil's national interests, but he was quick to suppress any social force that disagreed with him. He made overtures to Luís Carlos Prestes in 1930, offering him the position as head of the military, but Prestes refused. Striking out on his own ideological course, Prestes became the leader of the Brazilian Communist Party (PCB) which had formed in 1922. The PCB had a large following among urban intellectuals and the labor movement, but a communist-

electing Juscelino Kubitschek in 1955. In fact, the communists had broad support during the early 1960s and pursued a moderate path of seeking political reform. Many younger activists rejected what they saw as the pro-Moscow PCB's accommodationist stance. The left was badly split, with a section formed into the pro-China Communist Party (PC do B) while others opted for urban guerrilla groups, small clandestine organizations, and support for peasant movements. Splits among the left matched the polarization of left from right. Both factionalism within the left and the extreme political divisions in society helped to create the atmosphere that allowed the military to successfully launch a takeover in 1964.

The PCB, along with other leftist groups, was forced underground after 1964, and Prestes went into exile abroad. During the long period of military rule from 1964 until the early 1980s, the PCB was a significant force, operating through clandestine cells, stimulating debate when possible, and holding the allegiance of oppositional members of the intellectual and artistic community. Several well-known artists, writers, and musicians were at various times members of, or close to, the PCB, including the current president of Brazil, Fernando Henrique Cardoso.

Luís Carlos Prestes returned to Brazil under an amnesty in 1979 and the PCB became more active in the 1980s. While visible on the political stage, and holding some influence in Congress as a deal-maker with other left and liberal parties, the PCB does not now have the widespread following among labor and progressive groups that it enjoyed in earlier periods.

led revolt in November 1935 was immediately and severely repressed. Vargas suspended civil rights, jailed the opposition trade unionists, and strengthened police powers. He opportunistically used a rumor of a communist uprising on November 10, 1937, to stage a coup d'etat and launch his corporatist Estado Nôvo, or New State, which lasted for the next seven years.

The Estado Nôvo, or New State (1937–1945)

The early years of Vargas's presidency were marked by hot ideological debate (and occasional hand-to-hand combat) between those with conflicting political tendencies. Communists, neofascists, and liberal democrats competed for followers, all claimed a part of the Vargas political agenda as their own, and they grew increasingly discontent with the administration's inability to be all things to all political perspectives.

Getúlio Vargas stepped in to put an end to the disruption that threatened his rule.

Beginning in 1937, Vargas effectively ruled by decree. This authoritarian rule culminated in a totalitarian constitution that created the Estado Nôvo, or New State, that lasted until 1945. The Estado Nôvo curtailed states' rights and favored regional oligarchies, banned strikes and lockouts, and centralized Vargas as the center of all decision-making in the government. To avert class conflicts, Vargas promised something for both workers and employers, incorporating them into *sindicatos,* or state-regulated interest groups. In this way, the president was able to establish a pattern of leadership that claimed to place national interest above regional or class-based interests. Labor and political historian Barbara Weinstein points out that what Vargas actually did was join the interests of the industrialists with the state and decree them as one. He was also able to increase the role of the state in economic development and to create a stable domestic environment meant to attract foreign investors.

The Estado Nôvo borrowed elements from European fascism current at that time. Unlike Benito Mussolini in Italy and Adolf Hitler in Germany, Vargas did not build his base in a political party. Rather, he relied on support from the army to maintain order. When the political climate changed in 1945, he organized the Brazilian Labor Party as a base of support. Because the major social reforms of the Estado Nôvo were enactment of a minimum-wage law and the codification of all labor reforms since 1930 into a single labor act, Vargas was able to win to his party the devotion of the urban workers.

During the Estado Nôvo, the Integralist Action Party, or AIB, articulated a fascist agenda. This party was formed in 1932 by Plinio Salgado as a Brazilian counterpart to the powerful fascist movements in Italy and Portugal. Under the motto "God, Country, and Family," the AIB organized demonstrations with members sporting green shirts that bore the Greek sigma, Σ, as their identifying logo. Their propaganda attacked communists, foreigners, liberals, and Jews. Fascism's chief ideologue in Brazil was Gustavo Barroso, who was president of the prestigious Academy of Letters. He published strident anti-Semitic tracts warning of an impending Jewish takeover, despite the fact that the Jewish population in Brazil was exceedingly small and he had no evidence for these wild allegations. Just as Vargas used the labor movement and parties on the right when it was expedient, Barroso drew on his support among the AIB. When the ideological wars became too intense in the late 1930s, Vargas outlawed all parties, including the AIB.

Indicative of his flirtation with fascism, however, Vargas toyed with supporting Germany during World War II both in deference to the German-trained Brazilian military and in repayment for German investments and loans. In spite of some of Vargas's advisers' affection for fascism, the Germans sank a Brazilian submarine in 1942 and Brazil entered the war on the side of the Allies. In 1944, a contingent of the army fought in some particularly crucial battles during the invasion of Italy. The army's heroic showing in the Italian campaign served as the source of considerable Brazilian pride in its role in the war and also helped to consolidate the nation's antifascist reputation.

Cultural Transformations under Getúlio Vargas

A significant feature of the entire Vargas era was the extent to which new segments of the population contended for a voice and political space. Especially before 1937, segments of the Brazilian majority began elbowing in on the turf previously under the tight control of planters, industrialists, and commercial interests. Breaks in the old order could be seen in both politics and culture.

In the first place, newly empowered and growing sectors of professionals, entrepreneurs, members of the military, and the expanding middle class chafed under the domination of the planter aristocracy. They objected to the stranglehold the Minas Gerais and São Paulo planters exerted over the political culture and they sought a greater role in decision-making. Vargas drew his political capital from the long-standing discontent that had characterized the years before 1930. He sought, with considerable success, to fill the political vacuum left by the discredited oligarchy with his own brand of nationalism.

Second, within this changing political climate a kind of political and ideological space opened for greater democratic rights in Brazil. Previously unheard or marginalized segments of the polity organized in trade unions, in women's organizations, in student groups, writers' circles, ethnic, racial, and religious organizations. Women, Afro-Brazilians, and new intellectual forces raised their voices in the political and cultural arena. The end result of this turmoil was a new formulation of Brazilian identity, a sense of nationalism, and intellectual discussion over the influence of Afro-Brazilian culture on the national culture. Although the vast reaches of the interior remained much the same as in the past, political discourse began to change in the growing urban areas. President Getúlio Vargas himself played a decisive role in occasionally allowing and stimulating debate, and then prohibiting it when it raised criticisms he refused to consider.

137

Changing Roles for Women

Struggles over gender and what defined roles for women and men assumed a heightened importance during the 1920s and 1930s. In the 19th century free women had worked in the first factories, forming the backbone of the textile industry by century's end. Women in needle trades led the walkout that grew into São Paulo's general strike in 1917. This was an exception, however, since working women were usually ignored by the male-dominated trade unions and were segregated into the least-skilled and lowest-paid positions. Women suffered from a lack of education and educational opportunities that prevented them from seeking higher-paying and skilled positions. Employers, usually male, held to sexist views that saw women as incompetent, a view that fit with their overriding goal of securing a low-wage workforce.

Finally, the employment of women in factories and other workplaces was based on the availability of an even lower-wage workforce of women to work as maids to help maintain a household. Usually brought from the impoverished backlands of the Northeast to the cities, maids were paid miserably low wages. Often a family did not have even a room or a bed for a live-in servant, and would provide the maid with little more than a space on the kitchen floor to roll out a sleeping mat. Maids were, however, a necessary institution in a country that relied on low wages for women and men working outside the home. No matter how little a worker earned, the wages for domestic servants were so much lower that even working-class families relied on maids to cook and clean.

In the years after World War I, women, mainly from the middle-class urban sectors, sought a wider role in society. The women's movement agitated for the vote and finally succeeded in pressuring the government to pass a suffrage bill for women in 1932. Because suffrage was limited to literate women over the age of 21, only about half of the Brazilian women were enfranchised. The rise of a consumer culture and an expanded urban service sector provided women with more employment in stores and in the government bureaucracy, opening up places for women to work besides industry. Less reliant on fathers or husbands for their support, marriage rates fell and women began marrying at later ages. Middle-class women out alone and in groups became a more common sight on city streets, while the image of the flapper and the successful working girl in foreign movies and magazines was visible everywhere. The same year as the Rio de Janeiro *tenentes* revolt, 1922, women's rights activist Bertha Maria Julia Lutz (1894–1976) organized the Brazilian Federation for the Advancement of Women (FBPF) calling on the government to pass legislation to protect women from the exploitative working conditions they endured in factories. Lutz's action was the first in what would become a more directed campaign to win female suffrage and other rights in the next decades.

Lutz was from São Paulo, the daughter of a Swiss-Brazilian father and an English mother. She was educated in Brazil, sent to France for an advanced degree from the Sorbonne, and earned a law degree from the Rio de Janeiro law school in 1933. In 1920, she served as Brazil's representative to the Pan American Conference of Women in the United States, and in 1922 she linked the FBPF with the International Women's Suffrage Alliance. Although Lutz was a main advocate of women's suffrage, she was also aware that winning the right to vote was not the only means to women's equality. She campaigned for women's economic and political equality, for educational opportunities, and for social equalities on all levels of society. The signing of the 1932 civil code that granted women the franchise was, in Lutz's view, only the beginning of a long campaign to win equal rights for both genders.

In 1936, she ran for office and was elected as an alternate and, eventually, a full delegate to the Chamber of Deputies. While in Congress, she was instrumental in pushing for legislation that granted women full social and legal rights. These political gains for women were cut off, along with political rights for all Brazilians, when Getúlio Vargas assumed dictatorial powers in 1937. Bertha Lutz remained active in feminist politics throughout her life and was a delegate to the 1975 International Women's Year Conference in Mexico City. She died the following year at the age of 82.

Bertha Lutz was the most outspoken advocate for women's rights, but she was not the only one. Historian Susan Besse notes that Brazilian women were everywhere in public life and in print. "Dressed in the most modern styles imported from abroad, they adorned the covers of the abundant new glossy magazines, and their snapshots were sprinkled throughout the inside pages. Advertisers used their bodies to sell products and exploited their anxieties to increase sales." (Besse 1996:1) The seeds of a new ethic began to govern the interaction of men and women in the family and in the workplace. Women were now seen as consumers in society, as arbiters of culture, as members of the educated society at large. The era was marked by what Besse has called a restructured patriarchy. No longer under the strict control of fathers and husbands, and visible now in the public sphere, women still operated under the confinements of home, motherhood, and second-class status in the workplace.

The new ethic had its detractors. A powerful right-wing movement, among Integralists and others, feared that newly enfranchised women would bring about the destruction of society. Conservatives in the Catholic Church expressed fears that women were abandoning their roles as mothers and housekeepers, and thus, in their view, pushing society to the brink of anarchy. The changes in society were threatening the traditional order that had ensconced men firmly in charge of the household. Some men themselves felt uneasy with the knowledge that women were no longer dependent on them for their livelihood, that women could now influence the political process with their votes, and that women could begin to make decisions for themselves.

Not only did working and politically active middle-class women threaten the traditional relationships of power within the family, they transferred that upheaval to the society as a whole. Urban Brazilian men and women (remote and rural areas were little affected) were confronting fundamental changes in one of the most basic institutions of society. What was being transformed was not simply the lives of women alone, but the gender balance of society, or how men and women thought of themselves and sought to live their lives as individuals and as couples.

Racism and Racial Democracy

Besides gender, another of the hallmarks of stability upon which Brazil had relied since its earliest days was racial hierarchy. This hierarchy was based on the general acceptance of the superiority of lighter skin over darker, of European over African and Afro-Brazilian culture, and the association of whiteness with the elite's definition of civilization. The influx of immigrants had not destroyed the hierarchy but simply replaced the biracial continuum with a multiracial one, preserving the supremacy of white European culture over all others.

While there have been frequent challenges to the notion of white superiority at various times in Brazilian history, the absence of strong "black power" ideologies and of social movements based on Pan-Africanism are a striking testament to the pervasiveness of the whitening ideal. Thus, whereas whitening has been analyzed, quite correctly, as a racist policy, a counter-ideology extolling blackness has appeared only on the margins of Brazilian society. For example, Brazil has never had a civil rights movement comparable to the one in the United States that challenged discriminatory laws. Brazil also differs in that many school children in North America learn about black leaders such as Martin Luther King Jr., Malcolm X, or Rosa Parks along with their

Traditional baiana *(Bahian) dress, common for women street vendors of the Northeast.*
(Meade-Skotnes Photo)

study of recent history. In Brazil, children learn of great artists and writers, such as Machado de Assis, who happened to be a mulatto, but whose race generally passes unmentioned.

Considering that Brazil is a society in which about half the population probably can trace a part of its roots to Africa—Brazilian commentator Luiz Edmundo referred to Brazil as more a corner of Africa than a nation of the New World—the pervasiveness of discrimination against Afro-Brazilians is no small matter. Nonetheless, Brazil does not have the history of violence against blacks, of lynchings and organized terror to maintain white supremacy promulgated by organizations like the Ku Klux Klan, as does the United States. Some would say that in Brazil race is a nonissue. They contend that there is class oppression but not racial discrimination. Racism, they say, can be addressed through the correction of class inequalities, a view that is shared by members of the entire political ideological spectrum.

Brazil's conformity to the idea of "racial democracy" can be attributed to the long history of rigid social hierarchy in which class, family, and wealth determined a person's status. By this logic, Afro-Brazilians have been discriminated against, denied jobs or housing, and so forth, because they are poor, not because they are black. Others argue that this is a myth, because poor immigrants of European background have found greater acceptance in Brazil and prospered more than has the population of former slaves. Nonetheless, the myth of racial democracy, many would argue, has become one of the most deeply ingrained elements of the Brazilian social consciousness, accepted by many blacks as well as whites.

The idea of Brazilian "racial democracy" became an official doctrine during the Vargas regime and has lasted in modified form through its successors. Initially Vargas's leadership received support from the large Afro-Brazilian population because of the perception that the new era would loosen the control of the rural oligarchs and produce new opportunities for all marginalized groups to participate in the political process. Vargas hoped that Brazilian cultural nationalism would unify the diverse political and economic interests among the various factions in Brazilian society. He became a major proponent of a kind of race relations school of thought promoted by intellectuals like sociologist Gilberto Freyre. In reality, however, racism did not go away simply because the state decreed its absence or simply made racial discrimination illegal. What it did instead was pull the rug out from under attempts to correct discrimination against Afro-descendants.

On the other hand, while North American social scientists have been quick to criticize Brazilians for minimizing racial oppression, one might argue that people in the United States are similarly blind to class divisions in their own experience. Well over half, some estimates have even said three-quarters, of the residents in the United States claim to be middle class, despite statistics that show very little class mobility through most of U.S. history. Similar to the way Brazilians eschew racial divisions, Americans boast that the United States is a land devoid of class divisions, because of the relative absence of the rigid class barriers that historically operated in Europe, Latin America, and other parts of the world. The statement that "all men are created equal" has served to mask income inequalities in the United States, just as the notion of "racial democracy" has covered over racial inequality in Brazil.

The Frente Negra Brasileira

The 1920s and 1930s stand as the time when black identity was asserted strongly; and a movement developed to challenge racism. Despite the officially endorsed doctrine of racial democracy, Afro-Brazilians initiated efforts to develop a political presence and bring about real changes in the oppressed conditions black Brazilians endured. The Frente Negra

Brasileira (FNB, or Negro Front) was organized in September 1930 in São Paulo. According to historian Darien Davis, the FNB's principal aim was to push for greater civil rights, including equal treatment under the law and the right to work free of discrimination. This was Brazil's first national civil rights organization, and one of the first to see race and gender rights as intimately related. A woman's department was created within the movement that pushed for the FNB to adopt measures opposing sexual discrimination, harassment, and exploitation.

The organization's newspaper, *A Voz da Raça* (Voice of the Race) had a short life, with only a few issues published. Regardless, the Frente Negra enjoyed considerable support from blacks in São Paulo, Minas Gerais, and Espírito Santo, while in Bahia and Rio Grande do Sul other similar groups sprang up. The Frente and other organizations like it devoted their efforts toward addressing the racial injustices occurring in Brazilian society, sponsoring literacy and vocational training, medical treatment, and legal counseling for Afro-Brazilians. The Frente Negra however, was unable to establish itself as an effective political force or political party to run candidates for office. In 1933, Arlindo Veiga dos Santos, one of the movement's major organizers in São Paulo, ran for city council and was defeated. Between 1931 and 1937 the organization's voter registration drives could not muster enough voters to elect candidates to office. In 1937, when Getúlio Vargas shifted to the right and effectively ruled by decree, the Frente Negra and all political parties were banned. All electoral politics in the nation ended until 1946.

The banning of the Frente Negra also meant a temporary end to public discussions of race. The government argued that the suppression of the Afro-Brazilian political movement and public discussions of race and race-related issues was necessary to stabilize the political environment in order to attract foreign investment capital. While promoting the public myth of racial democracy, the Vargas regime projected the white image of Brazil to the world. The policy of whitening the population through increased European immigration continued during this era. In 1945, the Vargas government issued Decree No. 7967 to establish a criteria for immigration in which immigrants would be admitted only in conformity with the "necessity to preserve and develop, in the ethnic composition of the population, the more desirable characteristics of its European ancestry." Afro-Brazilians did not openly oppose Decree 7967. The political scientist Michael Hanchard notes that during the period of the Estado Nôvo, the black movement leaned toward accommodation rather than confrontation. Vargas's decree remained in force well into the 1980s, until the ratification of the Constitution of 1988.

COMMENTS ON BRAZILIAN RACE RELATIONS

There has been considerable debate over the extent to which black Brazilians have accepted the view that class oppression, as opposed to racism, is the dominant form of discrimination in modern society. The aversion to militant protest against racial discrimination may in part stem from the emergence in the 1920s of an Afro-Brazilian middle and professional class in São Paulo and Rio de Janeiro. According to some social scientists, Brazilian blacks have been inclined to support strategies to uplift the race one person at a time, not unlike the approach Booker T. Washington advocated in the United States at the turn of the 20th century. The loss of an organizational basis from which to propose real changes in Brazilian race relations never moved forward after the demise of the FNB.

Despite some efforts recently to build Afro-Brazilian organizations, there has been little uproar over some fairly blatant racist practices, while derogatory images of blacks still pass uncontested in movies and in popular culture. In the late 1990s a song by singer/composer Tiririca provoked such an outcry it was censored. In *"Veja os cabelos deja"* ("Take a Look at Her Hair") the singer described a black woman who "stinks like a skunk." Not only was the song censored but Tiririca, a white circus clown from the Northeast who cannot read and write, was also sued. Even more revealing of divided sentiments over racial stereotypes was the response. According to surveys, many blacks as well as whites argued that the song was not racist. For example, a popular black television comedian said in *Veja,* Brazil's leading news and entertainment magazine, that he did not find the song offensive and that people stink regardless of their race. Another commentator noted that Tiririca's song was no more offensive than many popular Carnival sambas, including *"O Teu Cabelo Não Nega,"* meaning "Your Hair Can't Deny It" and *"Nega do Cabelo Duro,"* meaning "Little Black Girl with the Stiff Hair."

On the other hand, because Brazil has so many people of African descent, its mainstream culture has a decidedly African influence. The historian Lisa Brock has remarked in comparing the position of African Americans with Afro-Brazilians that being black in Brazil is being on the bottom looking up, whereas being black in the United States is being on the outside looking in. The music hits mentioned above were, after all, the songs of black samba schools performed by black and mixed-race artists. Some have argued that Tiririca's song and others like it simply reflect an individual artist's problems with accepting a true black identity and need to be critiqued on a case-by-case basis as one does with all art.

Intellectual Trends

A key feature of Brazilian intellectual and cultural history has been the process of coming to terms with its African past. In contrast with the United States, which for much of its history has sought to hide and repress its African cultural heritage, Brazil has struggled to come to terms with what Africa has meant to the development of the national identity. While it is impossible to deny the persistence of racism in Brazil's history, it is likewise impossible to deny the pervasive acceptance of African culture. Note, for example, the widespread practice of African religions in many Latin American societies. In Brazil, slaves carried the rituals of *candomblé* and *macumba* from bondage to freedom, relying on the *orixas,* or gods, to provide comfort or even bring harm to enemies of the devout. As late as the early 20th century, Brazil introduced a new African, Yoruba-inspired religion called *umbanda.*

Founded in 1904, a decade after slavery was abolished, *umbanda* combines elements of African beliefs with Buddhism and Hinduism. *Umbanda* differs from *candomblé* in that the gods are directly symbolized by Catholic saints and are referred to by their saintly names, such as Saint George, Saint Catherine, and so on. Of all the African religions, it may best approximate Christian symbolism.

These religions, which came to Brazil in successive waves over several hundred years, enjoy a widespread following in Brazil today, not only among those of African descent, but by Brazilians of all backgrounds. Anthropologists and other social scientists contend that there are as many practitioners of African spiritism as there are Catholics, with a majority of the devout partaking in both religions.

Stores such as this one in contemporary Copacabana, Rio de Janeiro, sell religious articles for use in candomblé and umbanda rituals. (Meade-Skotnes Photo)

The late 1920s ushered in a period of intellectual ferment among academics, artists, and writers and an intense debate over the place of Europe and Africa in molding Brazil's culture. Coming to terms with what it meant to be Brazilian had been a key concern of the intellectual strata for much of Brazil's history. After the Week of Modern Art in 1922 had launched the modernist movement, more and more writers set about attempting to define a new Brazilian national identity. They sought to draw a clear cultural distinction between the European/ Portuguese legacy and the modern "new world" Brazilian reality. Picking up on themes outlined by Euclides da Cunha, the generation of writers from the 1920s through most of the Vargas era produced a body of literature and scholarship that has influenced Brazilian letters ever since.

Two figures, Gilberto Freyre and Jorge Amado, provide a window into the debate over Brazilian national identity. Gilberto Freyre in sociology and Jorge Amado in literature produced a large body of work that sought to demarcate the singularity of Brazil's racial and gender history from the experiences of other nations. Their work on the interplay of race and gender established criteria for how the nation viewed its past, its culture, and its place in the world. Freyre and Amado shared some concepts and their conclusions at times overlapped, but ultimately they stood at opposing poles. Regardless of their political and ideological differences, both have been enormously influential.

Gilberto Freyre, Twentieth-Century Sociologist (1900–1987)

Gilberto Freyre was the pioneer of Brazilian sociological studies. His most famous works, *The Masters and the Slaves* (1933), followed by *The Mansions and the Shanties* (1936), and dozens of other writings, examined the relationships between the Portuguese colonizers and their African slaves. Freyre argued that Brazilians formed a "new race" in the tropics, a "new people" of mixed origins.

Freyre's theory of Lusotropicalism and Lusophonic exceptionalism maintained that Portuguese culture and racial tolerance were responsible for the development of a Brazilian racial paradise, (*Luso,* derived from *Lusitania,* refers to Portugal and generally to the combination of Portuguese and New World people and culture.) He highlighted one of the key aspects of Brazilian slavery, and subsequent race relations: the pervasiveness of race mixture and the middle position between blacks and whites occupied by the mulatto. Along with many other mainly male writers, he saw the attraction of white male planters for black female slaves as a sign of the master's affection for his slave, as opposed to his lust and dominance over women.

In his writings, Freyre sought to establish the notion that slaves, no matter how badly treated, emerged from slavery unharmed and even forgiving of their masters. Most disturbing was his argument that Brazilian black and mulatto women craved the sexual favors of whites, and cunningly seduced their masters. Rather than victims of rape, black women were seen as inviting it. Although widely discredited by modern sociology and historians, especially the anthropologist Marvin Harris, Freyre's work was very popular in some circles throughout the Americas until the late 20th century. He made whites comfortable with slavery, arguing as he did that it was the basis from which a "racial paradise" could emerge.

Freyre was, however, reacting against the "scientific racism" of the eugenists a generation earlier. While asserting the biological inferiority of Africans, the Eurocentric eugenists had seen no benefit for Brazil from the nation's long contact with African culture. Freyre, by contrast, celebrated the African aspects of Brazil. Thus at the time his writings breathed fresh air into the stultifying Eurocentrism that earlier had characterized much of elite culture. In addition, Freyre's miscegenated "paradise" contrasted with the fears that Euclides da Cunha had stoked in his account of the Canudos uprising at the turn of the century. Da Cunha took stock of urban and rural Brazilian life and found them both wanting, but lay much of the blame for Brazil's backward interior on the effects of race mixture among indigenous people, Africans, and Portuguese settlers. If da Cunha's vision of Brazil's future in his masterpiece, *Rebellion in the Backlands,* had been pessimistic, Freyre's was optimistic from an entirely opposing perspective.

In the 1950s and 1960s, Gilberto Freyre became more closely associated with conservative politics, embracing the need for a strictly enforced orderly (read "dictatorial") system as the only way for the state to discipline the unwieldy, largely mixed-race, population. He began to articulate these views in *Ordem e Progresso* (1959) and moved to fully supporting the military dictatorship and writing parts of the military platform in the early 1960s. It would, however, be difficult to draw a direct line between Freyre's racial theories and his later conservative political views. His impact was enormous, and he had admirers of his racial theories on the left and the right, both at home and abroad.

Jorge Amado, Twentieth-Century Novelist (1912–2001)

One of the most successful writers of Latin America, and one of the most widely translated writers in literature, Jorge Amado wrote of life in his native state of Bahia at the beginning of the 20th century. Likewise he took up the key themes of race mixture and the influence of Afro-Brazilian folk culture on the broader society.

In his books Amado depicted a time when wealthy cacao planters dominated the land, as in *The Violent Land* and *Gabriela, Clove and Cinnamon*. In other works set in urban Salvador, such as *Dona Flor and Her Two Husbands* and *Jubiaba*, Amado delved into the Afro-Brazilian world of music, *capoeira*, and the African religious cults of *candomblé, macumba,* and *umbanda*. A masterful entertainer, humorist, and social critic, Amado gained enormous popularity for his sympathetic portrayal of the lives of a range of downtrodden and idiosyncratic characters in the villages and plantations of Ilheus in Bahia and its surrounding region.

While Amado's books usually feature memorable female protagonists—Gabriela, Dona Flor, Tereza Batista—he has been criticized for feeding the stereotypical view of the Brazilian mulatta as a sensuous and alluring "natural" character. Despite his leftist politics and generally sympathetic portrayal of poor and working-class people, shades of Gilberto Freyre's notions of a "racial paradise" seep into his work. In contrast to Freyre, Amado was uncompromising in his view of racial, class, and even gender oppression. Homosexuals and women of all social classes are frequently the voices of reason and of civilization in his writings. He gives these characters a voice within a cultural landscape that historically privileged masculinity. Afro-Brazilians, the poor and the working class in general are depicted sympathetically while no quarter is spared in showing the brutality of the planters and the hypocrisy of the urban elite who turned a blind eye to race and class oppression. Well-known for his leftist sympathies and active as a longtime member of the Communist Party, Amado spent many years in exile during the periods of intense political repression under Vargas and later.

Amado managed to return to Brazil sporadically and maintained close ties with the Brazilian left, as well as with its popular culture. If he suffered during the 1950s and was exiled in the late 1960s for his communist views, his outlaw status has never hurt sales of his books, nor the popularity of the many TV and film adaptations of his works.

Both Gilberto Freyre and Jorge Amado contributed in significant ways to the flowering of nationalist sentiment from the 1930s onward.

STRUGGLE AND CONFLICT IN THE NOVELS OF JORGE AMADO

Although a work of fiction, Jorge Amado's novel *The Violent Land* has been heralded as a source that captures the essence of the conflicts in the backlands. The book depicts what passes for law and order in Ferradas, a fictional town deep in the untamed frontier of the Northeast cacao country. As is typical of Amado's plotlines, a power struggle pits the townsfolk against the planters and their surrogates. In a subplot to the main saga of contested landownership, Amado inserts a conflict between the local doctor and priest (lackeys to the planters) and the townspeople, who have begun to rely on the expertise of a poor Afro-descendant woman.

...if the brand of Catholicism represented by the monk had little appeal for the residents of the town, spiritualism on the other hand flourished. The "believing ones" were in the habit of meeting at the house of Eufrosina, a medium who had begun to acquire a reputation in those parts; it was there that they assembled to listen to messages from dead relatives and friends. Seated in her chair, Eufrosina would begin stammering unintelligibly, until one of those present recognized the familiar voice of the dead. It was said that long ago the spirits—and especially the spirit of an Indian, who was Eufrosina's "guide"—had predicted the trouble that was to occur over the forest of Sequeiro Grande. These prophecies were much talked about, and no one in Ferradas was surrounded with so much respect as was the mulatto with the skinny figure as she made her way through the muddy streets.

Her "séances" having proved so successful, Eufrosina then began treating diseases by spiritualism, with comparative success. This was an encroachment on the domain of Dr. Jessé Freitas, the physician at Tabocas, who came over to Ferradas once a week to look after the sick and who was also called in on nights of gun-play; and he now joined forces with Friar Bento against Eufrosina. For she was taking his patients away; fever sufferers were now going to the medium instead of the doctor.

Source: Amado, Jorge. *The Violent Land.* Translated by Samuel Putnam. New York: Avon Books, 1945, pp. 120–121.

Their exact positions on Getúlio Vargas are of less importance than the way in which their work elevated to the national consciousness a conception of Brazil as a unique society based on its particular racial and gender configurations.

National Identity and Twentieth-Century Writers

In many ways, the Vargas period helped many writers to mature, but can be most credited with the promotion of a nationalist sentiment that served to build pride in all things Brazilian. Literature was a form of oppositional writing during the repressive period of the Estado Nôvo and under subsequent military governments. Artists argued that political freedom was essential to the spread of a self-defined artistic aesthetic.

Great fiction writers and poets of the 20th century include Carlos Drummond de Andrade (1902–87) who many consider Brazil's greatest modern writer. His poetry and prose reveal a deep dissatisfaction with the waste, banality, and superficiality of modern life. Clarice Lispector (1925–77), the daughter of Ukrainian immigrants to São Paulo, is credited with creating national characters and not simply regional ones, as had been Amado's forte, while Raquel de Queiros (1910–2003) another prominent female writer, continues the tradition of the regional narrative in the style of Jorge Amado. Having grown up in the backlands herself, Queiros describes the hardship of life in the drought-stricken regions. She incorporates female characters who question their place within society into plots that break with societal conventions. Many of her essays have appeared in newspapers and magazines, since her work combines journalism with social commentary.

Many Latin American writers and authors have a strong political focus, have participated in the political life of their countries as ambassadors or representatives in Congress, and have been frequent critics of authoritarian regimes. Brazilian writers are no exception. The nationalism that Vargas fostered was not unimportant in fostering a critical stance toward the military government and its primary backer, the U.S. government, and multinational corporations in subsequent decades. The generation that produced a large body of literature in the 1960s grew up in the last days of the Vargas years and bore the stamp of that era's contradictory trends, suffering from censorship but also blossoming in the wake of Brazilian nationalism.

Getúlio Vargas Overthrown

The contradiction between the government's position abroad in support of democracy and its authoritarian politics at home gave rise to increasing discontent once World War II ended. Forced by prodemocracy demonstrations and a growing political movement, Vargas abolished censorship in 1945, released a number of opposition political prisoners, issued a new electoral law, and authorized the formation of new political parties, including the communist PCB. He relied on the Brazilian Labor Party for support, but also toyed with the left when it suited his interests.

Fearing an imminent move by Vargas to usurp all power in his own hands, the army launched a counteroffensive and deposed him on October 29, 1945. In a departure from other such military actions, however, Vargas was not censored, could participate in the elections, and could even continue to hold lower office. He was elected to the Senate, but refused to serve and instead retreated to his estate in São Borja in Rio Grande do Sul, where he led a private life for the next five years. In 1950 he returned to politics, ran for president, and was elected by a wide margin.

The political and economic scene of the 1950s was not, however, conducive to rebuilding and sustaining either Vargas's own personal popularity or his ultranationalist program. Congress was divided and much of it opposed to him, inflation was out of hand, and a newly powerful North American business community was strong-arming its way into Brazilian industry and investing on its own terms. Corruption, graft, infighting and criminal activity characterized nearly all branches of the government. In 1954, the military again stepped in and demanded his resignation, which Vargas granted on August 24, 1954. Later in the day, he took his own life, leaving behind a suicide note blaming "outside powers" and indicating that his office was undermined by the forces of economic and political imperialism. If fingers could be pointed, they were directed toward the newly emerging power to the north: the United States. Getúlio Vargas attempted in his death note to depict his suicide as a necessary step to maintain Brazilian integrity and sovereignty in the face of outside pressures.

The Political Record of Getúlio Vargas

What did Getúlio Vargas accomplish? What is his legacy? Although the early years of Vargas's leadership, before 1937, were a period of intense political debate and organizing, most of the gains for women, minorities, and the working class came crashing to a halt in 1937. The working class was purged of any but its most compliant leaders and liberal modernizers who had supported the attack on patriarchal traditions in the early 1930s. By now they were content with the few gains, mainly suffrage, that women had achieved. Some among the white liberal elite who disapproved of the dictatorial rule of the

This statue of Getúlio Vargas is completely covered with flowers, notes pleading for assistance, and accolades. The statue bears a copy of Vargas's suicide note that was addressed to "The People of Brazil." (Meade-Skotnes photos)

Estado Nôvo nonetheless breathed easier now that Afro-Brazilians were no longer demanding greater equality. For many, the instability that democracy brought with it was frightening, and the old order of patriarchal authority in which the working class, women, and blacks "knew their place" was appealing. In that respect, Getúlio Vargas's reign had set the clock back.

On the other hand, Vargas probably did more than any leader before him, and maybe since, to bolster Brazilian nationalism. The expansion of the federal bureaucracy, the creation of national oil, steel, and chemical consortia, and the fostering of a sense of Brazilian pride can be attributed to him. He can be credited with promoting a model for independent capitalist development. Different also from other presidents, Vargas promoted, demagogically for sure, a populist image. Many ordinary Brazilians saw him as a defender of their interests. He claimed to care for the common man and woman, despite the fact that he strictly controlled society. On a bust of President Vargas that stands in a plaza in central Rio de Janeiro, people leave flowers, burn candles, and attach notes, some asking "Dom Getúlio" for help. The messages are very personal: a plea for running water in a house; protection from an eviction; money to pay for a child's medical care. These messages indicate that many Brazilians saw Vargas as a "man of the people." Even if he did little to resolve the entrenched poverty of Brazil, he did at least *say* that something should be done. For that alone, large segments of the working poor believed in him, and probably still do.

When sentimentality and self-promotion are stripped away, Getúlio Vargas's actual record shows less sympathy for the poor. He reformed the election laws that granted a secret ballot and extended suffrage to women, but the literacy requirement still left large numbers of Brazilians without the means to vote. The 1934 Constitution created a system of labor tribunals, guaranteed the right to strike, and established an eight-hour day, minimum wage, social security system, paid vacations, and set safety and health standards. In exchange, however, the unions came under the control of the Ministry of Labor and lost their independent standing. If employers cut wages or extended the working day, labor was not able to strike without government permission. During hard economic times, the government was reluctant to allow strikes and quick to send in the police to break up picket lines. The system became subject to corruption, with industrialists buying political influence among the vast bureaucracy and calling on the police and military to shut down union meetings and confiscate newspapers and leaflets for little reason at all.

Juscelino Kubitschek and the Post-Vargas Era

In the year after Getúlio Vargas's suicide, political life existed in a precarious balance between a military takeover and democratic government. In 1955, Juscelino Kubitschek, a political figure who had risen from humble origins in Minas Gerais, was elected president. An advocate of the U.S. political scientist Walt W. Rostow's economic theory of the "Five Stages of Development," Kubitschek concentrated investments in those regions where the preconditions for development already existed: Minas Gerais, São Paulo, and Rio de Janeiro. The plan successfully pushed industrial production ahead, and it increased 80 percent between 1955 and 1961, with a per capita growth rate of 4 percent a year from 1957 to 1961. Critics argue, however, that Kubitschek's policy was successful in the already dynamic regions in the Southeast, while the poverty-stricken Northeast remained even further behind.

153

Brasilia

The main accomplishment of the Kubitschek era was the movement of the national capital from the port city of Rio de Janeiro to the newly designed capital of Brasilia in the country's distant interior. The capital's relocation to the interior had been discussed as far back as the late 18th century, and a 5,500-square-mile site for the future Federal District was set aside in 1891. Kubitschek was the first president to campaign on making Brasilia a reality and the one to actually carry it out. The futuristic capital was the brainchild of a team of top modernist architects and urban planners headed by the Rio-born Oscar Soares Niemeyer, whose work before Brasilia included being a part of the architectural team that designed the United Nations buildings in New York City in the 1940s. Niemeyer's longtime close associate, Lucio Costa, laid out the streets and drew up the physical plans for the new capital. The Swiss-born French architect Charles-Édouard Jeanneret, better known as Le Corbusier, worked closely with Niemeyer and Costa on the design.

The three were joined by their love of modern architecture and by a desire to bring a socialist vision to urban planning. Government buildings were placed around a central plaza in the style of the traditional Iberian city, with water surrounding the Itamariti Palace which housed the Ministry of Foreign Affairs. A long column of white towers led up to Congress, housed in two opposing white towers offset by two bowls—one face up and one face down. The design was reminiscent of the United Nations buildings but on a much larger scale.

It was in the residential quarters that Costa and Niemeyer installed their egalitarian vision. They wanted buildings where all social classes could reside together, where shopping areas, schools, day-care centers, and recreation areas were incorporated into the apartment zones. On the outskirts they planned a large park and open green space, supposedly where the members of government would recreate along with white-collar and blue-collar workers, intellectuals, and all social classes.

The end result fell short of Niemeyer and Costa's utopian vision. The modernist towers, sculptures, and walkways of the government zone were completed, but the residential areas were not built according to the designers' plans. Apartments were sold on the open market after 1960 for prices that no worker could afford. The area designated for a park was subdivided and sold to wealthy Brazilians and foreign diplomats for luxury housing. The pedestrian walkways designed to connect

In 1987, UNESCO designated the city of Brasília as a World Heritage Site. These photos of national government buildings and the National Cathedral display architect Oscar Niemeyer's modernist vision. (Claire Skotnes photos)

the various parts of the city proved impractical and soon became transformed into a maze of roads and on- and off-ramps for highways. The working class, unable to afford the real estate and generally high consumer prices in Brasília, moved to satellite towns on the outskirts from which they travel long distances to work each day. Niemeyer himself denounced the outcome of his architectural plan, accusing the government of failing to provide the affordable housing and living subsidies it had promised in order to make his and Costa's utopian city a reality. Today Brasília stands as a monument to a modernist architectural vision, but critics are not wrong when they complain of its sterile and isolating atmosphere.

The Clash between the Left and the Right

The other main accomplishment for which Kubitschek is noted is that he both came into and left office legally and peacefully. After 1961, a series of conflicts over the ideological direction of the government marred the presidential succession. Brazil, like many countries in Latin America, endured heated struggles between the left and right in the 1960s. Radical forces in the union movement, leftist students and intellectuals, and liberal sections of the Catholic Church criticized the government's main concern with protecting the business environment and doing little to resolve the poverty of the majority of the population. The country's close political relationship with the United States and favorable investment climate for U.S. multinational corporations also came under harsh criticism. When in 1959 a small guerrilla army overthrew the long-standing dictatorship of Fulgencio Batista in Cuba, nothing in Latin America was ever the same again. The romantic Argentine figure Ernesto "Che" Guevara, along with the new Cuban leader, Fidel Castro, inspired a generation of young Brazilians to reenact the model of socialist revolution that seemed to be evolving in Cuba.

For its part, the right, concentrated among the military forces, large landowners, and heads of multinational corporations, began to see even the most feeble attempts at reform as "communist inspired." The society of the early 1960s became increasingly politically polarized. A period of exciting debate nonetheless characterized the early 1960s, and meaningful steps were initiated in bringing about a more equitable distribution of wealth. In that regard, the city of Brasília stands as a kind testament to the attempts—and the ultimate failure—of the era.

Social Activism, the Church, and the Struggle for Justice

The activists in the early 1960s were located in a number of areas. The communist-inspired Peasant Leagues were the closest counterpart in Brazil to the guerrilla movements that sprang up in other Latin American countries. In the early 1960s, the leagues (or *ligas*) achieved a national reputation under the leadership of Francisco Julião. They were intent on forcing land reform and obtaining rights for rural workers in a country that had ignored equality in the countryside since colonial days. Initially quite successful, the *ligas* expanded into 13 of the 22 states by 1962. This was Brazil's best-known rural trade union movement. Dedicated to land reform "by law or by force," the Peasant Leagues followed a variety of strategies. In some areas the followers seized land and occupied it in defiance of absentee land-owners or local authorities. In other areas, the *ligas* were organized as a trade union, with rural workers demanding higher wages, better living conditions and shorter hours, while in still other states there were armed rebellions.

The Peasant Leagues received support from Catholic priests and lay militants who joined the radical cause of land reform. Through the Frente Agrária (FA, or Agrarian Front), founded in 1962, radical and socialist-leaning members of the Catholic clergy worked in many areas of the Brazilian countryside to promote rural labor unions. Inspired by the teachings of Pope John XXIII in Rome and the movement toward liberation theology, the FA was organized by young priests who worked with the Peasant Leagues to bring justice to the impoverished back-landers. (See "The Beginnings of Opposition" in chapter 8 for more on liberation theology.) When the military took over in 1964, the Peasant League leaders were jailed or forced into exile. Moreover, the military pointed to the activities of the Peasant Leagues as justification for their intervention, claiming that radical elements were supporting the invasion of private estates. Since no government in Brazil's history had ever proposed or carried out any significant land reform measures, the destruction of the Peasant Leagues brought an end to one of the few moments when agrarian policy and real change was at least placed at the center of the national agenda.

The involvement of the Catholic priests with the Peasant Leagues was only one cause in which the church became increasingly active. By the early 1960s, the National Conference of Brazilian Bishops (CNBB) began to function as an important organization for inserting the voice of the Catholic Church into politics on the side of social justice. Founded in 1952 by one of Brazil's most outspoken clerics, Dom Hélder Câmara,

In the drought-stricken rural backlands, villagers eke out a living fishing in rivers and growing a few crops on the irrigated banks. (Meade-Skotnes photo)

archbishop of Recife, the CNBB supported trade unions and organizations designed to help the rural and urban poor.

The social activism of a sector of the Catholic Church mirrored promises of social reform and renewed prosperity from the political front. In 1959, Jânio da Silva Quadros (1917–1992), the governor of São Paulo, campaigned for president on the National Democratic Union (UDN) ticket. Quadros called for a series of reforms, including a neutralist stand in foreign policy, increased industrial growth, and moderate social reforms. He won the presidency, and in 1961, along with the vice president, João Belchior Marques Goulart, became the first Brazilian to be sworn into the highest office in the new capital, Brasilia. Quadros raised the ire of conservatives, as well as drew the wary eye of the United States, because he refused to break diplomatic ties with Cuba after the U.S. issued a mandate to all Latin American nations to isolate the communist government.

In an attempt to leverage more support from opponents in the military and political conservatives, Quadros resigned the presidency in August, after less than a year in office. Ostensibly, Quadros assumed that the right-wing opposition would rally, if begrudgingly, to his support because they distrusted even more Vice President Goulart, who was known to be to the left of the president. But the conservatives called his bluff, and to Quadros's surprise, Congress accepted his resignation. The motives of the conservative opposition in this move have been unclear. Most likely, they were planning to prevent Goulart from assuming the presidency. In that, however, they were not successful.

João Goulart's Disputed Accession to the Presidency

Conservatives in Congress and their friends in the military viewed the vice president, João Belchior Marques Goulart (1919–76) hostilely from the moment he entered national office. Despite his reputation as a reformer, "Jango" Goulart, as he was called, was not a maverick politician. To the contrary, he had matured under the reign of Getúlio Vargas. Goulart was from the same small town in Rio Grande do Sul as Vargas. In fact, he had benefited from his long association with the political machine and from his marriage to the sister of the powerful gaucho political boss, Leonel Brizola. He had been a local leader of the Brazilian Labor Party, founded as Vargas's base of support from the early 1950s, and he had served as labor minister in 1953 under Vargas.

As vice president under Jânio da Silva Quadros, Goulart had advocated discussions with the groups calling for land reforms and favored higher wages for urban workers. Like Quadros, he favored a more independent foreign policy and visited China to investigate the possibility of closer diplomatic and trading relations with the Communist country. Goulart was in China when Quadros resigned in August 1961. Although originally prevented from assuming the presidency by hardline conservatives in Congress who were associated with the military, Goulart's old friend Brizola threatened civil war if the vice president was not allowed to succeed to the presidency in accordance with the Constitution. In a brokered deal with the military, Goulart took office under a system of reduced power that allowed Congress to hold him in check. The arrangement was abandoned after a plebiscite two years later restored Goulart to full presidential powers.

8

FROM MILITARY DICTATORJHIP TO DEMOCRACY (1964-2002)

The main opposition to Goulart came from conservative business interests in Brazil and in the United States. Landowners also opposed Goulart's attempts to reform the unequal system of land distribution. The powerful rural bosses called on their allies in the military and police to crush rural workers, independent small landowners, and impoverished peasants who occupied disputed landholdings.

The U.S. Business and Government View of Brazil

Business interests in Brazil and in the United States viewed the political situation as unstable. Multinational companies counted on a compliant workforce that would tolerate the low wages and poor working conditions that their counterparts in the developed world shunned. Moreover, the business community was used to favorable tariff agreements, low taxes, and lax enforcement of health and safety laws in Brazil to keep profits high. Industrialists feared that Goulart's base among the trade unions, which he had cultivated as minister of labor under Vargas, would cause him to listen to labor's demands. The business community in the United States communicated its concerns to the U.S. Congress and the White House through lobbyists, alerting the U.S. government to possible changes in store for Brazil. For their part, after the failed 1961 Bay of Pigs invasion of Cuba, and facing an escalating war in Southeast Asia, the John Kennedy and Lyndon Johnson administrations both looked very unfavorably on any assertion of Latin American nationalism or reform.

The 1964 Military Takeover

In March 1964, Goulart feared that the military was planning to move against him. In response he sought to win the support of the working class, the rural poor, and the left through the announcement of a comprehensive reform package. The plan included provisions for rural workers to form unions, voting rights for illiterates, and a mild land reform, among other measures. It was by this time much too late. Convinced of an imminent coup, Goulart made a final attempt to rally democratic forces within the military to his side. On March 30, 1964, he called on the rank-and-file soldiers to disobey any orders from their commanding officers to unseat the constitutional government. This only antagonized the military more, and on March 31 General Olimpio Mourão Filho marched on Rio de Janeiro, setting the coup into motion. Other branches of the military joined within hours. Under the leadership of General Humberto Castello Branco, the legal government was deposed. João Goulart flew into exile in Uruguay where he died of a heart attack in 1976.

Many quarters greeted the military intervention enthusiastically, including most of the media, the hierarchy of the Catholic Church, the business and political elite, the national bar association, and even a group of conservative, prosperous women who had feared that Goulart's reforms would result in higher prices on consumer goods and increased rights for their maids. Most of those who immediately endorsed the "Revolution," as the military labeled the 1964 coup, had feared the upheaval and social destabilization that Goulart's reforms seemed to signal. In that regard the coup was a preemptive move, intent on cutting off debate, stopping disenfranchised and marginalized groups from bidding for power, and eliminating the possibility of meeting the demands of the rural and urban poor, as well as of liberals and progressives. For example, a group of important Catholic bishops issued a statement in the month after the April takeover, applauding the armed forces who "came to the rescue in time to avoid the implementation of a Bolshevik regime in our country." (quoted in Skidmore 1988:27) Some sectors fell into line behind the military initially, then drew back when the extent of the military's repression, especially the arrest and torture of thousands of citizens, became clear. A leading Rio de Janeiro newspaper, *A Correio da Manhã*, reversed its initial endorsement of the military and opened its pages to critics of the government as accusations of human rights abuses began to mount.

BRAZIL AND OPERATION CONDOR

Brazil's role in Operation Condor, and the degree to which the United States was aware of the coordination among the Southern Cone nations, has been verified in recently declassified U.S. State Department documents. These documents validate the assertion that the repression and human rights abuses that occurred in Argentina, Uruguay, Chile, and Brazil were part of a coordinated strategy. In addition, critics have questioned the role of the United States in supporting and even aiding the repression. Paraguay, long under the tight military dictatorship of Alfredo Stroessner, was a center for this coordination and the conduit between the military states and the United States. In a cable from U.S. ambassador to Paraguay Robert White to Secretary of State Cyrus Vance, sent October 20, 1978, the ambassador states in part:

> On October 1 I I called again on Chief of Staff (Paraguay) Alejandro Fretes Davalos. He read me the Acta or Summary Minutes resulting from the visit of General Orozco, Chief of Intelligence to Asunción. . .
>
> The document is basically an agreement to coordinate all intelligence resources in order to control and eliminate subversion. It speaks of exchange of information, prompt use of communication facilities, monitoring of subversives and their detention and informal hand over from one country to the other. It repeats over and over the need for full cooperation and mutually facilitative acts in the context of a fight to the death against subversion. . .
>
> Brazil, Argentina, Chile, Bolivia, Paraguay and Uruguay make [up] the net, although Uruguay is now almost on the inactive list. . . . They keep in touch with one another through U.S. communications installations in the Panama Canal Zone which covers all of Latin America. The U.S.

In the United States, the Lyndon Johnson administration had never viewed Goulart favorably. In an era of intense cold war rivalry between the United States and the communist nations of the Soviet Union and China, exacerbated by the successful Cuban Revolution and widening conflict in Vietnam, the United States distrusted any political leader who sought to maintain a middle ground. The United States rejected Goulart's explanation that his trip to China was an

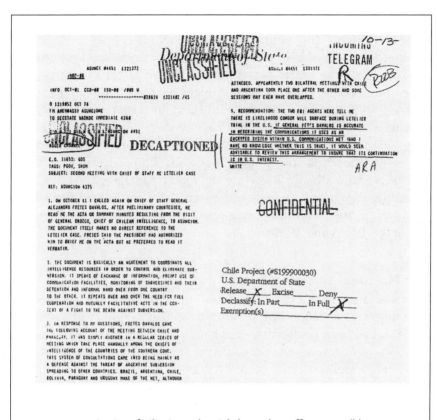

communications facility is used mainly by student officers to call home to Latin America, but it is also employed to co-ordinate intelligence information among the Southern Cone countries. They maintain the confidentiality of their communication through the U.S. facility in Panama by using bilateral codes...

Source: These materials are reproduced from www.nsarchive.org with the permission of the National Security Archive.

attempt at nonalignment (ignoring the fact that he had been sent to China by Quadros) and used that as one of a number of reasons for lending support to the military government. Other issues were the emergence of a more powerful trade union movement under Goulart, a law the government had recently enacted that restricted the rights of foreign businesses to repatriate their profits, and a high inflation rate.

The U.S. embassy and the Central Intelligence Agency were no doubt aware of the impending military coup in the months before it happened. Whether they helped plan it or not, the Brazilian military knew that it could count on the hearty support of the United States and immediate recognition of a new government. Moreover, in the subsequent years, despite widespread and highly publicized human rights violations, the United States supported the string of dictators who ruled Brazil from 1964 until democracy was restored in 1988. Recently declassified documents show that the United States was supportive of Operation Condor, a secret alliance involving the military dictatorships of Chile, Argentina, Paraguay, Uruguay, and Brazil that coordinated the arrest, detention, torture, and disappearance of dissidents in these countries during the 1970s and 1980s.

The National Security State

The 1964 coup d'etat ushered in a new era of military rule. In the first place, previous dictatorships, in Brazil as well as in other parts of Latin America, had been personalist, or what Spanish America calls *caudillo*. *Caudilho*, in Portuguese, or *caudillo*, in Spanish, means "strongman." They were a well-known feature in Spanish America, where dictators used the armed forces as a kind of personal tool to win power, especially in the era after independence in the 19th century. With the possible exception of Getúlio Vargas's Estado Nôvo, Brazil did not have a history of personalist dictators. The coup of 1964 was not a personalist dictatorship. Its ascendance represented a change from the politics of personal clientelism and corruption to a bureaucratic and institutional military rule. In contrast with the single, self-interested rule of Rafael Trujillo in the Dominican Republic, Anastasio Somoza in Nicaragua, or Fulgencio Batista in Cuba, for example, the Brazilian model demonstrated an ideological commitment by the full military bureaucracy to hold power.

Second, unlike earlier military governments, beginning in 1964 a coalition of generals sought to transform the state and society. It was the first of what came to be called the "national security regimes." The experiment in Brazil from 1964 until the early 1980s was followed by regimes in Uruguay (1973–85), Chile (1973–90), and Argentina (1976–83), all of which looked to Brazil as a model "national security regime." Intent on national economic growth in a controlled environment, they had as their basis the repression of human rights in sectors that disagreed with the military agenda.

Finally, during the following two decades the military coup in Brazil was followed by similar ones in Chile, Uruguay, and Argentina (known as the Southern Cone). These regimes followed in the path of the national security state pioneered in Brazil in 1964. Not only did they seek to repress subversion, censor the press, and jail dissidents in their respective countries, but they embarked on a plan, known as "Operation Condor," whereby they coordinated their actions so as to eliminate dissent among all the Southern Cone countries.

The national security state evolved over a number of years. From 1964 until 1967, the military junta ruled through a series of exceptional measures without changing the basic structure of the government. At the same time, the military leaders began a process of rewriting the national constitution. In 1967, a new constitution was ratified by a Congress from which any opposition had been purged. It stated that the president was elected by an electoral college, however only a military leader could be a candidate. It granted the president the right to govern through decree even when the legislature was in session, effectively overriding any disagreement with Congress. While on paper there were laws to protect individual rights, they were either not enforced or constantly nullified by decrees to enforce "national security." What began as a "moderate" military dictatorship in 1964, based on purging the system of opponents while keeping some institutions of civil society in operation, turned more repressive in the midst of growing opposition a few years later.

Political Turmoil at Home and Abroad

Nineteen sixty-eight proved a pivotal year, both in Brazil and throughout the world. That year began with the Tet Offensive in which the Vietcong army shocked the world by showing its ability to overpower the U.S. forces in South Vietnam. Later, the year was marked by student protests in Paris and at many universities in the United States; it culminated in a bloody massacre of students before the opening of the Olympic Games in Mexico City. Students everywhere called for an end to the U.S. military presence in Southeast Asia, for greater democracy on college campuses, for a more equitable distribution of wealth, and increasingly condemned the U.S. role as the anticommunist policeman of the world. In Brazil students mounted huge demonstrations against the generals. Unlike their counterparts in North America, however, powerful sections of the industrial working class in São Paulo and Rio de Janeiro joined in support of the student uprising. Fearing the rise of an opposition movement among workers, intellectuals, and even some of the traditional elites, and equating any call for democracy with subversion, the regime fabricated a "communist threat" everywhere and cracked down.

Late in 1968, the military began to govern through a series of institutional acts added to the framework of the constitution. Institutional Act 2 allowed for indirect elections, dissolved all existing political parties, and created two new ones: the Brazilian Democratic Movement, or MDB, as the opposition party, at least on paper, and the National Renovating Alliance, or ARENA, as the progovernment party. Institutional Act 5 suspended the legislature, forced three Supreme Court judges into retirement, eliminated many of the lower court judges and suspended habeas corpus, the right to challenge a person's detention or imprisonment, for crimes against a broadly interpreted notion of "national security."

The Regime's Harshest Hours

In 1969, another "new" constitution was passed, but many interpret it as simply an extension of the 1967 Constitution in that it strengthened the executive's powers. Most individual rights were suspended, the executive was granted powers to levy taxes, create public jobs, set salaries, force bills through the legislature without debate, and enact a wide range of measures governing public life. The years from 1968 until 1975 were the darkest hours of the Brazilian dictatorship. The institutions of civil society either disappeared or were restructured under the military. Political parties and labor unions were outlawed or limited to associations in favor of the regime, the press was censored, Congress was marginalized and allowed to take action only when favored by the military government. Military officers presided over all the universities, student groups were closely monitored, and many of the country's leading intellectuals, artists, musicians, and writers went into exile abroad. The police and courts ignored due process, while torture, executions, and disappearances became common.

Whereas internal resistance was all but eliminated, exiles abroad and critics of the regime waged a constant struggle from outside the country. Internally, a small urban guerrilla movement comprised of students and young militants engaged in various acts of sabotage. Led by Carlos Marighela, the faction had split from the Communist Party in 1964 when the party ceased waging any significant opposition. Marighela, an architect born in Salvador of a mulatto mother and Italian father, was a leading proponent of waging urban guerrilla warfare against the regime. He founded the Action for National Liberation (ALN) in 1968 and led a group of students and young militants in various acts of sabotage, but with no great effect. He was killed in a shootout with the police in São Paulo in 1969. The only other resistance came from some priests and religious leaders at the local level who used their legitimacy in this overwhelmingly Catholic nation to criticize the regime.

Kidnapping the Ambassador

Probably the most spectacular, if not particularly effective, opposition to the military government was carried out by a small group of urban activists. On September 4, 1969, they kidnapped the U.S. ambassador to Brazil, Charles Burke Elbrick, in Rio de Janeiro. The group demanded the right to broadcast an antigovernment manifesto on radio and TV stations, the release of 15 political prisoners, and their safe passage from Brazil to Mexico. The government agreed, and Elbrick was released three days later.

The kidnapping was significant more as a news item in Brazil and around the world (no U.S. ambassador had been kidnapped before) than as an effective political action. Urban guerrilla protest did not grow as a result of the publicity, nor did this type of political activity reach the dramatic heights it did in neighboring Argentina and Uruguay in the following decades.

The Brazilian Miracle

The national security state sought immediately to improve the economic picture as a way of quelling dissension. Since it was the threat of working-class militancy, rising inflation, and fear of regulation that had led foreign and domestic businesses to support the coup, the military government was anxious to prove that it had created the conditions for economic revitalization. During the government of General Emílio Garrastazu Médici (1968–74), Brazil launched its economic "miracle." The Brazilian Miracle, called for the infusion of large amounts of foreign investment capital, under very favorable conditions for the investors, into basic industry, development of the infrastructure (roads and the Transamazonian Highway in particular), and military hardware.

The miracle, really a "quick fix" industrialization program, increased manufacturing but resulted in a staggering debt and inflation that has been with Brazil ever since. As an economic policy, it failed, and there is nothing miraculous about economic failures. Steel production jumped from 2.8 million tons in 1964 to 9.2 million in 1976; passenger car production grew from 184,000 vehicles in 1964 to 986,000 in 1976, many for export. Exports diversified, especially with the addition of a wide range of manufactured goods, so that Brazil was no longer dependent simply on revenues from the sale of coffee. On the other hand, income disparity increased decisively, poverty was widespread, and unchecked urbanization strained the already woefully inadequate electrical, water distribution, road, and sanitation systems in the cities. The existing infrastructure and resources were taxed far beyond their capacity to deliver. In 1950, 64 percent of the population was rural and 36 percent was urban; in 1980, 33 percent was rural and 67 percent was urban. It had turned on its head.

Finally, the miracle relied almost completely on the influx of foreign capital to maintain growth. Despite the military's public proclamations of nationalism and Brazilian autonomy, they were handing the most important part of the nation—its finances—over to foreign interests. In exchange the military got a defense budget of unprecedented proportions and huge increases in military hardware. This allowed Brazil to build a formidable armed force, which in turn generated concern among the other Latin American countries, always wary of Brazil's expansionist and domineering tendencies. Since there were no direct foreign attacks, one can assume that this build-up was to maintain internal order and for use against the Brazilian population. The dependence on foreign investment has yet to be undone, forcing Brazil into reliance on the International Monetary Fund to maintain the semblance of financial order. Brazil had a temporary "bubble" but no miracle.

"Pharaoh Projects"

Along with the construction of a massive hydroelectric dam at Itaipú, on the Paraná River between Brazil and Paraguay, the Trans-Amazonian highway was one of the major achievements of the Brazilian Miracle. The so-named Pharaoh Projects were grandiose in scope and were designed to attract the world's attention to Brazil's economic potential. Constructed in the 1970s but not yet complete at the end of the 20th century, the Trans-Amazonian Highway is a two-lane red-dirt road that stretches 3,400 miles from the town of João Pessoa on the Atlantic coast across the Amazonian plains. Named BR-320, the highway was one more in a long series of attempts to open the interior to settlement. The

The Itaipú Hydroelectric Project is a power station and reservoir located near the famous Foz do Iguaçu. Wheras the Foz (pictured above) are a major tourist attraction, and honeymoon site, on the border with Argentina and Paraguay, the Itaipú Dam is a gigantic power station located nearby. The dam project, completed in 1991, generates 77,000 gigawatt-hours annually. (Claire Skotnes photo)

road was meant to encourage migrants from the poverty-stricken lands of the old Northeast, Pernambuco and Bahia in particular, to move to the remote northwestern territory of Rondônia, and to the states of Mato Grosso and Acre. Six different companies have cooperated in its construction, all of which have been criticized for inefficiency and receiving government favors.

While the highway might be considered an engineering feat, and even another component of the successful public relations campaign for which the miracle was well known, it did not encourage migration to the interior. The new towns that developed along the highway grew up only to house the road construction crews while the work was in progress, but were then abandoned as the project moved to a new site. Moreover, migration throughout history has generally occurred as a result of "push-pull" factors. Dire economic conditions may "push" migrants from an area, but the possibility for employment or a better life "pulls" migrants to specific locales. Certainly the impoverished backlanders left the dry, jobless towns and countryside of the Northeast during the years

169

of the miracle, but they traveled to the cities of São Paulo, Rio de Janeiro, Belo Horizonte, Santos, and others where job prospects were better.

One of the direct effects of the military's exploration of the sparsely settled interior was the addition of a new state carved from the land bordering on Bolivia, Mato Grosso, and Amazonas. The area, known as Guaporé, was incorporated as a territory in 1956 and renamed in honor of Cândido Rondon (1865–1958), known for his efforts to protect the indigenous population of the region. Ironically, the new state, named for a protector of the Indians, was the home to the Urueu-Wau-Wau, Wayoró, and Tuparí Indian groups, whose incorporation into the Brazilian state led to greater exploration and deforestation of the region. In the late 19th and early 20th centuries, Guaporé was populated by rubber tappers who moved in to harvest sap from the Amazon jungle and railroad workers there to build the Madeira-Mamoré railroad, which stretches between the Guaporé and Amazon Rivers. Highway construction in the 1970s aided the government's plan to distribute large tracts of land to ranchers who, in turn, felled the trees to create pasture. The population soared from 100,000 to 750,000 between 1970 and 1985. The territory was admitted as a state in 1981.

The increases in human habitation met with a corresponding decline in the tree population, with corresponding deleterious effects on the indigenous people. By 1990, approximately 20 percent of the rain forest had been destroyed as a result of slash-and-burn deforestation methods that the government's land giveaway program encouraged. However, the area has not proven to be good for agriculture. As the farmers soon discovered, the soil of a rain forest is surprisingly infertile, fragile, and unable to sustain pastures for cattle or to grow many crops. Today, ranches continue to dot the region, interspersed with mining and some other extractive industries.

A Crisis-Ridden Economic Miracle

The rise of the industrial sector and prosperity, especially among the urban elite and new middle class, had helped legitimize the military government. Although critics argued that the Brazilian Miracle was built on weak foundations, so long as prosperity continued for a considerable sector of society, the military suffered no direct threat. In the crisis of petroleum in 1974, the house of cards upon which the economic miracle rested came tumbling down. As the economy soured and inflation began to rise, the working class, chafing under a system of rising consumer prices but static wages, began to voice its discontent.

In the isolated rural areas, families live in tiny houses with no modern amenities, such as the one shown here. Frequently facing starvation, migrants travel to distant cities in search of jobs and access to basic necessities. (Meade-Skotnes photo)

The miracle came under intense criticism for having staked so much of the development process on expanding the network of roads and creating a dependency on automobiles, buses, and trucks instead of building efficient rail and subway transportation systems. The price rise by the Organization of Petroleum Exporting Countries (OPEC) and the international oil shortage of 1974 had dire consequences for Brazil's economy. In addition, economic woes combined with ongoing criticisms of human rights violations, lack of political freedoms, censorship, overbearing police presence, widespread corruption, and an inefficient government bureaucracy based on rewarding supporters of the regime, began to open new routes of dissent.

The downward economic trend exacerbated tensions in a Brazil in which everyone had been feeling the effects of the military dictatorship. For most of the time since 1964 the very rich and those close to the military had enjoyed greater prosperity, while the majority of Brazil's poor and working class had sunk deeper into poverty. The middle class had prospered before 1975, but as inflation soared later in the decade, they saw their gains eroded.

The malnourished section of the population doubled in the years from 1961 to 1975. The number suffering hunger moved from 27 million people in 1961, or 38 percent of the population, to 72 million in 1975, or 67 percent of the population. By the mid-1980s, the richest 1 percent

Shacks built into an automobile overpass in Recife by poor urban dwellers who have fled poverty in the countryside for the city, but have nowhere to live in the city. (Meade-Skotnes Photo)

had increased its share of the national income from 13 percent to 17.3 percent, while the share of the poorest 50 percent had declined from 13.4 percent to 10.4 percent. The number of landless rural workers increased, and migrants poured into the cities, especially in the industrializing Center-South. Urban shanty towns, or *favelas,* rimmed the outskirts of São Paulo and climbed the steep mountain slopes (called morros) in Rio de Janeiro, and individual makeshift shacks could be found propped precariously under railroad bridges, along roadbeds, or on vacant lots. Children ran loose with no one to care for them, and hardened criminals among the very young flourished in an environment where schools either did not exist or were in such terrible condition that even the teachers seldom showed their faces. Thousands of migrants searched for jobs and a livelihood in the cities, eking out an existence on the margins of productive society.

Ten years into military rule, the middle class, which had initially prospered under the economic stability of the miracle, began to feel the effects of heavy borrowing. The generals had built the miracle, and financed the Pharaoh projects by running up a huge debt. In 1964, Brazil's foreign debt stood at $3 billion; in 1980, it was $100 billion. Indeed, the military had failed at its single most important goal: balancing the budget and restoring economic order. When the oil crisis hit in October 1973, Brazil was not only deeply in debt, it had built an infrastructure that relied on oil, 80 percent of it imported. In 1974 the generals were faced with borrowing more money to pay for oil at its escalating price. Monetary values plummeted and Brazilians faced triple-digit inflation.

Opposition from the Catholic Church

By the mid-1970s, many voices were joining to criticize the regime. A few members of the Catholic clergy had spoken out against the regime during even the darkest days of repression. Whereas the church hierarchy initially supported the government or remained silent, by the late 1960s it began to emerge as an outspoken critic of the government's use of torture, of the arbitrary arrest and detention of citizens, and of the restrictions on the organizations of civil society. In 1972, the popular Paulista prelate, Archbishop Paulo Evaristo Arns, and a leading Protestant minister, Jaime Wright, formed an organization called the Comissão de Justiça e Paz (Peace and Justice Commission, or CPJ), which sought to unite the human rights community.

The CPJ galvanized the opposition to the military after the death of journalist Vladimir Herzog in September 1975. A Yugoslav Jew, Vladimir Herzog had immigrated as a youth to Brazil with his family, attended the University of São Paulo, and eventually rose to a position of prominence on *O Estado de São Paulo,* Brazil's foremost newspaper, and as a correspondent for the British Broadcasting Corporation (BBC). He earned the enmity of the police for his criticism of the regime. After inquiries by the local police into his activities, Herzog voluntarily presented himself for questioning at a São Paulo police station. The next day, his body was returned to his wife with the explanation that he had hanged himself in jail. It was widely assumed that the journalist had been tortured and killed. As if to confirm this view, the police insisted that the coffin not be opened for public viewing and presided at the funeral to ensure that it was never opened. Herzog's death was a key turning point in bringing international criticism on Brazil's human rights record. Many prominent members of society from among the church, as well as the press and intellectuals, stepped forward to condemn human rights violations and the anti-Semitism of the military.

The role of the Catholic Church was a part of a larger movement that came to be known as liberation theology in many countries of Latin America. Liberation theology developed in the late 1960s and early 1970s as many priests and nuns increasingly took the side of the poor and oppressed against the tyranny of military rule. One of its foremost centers was Brazil, where it developed a strong following among the church hierarchy, as well as the clergy and lay population. Arguing that the church had for too long taken the side of the rich and powerful, liberation theologians called for the church to use its influence to protest against poverty, human rights abuses, and dictatorships. The devout were organized into *communidades ecclesiaticas da base* (Christian base communities), usually called CEBs.

During the 1970s, the bishop's council of CNBB and the Catholic clergy in general became prominent critics of the military government and champions of the rights of the poor. As leaders of the largest Catholic population in the world, the bishops and clerics of Brazil were able to exert considerable pressure on the military government in order to open up more political space in which other groups seeking human and civil rights were able to voice their views. As one of the three largest national conferences of Catholic bishops in the world, the CNBB played a key role in bringing to the attention of the world press and international organizations the plight of the Brazilian masses under military rule.

The *Abertura,* Political "Opening," Begins

In the face of international pressure and growing discontent at home, the government embarked on a less hard-line approach. Under the pragmatic general Ernesto Geisel (1974–78), a more subdued coercive environment, called the *abertura,* or political opening, began in 1976. Although the military regime was never united in support of the *abertura,* more moderate elements felt that a lessening of repression, an amnesty that allowed dissidents to return, and a stronger role for the opposition, would stave off the more radical opposition. The Brazilian Democratic Movement (MDB) was the main organ of the diverse opponents of the regime. When the regime reinstated political parties in 1979, the MDB formed itself into the Party of the Brazilian Democratic Movement (PMDB) and grew to be the largest and most widespread party to contest the military's own ARENA party.

The *abertura* did not, however, proceed according to the generals' plan. Initially the regime saw the lessening of political repression as a way of pacifying its opponents, but intensifying economic problems began to galvanize a broader section of the population into a more activist opposition role. In 1980, inflation surpassed 100 percent. Two years later, Brazil stopped payment on its foreign debt and barely made payments on the interest. Simply servicing the debt drained the economy of its resources, leaving nothing for social services, education, health, maintenance of the infrastructure, or even salaries for government employees.

The Labor Movement Spearheads the Opposition

Beginning in the late 1970s, a reinvigorated labor movement began to insert itself into the national political scene. This movement originated in the industrial circle around São Paulo known as the ABCD for its four most important cities: Santo Andrade, São Bernardo do Campo, São Caetano do Sul and Diadema. The shop floor–based factory commissions in the industrial town of São Bernardo do Campo spearheaded the movement. These shop-floor units drew together auto, steel, and other metalworkers into a single movement to demand higher wages, better working conditions, and the right to strike. Illegal strike waves spread through the ABCD region in 1978–79, eventually encompassing more than 15 states in 113 strikes.

The compliant government-sponsored trade unions were replaced by new militant unions made up of thousands of members. Union assemblies began to be held in soccer stadiums where thousands of workers and their supporters gathered to hear their leaders call for an end to the restrictions placed on labor by the military regime. At the invitation of the Catholic Church, the offices of these new militant unions were moved to the cathedral of São Bernardo. In a single year, even in the face of military repression, more than 3 million workers went out on strike. Completely caught by surprise, the corporations and military gave in to substantial wage increases. The Partido dos Trabalhadores (Workers Party, or PT) formed in 1980 under the leadership of the former president of the metalworkers' union, Luís Inácio Lula da Silva, and a group of intellectuals and workers involved in the opposition movement. The PT was the organization that served as the platform from which to launch both opposition candidates and formulate a pro-democracy agenda.

Lula, the person who most embodied labor's opposition to the dictatorship, was born in 1945 in Garanhuns, Pernambuco. When he was seven years old, his mother left the Northeast and brought the family south to Santos, where Lula's father was working as a longshoreman. Eventually abandoned by his father, Lula grew up in a household where his mother managed seven children, nearly all of whom had to leave school to work at a young age. From this background, Lula came to oppose the military's restrictions on working people. In a country known for a weak leftist tradition among the working class, when compared with neighboring Argentina in particular, Lula established himself as a major socialist trade unionist in the 1980s. He rose to prominence as head of the São Bernardo do Campo Metallurgical Workers Union in the ABCD industrial belt

175

Lula addresses other leaders of Latin American countries at the founding meeting of the Union of South American Nations (UNASUR), May 2008, in Brasilia. The former auto worker lost the smallest finger on his left hand while operating a factory press when he was 19 years old. Lula states that his concern for workers' rights stems from this accident and the fact that he was denied treatment at several hospitals because he was unable to pay. (Agência Brasil)

on the edge of the city of São Paulo and became well known for his dynamic speaking abilities, savvy organizing, and charismatic leadership skills in a series of strikes that brought the dictatorship to its knees in the 1980s.

The PT developed as one of the most formidable opponents of the military government, exercising a strength no other sector could touch: the ability to grind industrial production to a halt. In 1980 a new strike wave swept the industrial Southeast cities. Under the leadership of the PT, the strikes were better organized, involved large numbers of rank-and-file workers, and succeeded in winning higher wages, improvements in safety conditions, paid sick and vacation leaves, as well as a more democratic union structure.

Return to Democracy

In 1984, massive demonstrations calling for direct elections broke out in nearly every Brazilian city. The uprisings caused supporters of the government's ARENA party to defect, ushering in an end to military rule. In an upset in the electoral college, Tancredo Neves, a long-standing member of the MDB, powerful former governor of Minas Gerais, and cabinet minister under João Goulart before the coup, was elected president. In a compromise, ARENA party leader José Sarney was chosen vice president. Although the head of the government party in the Senate, Sarney had led the insurgent bloc in support of Tancredo Neves. After all the demonstrating, deal-making, and intense negotiating to bring Neves to power, the president-elect suffered a massive perforated ulcer and entered the hospital the night before he was to take office. After a month in intensive care, Neves died on April 21, 1985. Vice president designate Sarney was sworn in as president.

When the military stepped down in 1985, the Brazilian social structure and economy were in desperate circumstances. The generals' spending spree on military equipment, elaborate and inefficient energy projects, and the absence of any opposition to curb their profligate agenda, had left the country on the brink of bankruptcy. Sarney had little authority to enact change because he had no friends on either side of the political divide. The democratic forces distrusted him for being a longtime supporter of the military government, while the military

Street vendors selling outside Gloria Church on a Sunday morning. High unemployment in traditional jobs has forced thousands of Brazilians into the "informal sector," where they make a living selling goods on the street. (Meade-Skotnes Photo)

would have nothing to do with him because of his role in supporting the democratic opposition. The comedy of errors that had brought him to power was also his undoing. Nevertheless, the military had no other candidate and feared direct elections even more. After a short moratorium on debt payments, Brazil capitulated to an austerity program originating with the International Monetary Fund (IMF) in 1988 and began to walk a tightrope between appeasing domestic demands for better government programs and holding the international banks at bay. The country drifted down this stream for the next five years, until the first direct elections.

The Constitution of 1988

From 1985 until 1988, most of the political forces in Brazil were engaged in writing a new constitution. As opposed to many constitutions in Brazil or other countries that are written by a relatively small body of electors, the 1988 constitution was drafted by the entire Congress of 559 members. As a result, it stands as a document that expresses better the differences, negotiations, and jockeying for position, of widely disparate representatives than it does as an instrument for government. Its 245 articles and 70 transitory provisions (the meanings of which are debated) have yet to be fully implemented.

On the whole, the 1988 constitution weakened the executive and strengthened the legislative and judicial branches of the government. It outlawed government by decree, granted to Congress the right to create and oversee administrative agencies and placed the executive under the oversight of Congress, including the provision that allowed Congress to impeach the executive and members of the judiciary. The Constitution provided for extensive protections of legal rights and human rights, as well as an array of social and economic rights to an education, maternity leave, social security, labor and leisure guarantees, and much more. Lula, who had been elected deputy from São Paulo to the national government in 1986, played an active role in designing the 1988 constitution, winning important progressive additions pertaining to land reform and workers' rights. He advocated nationalization of mineral reserves, protective legislation for national enterprises, a 40-hour work week, and left-liberal reforms in support of women's rights, anti-poverty programs, and preservation of the environment. On paper, the constitution of 1988 is one of the most far-reaching progressive documents passed by any government of the world. Both the enactment and enforcement of its numerous provisions, however, have been less than effective. Brazil's many social problems cannot be resolved with the passage of a single constitution.

The Presidential Campaign and Election

In 1989, in the most intense showing of Brazilian democracy in its history, a wide field of candidates sparred for the presidency. The main contest pitted Fernando Collor de Mello (1949–) the centrist candidate from an old-line aristocratic family and governor of the tiny state of Alagoas in the Northeast, against Lula, the PT candidate and leader of the labor opposition. The election brought 80 million voters to the polls. In a run-off that narrowed the field of candidates to two, Collor beat Lula. Collor received early support from Roberto Marinho, the conservative head of the *Globo* media empire. Collor, 40-year-old, photogenic former karate champion, was good copy. Collor favored a laissez-faire economic program and beat back the Paulista head of the powerful metallurgical union, who advocated a leftist, social democratic program. Nonetheless, Lula's showing in the national election, along with a string of impressive PT victories in state governors' races, contests for mayoralities, and seats in the national Congress, signaled the terms of opposing forces in the years to come.

As a presidential candidate from the time of his first campaign, and in speeches that he delivers throughout the world, Lula has promoted the concept of empowering working people to take control of their political destiny. Inserted into the Workers Party program is the slogan "Without Fear of Being Happy." According to Lula, Brazilians have been disenfranchised and left out of the decision-making process for so long that they have become afraid to assert their rights. He calls for a strategy of overcoming society's fear, or what he refers to as "the fear of the new; the fear of change." (Sader and Silverstein, 1991:6)

Scandal and Corruption under Fernando Collor

Fernando Collor assumed the presidency in March 1990. After a quarter of a century, the long nightmare of military control over the democratic process had finally come to an end. Despite high hopes for the Collor presidency, his administration proved to be one of Brazil's worst. His economic shock plan, closely coordinated with the IMF and reliant on selling off state-controlled enterprises, failed to halt Brazil's out-of-control inflation. Although he had run on an anticorruption platform, and even established his political credentials while governor of Alagoas by cracking down on public employees who earned exorbitant salaries but never showed up for work, Collor's presidency was undone by corruption. The unraveling resembled the plot of a *telenovela*, or nighttime soap opera, of which the Brazilians are so fond.

The scandal began in mid-1992 when Pedro Collor, the president's brother, revealed that Fernando had used cocaine and was involved in an embezzlement/kickback scheme coordinated by his close associate, P. C. Farias. As the investigation over the succeeding six months uncovered, Farias was selling political favors to large corporations and some wealthy individuals in return for large deposits in clandestine bank accounts. Millions of dollars were funneled through these accounts to Fernando, his wife Rosane, and to Farias. With the money the Collors had furnished an elaborate mansion and landscaped the backyard with waterfalls, pools, and exotic plants. Rosane used her share for several plastic surgery makeovers, expensive orthodontia, a $20,000-a-month clothing allowance, and frequent European shopping sprees.

In the middle of the Brazilian summer, December 1992, Congress impeached and convicted Collor, who then resigned. This accorded him the dubious honor as the only president in the history of North and South America to be both impeached and forced from office. Vice president Itamar Franco served out the remaining two years of Collor's term.

Several aspects of the Collor impeachment are significant. In the first place, the extent to which the Collors were bilking the government, and the audacity with which they were doing it, shocked even Brazilians, a people fairly used to corruption in politics. Secondly, the sordid details of misconduct at the highest level of the government were revealed in the press and uncovered through a series of congressional investigations. This demonstrated the extent to which Brazil was operating with a free and uncensored press and under a government that took seriously congressional oversight. Finally, Collor was tried and convicted by the Senate, found guilty of abuse of power and lost his political rights for eight years. In the eyes of many, this placed the Brazilian system of justice even above that of the United States. Brazilians were able to take pride in the fact that the military stayed clear of the process, the mechanisms for pursuing justice endured, and, in contrast to the case of Richard Nixon in the United States, the president was granted no special favors or pardon to avoid prosecution. The political laundry was indeed quite dirty, but Brazil aired it in public and found its way out of the crisis, peacefully.

The Presidency of Fernando Henrique Cardoso

The most noteworthy event in Itamar Franco's presidency was his appointment in 1993 of Fernando Henrique Cardoso (b. 1931) to the powerful cabinet post of Finance Minister. Cardoso, who was elected president the following year and assumed office in January 1995, had taken bold steps as head of a team of economic advisers to rescue the country's ailing finances. His plan, the Plano Real (pronounced rey-al) was a total assault on inflation. He introduced a new currency, the *real*, imposed a series of measures to reduce inflation, and set in motion a mild austerity program. The rate of inflation dropped dramatically, from near 50 percent a month in 1994 to 1 to 2 percent over the next two years. The success of the Plano Real was an enormous boost to Cardoso's popularity and established him as a major contender in the presidential election in October 1994.

Before entering politics, Fernando Henrique Cardoso was one of Brazil's most well-known intellectuals. As a leftist critic of the government, he had been exiled after the military coup but returned to Brazil in 1968. A professor at the prestigious and decidedly left-wing University of São Paulo, Cardoso had coauthored with Enzo Falletto in 1967 a well-known text on dependency theory, *Dependency and Development.* Cardoso and Falletto were key exponents of one of the political arguments at the core of dependency theory. They revised the theory of the "development of underdevelopment" pioneered by Brazilian economist Celso Furtado, arguing that peripheral nations such as Brazil, along with other poor countries of what was then called the Third World, were kept in a state of perpetual dependency on rich nations in Europe and North America. Moreover, Cardoso contended in this and many other writings that members of the national bourgeoisie, made up of the industrial, commercial, and landed elite of the peripheral nations, enriched themselves at the expense of the impoverished lower classes of their own countries.

Although Cardoso built his intellectual reputation on the basis of critiquing the business class of Brazil and similar Latin American nations, he did not clash with either domestic business interests or the International Monetary Fund (IMF) while president. He remained a critic of inequality and advocate of broad democratic reforms, but argued that the road out of poverty was a program of development closely matched to attracting investment according to the structural adjustments outlined by the World Bank, IMF, and international financiers.

Current analysts are split in their appraisal of Cardoso's record. Some argue that his conversion to neoliberalism was rooted in the particular twist on dependency theory which he and Falleto developed in the 1960s. Others contend that as president he abandoned entirely his leftist concern for the oppressed and embraced the full slate of proposals emanating from the IMF and other international financial agencies.

The 1994 election that pitted Cardoso against the Workers Party candidate, Lula, was one of the most remarkable in Brazilian history. The key difference in this election was that both Cardoso and Lula had developed their political careers in opposition to the powerful right-wing military, and as foes of the industrial and landed elite. Cardoso won by forging a coalition of his own Brazilian Social Democratic Party (PSDB) with the conservative Liberal Front Party (PFL) and a number of other smaller parties. Although Cardoso no longer considered himself a leftist, he began his career as one of Brazil's foremost marxist academics. Lula had built his base of support among the rank and file of the trade unions, as an advocate for the poor, and as a key player in the demise of the military government. Both candidates had built their own parties. Cardoso had founded the PSDB and Lula the PT.

During the *abertura,* Cardoso had been a frequent critic of the regime, both inside Brazil and in his many publications and talks outside the country. As a highly respected academic whose writings had been translated into many languages, Cardoso was able to tap connections in intellectual and human rights circles in the United States, Europe, and throughout Latin America. As such, he served as a key conduit for criticism from abroad that severely damaged the government's reputation and helped bring about the end to the military dictatorship. When the generals stepped down in the early 1980s, Cardoso entered politics and became a senator from the state of São Paulo.

During the presidential campaign, Cardoso disassociated himself from his leftist past and disavowed many of his ideas about dependency, especially his harsh picture of the national bourgeoisie. He did, however, continue to support a broadening of social programs to benefit the Brazilian majority, favored environmental initiatives, and called for curbs on military spending. In the campaign, he won the support of the conservative business sector by convincing its members that he would keep the economy on track. No doubt many among the elite distrusted his leftist past, but they preferred him to Lula and the clear Left alternative.

Fernando Henrique Cardoso won with more than 50 percent of the vote, one of the widest mandates in Brazilian electoral history. When he took office in 1995, he was only the second president in 32 years who was elected by popular vote *and* allowed to take office. In 1997, an amendment, widely known as the "reelection amendment," was added to the constitution. It allowed Cardoso, as well as governors who had been elected at the same time as he was, to stand for immediate reelection in October 1998 for one term. Cardoso was reelected president with 53 percent of the vote.

Brazil and the Economy at the End of the Twentieth Century

At the end of the 20th century, economic analysts were unsure of Brazil's future. While developments in Brazilian politics in the 30 years from 1964 to 1994 had been dramatic, key changes in social forces and the country's economic problems had not changed much, and in some cases worsened. Since the end of World War II, Brazil's economy had grown in fits and starts. By century's end, it was the 10th largest in the world but still counted among the developing nations. Moreover, growth and

Gas station in Rio de Janeiro with both ethanol-based fuel and gasoline pumps. (Meade-Skotnes Photo)

technological change was exceedingly uneven. In parts of the interior of the Northeast and in Amazonia, farming and production methods have barely changed in 100 years, while in the industrial belt around São Paulo steel, chemical, and high-tech industries stretched as far as the eye could see. In 2000, Brazil boasted some of the most technologically advanced automobile plants in the world, a fact some blamed for high levels of unemployment. Brazil's capital intensive development has not provided the jobs needed by the millions of urban poor, many of whom continually migrate from the countryside in search of employment.

Brazil's industrial growth in the 1990s suffered from poor planning and the legacy of a tendency to concentrate on megaprojects or quick fixes to endemic problems. For example, during the military government a high priority was placed on developing nuclear power. In 1974, the government signed an agreement with West Germany to obtain nuclear technology in exchange for German access to Brazil's uranium reserves. Brazil developed a highly expensive, technologically sophisticated nuclear program, with German assistance and in the face of opposition from the United States. Nuclear power plants require enormous amounts of capital investment, absorbing money that might have been better spent in developing energy-efficient transportation and electrical power sources.

Similarly, a plan to reduce dependency on foreign oil centered on developing biofuels and ethanol-powered automobiles. The alcohol fuel program that was launched in earnest in the late 1970s was intended to provide a domestic source of fuel, drawn from Brazil's abundant sugarcane production, at a time when the international price for oil was about $40 a barrel. Although ethanol might appear to be a simple and renewable source of fuel, the cost of refining it and of converting engines to burn the fuel outstripped the cost of gasoline once the international price dropped. By the early 1990s, there was little interest in ethanol, and Petrobras, the state-subsidized refinery that processed it, turned to the government for a bailout. Needless to say, this investment subsequently placed Brazil at a tremendous advantage in 2008 as worldwide fuel prices skyrocketed.

At the time, however, the search for alternative fuel sources absorbed huge amounts of capital investment from abroad. By the end of 1985 Brazil had racked up $100 billion in foreign debt. The balance on paying the debt was maintained only through strict adherence to IMF austerity guidelines. The IMF, interested in ensuring the solvency of the worldwide banking system, especially the lenders from the United States and Europe, set Brazil on a plan of making payments on the debt, privatizing government enterprises, and keeping exports high and cheap so that they find a ready market in foreign markets. Privatized enterprises, then, became a key recipient of investment funds from abroad. Such a plan may work well for a period, but can fall precipitously if international demand for the goods Brazil has to offer falls off.

In the late 1980s and early 1990s, high inflation hindered economic activity and investment. Brazil and its international lenders, worried about a default with ripple effects throughout the world, concentrated on the financial picture. The Real Plan, instituted in spring 1994, sought to break inflationary expectations by pegging the real to the U.S. dollar. Inflation was brought down to single-digit annual figures, but not fast enough to avoid substantial real exchange rate appreciation during the transition phase of the Real Plan. This appreciation meant that Brazilian goods were now more expensive relative to goods from other countries, which contributed to large current account deficits. At first it seemed that Brazil would be able to weather the crisis and attract foreign investment, but investors became more wary of emerging markets during the Asian financial crisis in 1997 and the Russian bond default in August 1998.

Fearful of spreading the Asian and Russian crisis to Latin America, the IMF granted Brazil a $41.5 billion loan, with attendant payback and austerity program, in November 1998. In January 1999, the Brazilian Central Bank announced that the real would no longer be pegged to the U.S. dollar. This devaluation helped moderate the 1999 downturn in economic growth, about which investors had expressed concerns during the summer of 1998. Brazil's 1999 debt to gross domestic product (GDP) ratio of 48 percent beat the IMF target and helped reassure investors that Brazil would maintain tight fiscal and monetary policy even with a floating currency. The rosy picture rests on a growth rate of greater than 3 percent from 2000 onward and, despite setbacks, has held at 5 percent or better.

Throughout the 1990s, the financial balance sheet was maintained by exacting enormous concessions from the Brazilian working population in the form of cutbacks in social services and wage stagnation. At the end of the 20th century, as the United States entered the first stages of an economic downturn, Brazil's products were not in high demand abroad, and it became increasingly difficult to generate the capital needed to make payments on the huge debt. The only solution, therefore, was to keep production costs low by further reducing wages for an already strapped working class. One might think of the "trickle down" theory in reverse, as far as Brazil was concerned. Poverty trickled down from the middle through the working class and pooled among the urban and rural poor.

The economic crisis, the fall in the stock market, and the collapse in technology stocks that crept over the U.S. market in early 2001 affected most of the world. While Washington's attention was riveted on Japan, whose continuing economic decline threatened to stall any chance of recovery in the U.S. market, Latin America's economic problems began to surface. Brazil was not in a position strong enough to absorb ripples, much less the pounding waves of global economic crises. The crisis that swept Argentina at the end of 2001 temporarily bypassed Brazil.

Argentina absorbs more than 11 percent of Brazil's exports and ranks third behind China and the United States as the nation's most important trading partners. As Argentina's crisis deepened, it cut back drastically on imports, especially big-ticket items like machinery, technology, automobiles, steel, and chemicals that supply the industrial sector. By the end of 2003, Argentina's economy had stabilized. Under the leadership of Brazil's new president, Lula, and Nestor Kirchner, elected president of Argentina in May 2003, the two nations embarked on cooperative trade policies, seeking to develop greater unity to counterbalance U.S. demands that both countries consider detrimental to their autonomy.

As it turned out, Brazil's industrial, agricultural, and petroleum exports have been commanding very high prices. In the first decade of the 21st century, the economy has improved markedly as a result of diverse productivity in agriculture, industry, extractive, and service sectors. The international demand for food, especially soybeans and beef, both of which Brazil has in plentitude, in addition to the discovery of oil and gas reserves, has considerably upgraded Brazil's economic forecast. As the world's 10th-largest energy consumer, Brazil's investment in hydroelectricity and ethanol was fortuitous. By century's end, Brazil's prospects appeared so promising that an economist from the U.S. investment firm of Goldman Sachs posited the BRIC thesis. Brazil, Russia, India, and China (BRIC), the theorist claimed, were the four economies that would by 2050 be the most dominant in the world, surpassing in growth and wealth all existing world powers. No doubt there are those who disagree, and the world economic crisis beginning in 2008 could undercut any predictions, but Brazil's position economically and politically has changed dramatically since the return to democracy.

9

POPULAR CULTURE: MUSIC, SPORTS, TELEVISION, AND CINEMA IN TODAY'S BRAZIL

No history of Brazil, no matter how brief, should overlook that part of life that absorbs the attentions of many ordinary people outside their places of work during much of their waking hours. Very often it is popular culture, as much or more than impersonal political and economic events, that engross the people of a nation and help them to define who they are on a day-to-day basis. In this chapter, the histories of the key features of the Brazilian pastime will be examined: samba and Carnival, *futebol* or soccer, the nighttime television melodramas called *telenovelas*, or simply *novelas*, and finally, cinema. In the case of Brazil, periodically during the 20th century and on into the 21st, popular culture, including dance, music, and sports, has moved from the streets and neighborhood bars of Rio de Janeiro, São Paulo, and Salvador da Bahia, to the clubs, movie theaters, dance halls, music stores, and sports arenas of the world.

Samba, Soccer, Television, and Movies

In 1939, Carmen Miranda became the most widely recognized Brazilian entertainer abroad and, as a result of shrewd contract negotiations, the most highly paid woman in Hollywood. In subsequent years, musicians such as Caetano Veloso, Gilberto Gil, Maria Bethânia, Milton Nascimento, Antônio Carlos Jobim, and others have enjoyed huge popularity and exerted a definite musical influence both inside and outside the country, from samba to the bossa nova to *tropicalismo* to jazz and jazz fusion.

Of all the diverse types of Brazilian music, the best-known is the infectious samba. During the 20th century, samba catapulted from its modest beginnings as a music sung and danced in neighborhood bars in the poorest sections of Salvador and Rio de Janeiro to become the signature for the yearly Carnival, a pre-Lenten extravaganza that stands as one of the world's biggest parties and the most important tourist attraction in Brazil.

On the sports front, since the 1960s when Pelé first dazzled the soccer world with his agile ball handling and powerful offensive play, Brazil has been synonymous with soccer. Going into the 2002 World Cup competition, Brazil had participated in every World Cup playoff since the games were resumed after World War II and had won an unprecedented four championships (1958, 1962, 1970, 1994). The 2002 team turned a lackluster qualifying circuit and widespread accusations of fraud and corruption in the Brazilian Soccer Federation (CBF) into a brilliant finish to capture its fifth cup, or *Penta*. Reaffirming the sport's grasp on the national psyche, half a million fans wildly cheered the victorious team as it arrived in Brazil on July 2 after defeating Germany in the final, 2-0, in Japan.

Finally, most Brazilians watch soccer, as well as Carnival and the pre-Carnival festivities on television, just as they are glued to the set for nearly all their news and entertainment. Brazil's media giant, TV *Globo,* is the largest network in Latin America and fourth largest in the world, reaching 80 million viewers daily. The passion of Brazilian home viewers is the nightly *novela,* or soap opera. The media frenzy surrounding the death of Daniella Perez, a television star from a popular *novela, De Corpo e Alma* ("Body and Soul"), in 1992 exemplified the *novela's* place at the center of national popular culture. When the starlet's body was found on a roadside on the outskirts of Rio de Janeiro in late December 1992, the nation turned its eyes from the day's top story, the impeachment of President Fernando Collor de Mello, to soak up the details of the sordid crime instead. In a case of reality imitating art, Perez's death garnered even more attention when it became clear that her assailant, who had punctured her body with 16 knife stabs, was her costar, Guilherme de Padua.

This chapter explores various aspects of Brazil's popular culture as a vibrant blend of the nation's African and European heritages. To know Brazilian popular culture, is to know a bit of the Brazilian character.

Carmen Miranda

One of the first Brazilian entertainers to make a mark internationally was Carmen Miranda. Born in Portugal, Miranda became a popular

Carmen Miranda. (© Bettman/Corbis)

radio and film star in Brazil in the late 1920s. Despite her Portuguese past, Miranda had a decidedly Brazilian act, based on urban sambas, rotating hip dance moves, stylized and exaggerated hand, facial, and body gestures, all performed to an undulating conga drumbeat. Her trademark was to have her head wrapped in a turban topped with an elaborate fruit and flower arrangement. She sang and danced in an exaggerated headgear and attire based on that of Bahian market women

189

that dated back to the time of slavery. In movies and in her popular nightclub acts, the white, Portuguese-born Miranda, projected the Brazilian mixed-race woman with a tropical flavor to adoring audiences in the United States and Europe.

Some Brazilians argued that Miranda's bold, exaggerated style, the elaborate jewelry and costumes she performed in, were an embarrassment to a country trying to portray itself as a developing major power. Another faction of Brazilians rejected Miranda for leaving the country and building her reputation abroad. Apparently, for some she was "too Brazilian" but for many others she was "not Brazilian enough." For example, in 1940 when she returned to Brazil for a series of performances she was met with little more than polite applause and even criticism that her act had become "too Americanized."

When Carmen Miranda died in 1955, her popularity abroad was greater than in Brazil. Nonetheless, her contributions to the music and culture of Brazil should not be overlooked. Although she was accused of peddling Brazilian music and dance in a highly commercialized format, Carmen Miranda can be credited with bringing Brazil's national music, the samba, to a worldwide audience. In addition, she introduced the image of the *baiana* (Bahian traditional slave woman) with wide skirts and turbaned headdress as the "showgirl" of Brazil at home and abroad. The *baiana* costume was adopted as the central feature of Carnival for women and, especially, for men, who famously dress up in elaborate Carmen Miranda style and parade through the streets of Brazil's cities during Carnival.

Samba

Samba refers to both a rhythmic music and a dance born in the slave quarters of the Brazilian Northeast and spread to the cities of the coast, especially Salvador da Bahia and Rio de Janeiro. Samba had its beginning among the slave population of Bahia, having been imported in a varied form from Angola. It flourished in the social milieu of the freed persons during the early decades of the 20th century after the abolition of slavery in 1888. In the *favelas* and working-class neighborhoods that cropped up in the expanding urban centers, blacks came together in private parties and outdoor bars, affectionately called *botequims*, to play music on their assortment of homemade instruments. Most of these instruments were passed down from the time of slavery into the communities of freed persons. They had been fashioned from found objects and scrap materials.

The blocos, a loose network of street musicians and dancers, were the precursors to the modern samba schools. They continue today, ranging from young boys such as these in Salvador, to the famous Bloco de Ipanema in Rio de Janeiro, that hundreds of revelers join during the Carnival season. (Photograph by Erich Goode)

The dominant feature of these parties was the *roda de samba*, an arrangement of samba dancers in a circle, swaying and stepping to a steady drumbeat, with at least one, and sometimes more than one, dancer in the middle. The dancers moved to the mesmerizing beat, while local composers chanted out verse after verse of an improvised refrain. The party, simply called a *roda* (circle), typically stretched from late evening until the next morning.

The first formal organization of samba dancers, singers, and instrumentalists formed in 1928. The organizers called it an *escola de samba*, or samba school. Most likely they chose this name as a way of establishing legitimacy for the dance and musical form by associating the concept of a dance hall with a school, a place of discipline, hard work, and learning. These clubs or schools became the foundation from which samba emerged as a major cultural force in all urban areas, but especially in Rio de Janeiro. The schools grew out of the loose network of revelers called *blocos de sujo*, literally "groups of dirty ones," who paraded through the streets at Carnival time. In the 1930s, the *blocos* and other groups, often made up of several generations of extended families, began to come together in the samba schools. As a musical form and popular entertainment, samba and the schools in which it was centralized flourished in the back alleys and local *botequims* from the late 1920s through the 1930s.

Carnival

The first recorded samba was *"Pelo telefone"* (On the Phone) which was registered to a musician named Donga in 1917. Other musicians added to the system of two-bar phrasing, slowed the tempo, and added notes. The modern samba developed in the 1950s, and has been added to by a host of well-known composers including Noel Rosa, Caninha, Heitor do Prazeres, Ataulfo Alves, Geraldo Pereira, Lamartine Babo, Braguinha, Dorival Caymmi, and Paulinho da Viola.

The rhythm is carried by a drum (the *batucada*) and many percussion instruments that do not have names in English, including *surdo, tamborim, pandeiro, frigideira, chocalho.* The music does not feature brass instruments, although some have been introduced for a style that imitates North American jazz, but there is often a guitar.

To the unstudied ear, samba can appear to be a single rhythmic song and beat, but there are actually many variations that have developed over the years and have been recorded by many of the best known *sambistas*. In addition to the long-standing *samba de breque* (samba in which the singer "breaks" into a dramatic story), *samba de enredo* (samba with a theme, as in Carnival), *samba de roda* (samba in a circle with hand-clapping), there have been recent additions that reflect international influences. In the 1980s a *samba tan-tan,* featuring a banjo, became popular, as did *samba-reggae,* influenced by West Indian music, samba with "cool jazz" influences from the West Coast of the United States, and *samba rap,* that incorporates American rap and hip-hop. As a musical form samba itself continues to evolve and mutate as it comes into contact with new musical trends and international influences.

As Afro-Brazilian musical culture grew, it attached itself to the pre-Lenten parties that were a tradition among the Portuguese, Italian, and other Catholic immigrants from Europe. The entrance of Afro-Brazilian culture on the national scene was not welcomed by everyone from the white elite and immigrant communities. In the face of a growing Afro-descendant urban population in the 1920s, a backlash against black culture took hold among some sectors of the white population. The latter argued that blacks, most of whom were poor, lacked education and skills as a result of slavery and were to blame for the nation's backwardness. This "blame the victim" syndrome gave rise to a number of laws that sought to prohibit the practice of non-Christian religions and any public expression of black music and dance. This prohibition coincided with the efforts of immigration authorities to exclude where possible, and otherwise actively discourage, nonwhite immigrants from entering the country.

The practice of African religious cults of *candomblé, umbanda,* and *macumba* was driven underground and police informers infiltrated the *rodas de samba* and rounded up participants when a party or street dance began. In one case, a black actor practicing a play that featured a *candomblé* scene was arrested in his boardinghouse after being turned in by his neighbor who accused him of practicing witchcraft. In historian and political commentator Alison Raphael's study of samba in Rio de Janeiro she reports that an elderly black man claimed that "it was enough to be seen walking with a tambourine under your arm to be beaten and arrested by the police." (*Brazil Herald,* January 30/31, 1977)

Despite this harassment, in the early 1930s, the samba schools were officially recognized as participants in the citywide Carnival festivities. The mainly black and poor *sambistas,* organized in the samba schools, joined the citywide party dominated by the mainstays of Carnival: the *grandes sociedades,* or great societies. The *grandes sociedades* were clubs made up of the city's most affluent residents, businessmen, and professionals. On the Sunday before Ash Wednesday, some of the most prominent citizenry dressed in elaborate costumes and paraded through the streets either perched on top of or walking alongside richly festooned floats. Drawing on direct or indirect government connections, the elite societies garnered substantial funds to help defray their expenses.

By contrast, the samba schools received no subsidies and their members lacked any sources of cash beyond a few contributions to pay for floats, costumes, or musical instruments. As a result, school members sewed their own costumes, created instruments, and decorated floats with found materials. Relying on the skills of local craftsmen, seamstresses, and a host of volunteers, preparations for Carnival involved a massive effort, turning the months and weeks before Carnival into a frenzied outpouring of cooperation and recreation in the city's poor neighborhoods. In fact, it was this sense of community that would be lost in later years as the samba schools garnered more attention, drew on more lucrative resources for funds, and began to engage in fierce competition to win prizes and acclaim as the top schools of the season.

Official Recognition of the Samba Schools

In 1933, President Getúlio Vargas officially recognized the samba schools. Vargas's recognition of the schools can be seen as a part of his overall policy of winning the loyalty of the urban working classes and poor. In addition, legalizing the samba schools contributed to Vargas's strategy of unifying the country's citizens around a nationalist and populist base in support of his political goals. Once the schools were officially authorized, they became subject to greater government scrutiny and censorship. Recognition was not, however, a single top-down process. As anthropologist Hermano Vianna points out, official acceptance was the culmination of years of give-and-take, when respect frequently alternated with dismissal, before the mainstream audience eventually embraced the samba schools as the mainstay of Carnival.

The samba schools began to employ skilled professionals to design the floats and costumes. They vied for the best choreographers to arrange intricate samba routines. The samba schools began to enjoy a heightened prestige, *sambistas* attained celebrity status around the country, and the process of mounting the elaborate productions became less of a financial burden on the shantytown dwellers. At the same time the schools' relationship with the residents of their local neighborhoods grew more remote. The community spirit that had united the

Baiana *contingent of samba school in the Carnival parade.* (Photography by Erich Goode)

poor Afro-Brazilian population and had been responsible for launching the early parades and the *rodas* increasingly waned as samba lost touch with its roots.

Before they were admitted to the yearly Carnival, the schools had to register with the police and obtain a license to parade. In addition, the government required that the schools' *enredo* (theme) and the float reflect a page out of Brazilian history or depict a famous historical personality. Vargas's intention was to use Carnival, just as he was using other mediums such as national education, social welfare, and political discourse, to construct a unified nation-state. Carnival was just one part, albeit an important one because of its widespread popularity with all social classes, of the president's overall plan to forge a national consciousness and national unity out of the loosely knit federation of states that had characterized Brazil from the colonial period through the First Republic.

Carnival and National Identity

The Carnival themes increasingly celebrated national development and progress. Getúlio Vargas's goal of building national unity through an accelerated plan of increased production and industrial efficiency relied on a unified workforce with a single national identity. Vargas's vision of Brazilian identity included Afro-Brazilian culture. The legitimacy of the Afro-Brazilian samba schools, therefore, served as a powerful centerpiece for the promotion of a new racial ideology. Vargas pointed to the importance of samba and Carnival to show that Brazil had escaped the ravages of racism that separated people in the United States and elsewhere. To stem the effects of racial antagonism, Vargas envisioned Carnival as a place in which the heroic efforts of both blacks and white immigrant workers stood at the apex of Brazil's "racial paradise." A 1941 article stated that one of the "most characteristic features of Brazilian democratic formation is the non-existence among us of racial prejudice." A government publication in 1942 explicitly linked this egalitarian racial philosophy to Vargas's vision of Carnival. It proclaimed, "samba has come down from the morro to the paved streets of the city. . . . The personalities of our songs today bring their activity to bear in our factories and shops." (Vianna 1999:91–92)

As with all popular culture, Carnival themes have fluctuated to reflect changes in the nation's broader political reality. In the 1970s and 1980s, *samba de enredos* celebrated the famous rebellions of Brazil's past, such as Canudos and Palmares, adding not-so-veiled calls for

Allegorical float and samba school in the Carnival parade. (Photograph by Erich Goode)

resistance to the military regime. Today the samba schools have sought corporate sponsorship as a way of paying for the exorbitantly expensive floats and costumes. A current complaint of Carnival observers is that the parade is one long advertisement, with corporate logos and slogans taking the place of indigenous cultural themes.

In a process that began in the 1930s and has continued since, the samba schools have been instrumental in integrating, especially, Carioca (or Rio) society and providing a cultural symbol for all Brazil. Black *sambistas* began to enjoy widespread fame and acceptance as the samba, initially feared and relegated to the margins of society, came increasingly into style. One man commented: "When I saw, in 1933, that parade of black people, with the crowd clapping for our sambas, I realized that the black man is important for Brazil." (*Brazil Herald,* February 13/14, 1977) Since Afro-descendant Brazilians comprised key segments of the workforce, governmental declarations of racial accord and respect for workers did win Vargas support among the working class. However, words, even songs, parades, and dances, no matter how popular with white tourists, upper- and middle-class Brazilians, could not erase widespread discrimination and class inequality.

By the 1940s and 1950s, Carnival emerged as a major Brazilian tourist attraction and source of both foreign and domestic revenue. The legitimization of the samba schools under Getúlio Vargas's presidency continued after his death. The samba schools moved from the margins to the center of Carnival celebrations. Professional artists and choreographers replaced amateur artisans as the schools began to compete for the favor, prestige, and cash prizes accorded the best floats, music, and dance routines. Carnival transformed into a performance in which the mainly black and mulatto poor people paraded before mainly white tourists and wealthy Brazilians who looked on from spectator stands.

In 1963, Rio's tourism authorities began to sell tickets for the best seats in the prime locations to tourist agencies who in turn used them to attract not only tourists but international personalities from abroad. The price of admission to any seat in the grand stand rose to a level unattainable for all but the affluent. Record companies began to market the *samba-enredos* (songs) on the airwaves and in records sold abroad. Brazilian singers and TV and media stars paraded with the most prestigious samba schools.

At every turn samba became a commercial enterprise, pitting the old neighborhood groups into fierce competition with each other in order to pay for the expensive costumes, professional expertise, and advanced recording equipment. Finally, in the 1980s the Carnival parade was moved into a 10-block long staging ground in central Rio.

Mangueira, one of the largest favelas in Rio de Janeiro, extends from the top of the high hill (morro) to the street. Mangueira is famous for its spirited samba school. (Meade-Skotnes Photo)

197

The *Sambódromo*, as the area is called, can accommodate the international tourist, upper- and middle-class Brazilians, and the media, far from the threat of pickpockets and street beggars, even isolated from much of the real city. Whereas Carnival has become a parade of spectators far detached from the neighborhood people who are yet the heart and soul of samba, parties in the samba schools and local clubs located in the poorest areas of the city still dominate the social scene.

Carnival and Gender Roles

Carnival also projects a different sexual aesthetic. At its core, the pre-Lenten parties have always been a time to throw aside for a short while the constraints of engendered behavior. Carnival in Brazil features men dressed as women, and perhaps plays more decidedly than any of the other celebrations in the Caribbean and the United States on gender categories. Carnival showcases two sexual sensibilities. On the one hand, the majority of men who participate are "ordinary married men dressed in drag, flaunting jewelry and finery borrowed from their sisters, mothers, and girlfriends in order to engage in three days of uninhibited revelry." (Green 1999:1) These groups of middle-class (presumably heterosexual) boys and men turn out for street dances and roam the buses and public plazas dressed as elaborately bosomed, wigged, and made-up women.

Another sexual sensibility is equally ubiquitous, as any observer of Carnival can testify. Carnival, especially in Rio de Janeiro, is also a "public forum for both humorous and serious manifestations of gay pride." (Green 1999:2) Carnival festivities include large *transvesti* parties, gigantic street and ballroom celebrations for the international gay community that converges on Rio de Janeiro and Salvador da Bahia for the yearly celebrations. (*Travesti* translates literally as "transvestite" but the media uses it to refer to the "drag queen" contingent of the samba-school parade. It was used to refer to male homosexuals until the more common English-language term *gay* came into use in the 1980s.) Tourist brochures from Rio's official tourist agency distributed in major cities of the world invite gay tourists to partake in Rio's Carnival celebration.

A particular feature of gay pride can be seen in the *bandas. Bandas* are contingents of dancers, musicians, and assorted revelers who take to the streets of local neighborhoods and perform throughout the city in the days before Carnival. In 1984, the Banda de Carmen Miranda split off from Rio's most famous street revelers, the Banda

Revelers pose for a photo during the Banda de Ipanema carnival parade in Rio de Janeiro.
(AP Photo/Silvia Izquierdo)

de Ipanema. The Banda de Carmen Miranda, named for Rio's most famous international celebrity, was formed by gay men who adopted Carmen Miranda, long an icon of gay culture in Brazil and abroad, as their symbol.

In the hot summer months from the beginning of the year until the start of Lent in late February or March, Carnival tweaks traditional gender roles, brings the rich and poor into the same celebration, and celebrates the African soul of Brazil's music. The week of Carnival celebration, especially the last three days, when it reaches its most frenzied level, overturns the traditional race, gender, and class hierarchies. When Carnival ends, however, things go back to how they were. Although there are active and visible gay and lesbian communities in many cities, most Brazilians are homophobic, or at least not particularly accepting of gay sexuality. Racially, whites hold dominant positions in society, and people of European ancestry enjoy the highest economic status. Carnival, therefore, is a kind of cultural "time-out," when fixed social conventions turn upside down. For a week or more one can hear the pulsating beat of the *batucada* drum ring out from the hillside *favelas* as the sounds of samba envelope the nation in uniquely Brazilian celebration.

199

Bossa Nova and Other Musical Genres

In the 1950s, a new type of samba, called bossa nova, spread from Brazil to the United States and Europe. It was popularized in the United States by Frank Sinatra and immortalized in the English version of the song "A garota de Ipanema," or "The Girl from Ipanema." Recorded by Brazilian artists João Gilberto and Antônio Carlos Jobim, the song became an international hit and is today said to be among the top five most recorded songs in music history. Bossa nova was pop in some hands, and jazz in others.

In the 1970s and 1980s, music began to play an important role as a tool for opposing the conformity of the military government. Artists such as Milton Nascimento, Gilberto Gil, Chico Buarque, Maria Bethânia, and Caetano Veloso played with words and themes in songs as a way of resisting the military censors, extolling the African roots of Brazil's culture, and celebrating the hardworking and oppressed rural and urban workers. These artists, many of whom had been in exile for a time in the late 1960s and early 1970s, had met up with and learned from musicians abroad. They saw their music as linked with the international struggles for civil rights in the United States, for the goals of youths throughout the world, and especially with the struggle for freedom in much of Latin America.

There are critics who argue that the current generation of Brazilian youth is more pessimistic than its 1960s and 1970s predecessors, that they have retreated from rebellion into nihilism. It would be dangerous to draw this conclusion on the basis of a few songs, but it is true that a strain of pessimism runs through Brazilian rock in particular. Whether that is any different from the refrains in rap and hip-hop in North America and Europe would be hard to say.

The Brazilian anthropologist Hermano Vianna argues in his study of popular music that the vision of Brazil contained in modern rock lyrics is "unabashedly pessimistic." (Vianna 1999:99). A popular 1980s song, "What Country Is This?" by Legiao Urbana, proclaimed, "In the *favelas*, in the senate, filth is everywhere." The band, Paralamas do Sucesso shout out in their song "Perplexed" that Brazilians are "unemployed, cleaned out, without even a place to drop dead, indebted without a way to pay, this country, this country that someone called ours." In "Brazil" the singer Cazuza declares, "Great insignificant country, I'll never betray you." The band Ultraje a Rigor in its darkly titled song "Useless," rolls the lost generation of youth into the national image: "We don't know how to choose a president, we can't take care of ourselves, we can't even brush our teeth, we borrow money and then can't pay, we are useless." (quoted in Vianna, 1977:101) By contrast, however, an infectious optimism and racial inclusiveness is still apparent in some areas. The beat and refrains of the *blocos afros* such as Olodum, popularized in North America by the musician Paul Simon, reflects a more positive and upbeat reality.

Although there is an official police presence at some of the funk parties, which regularly attract from a few hundred to thousands of revelers, the most common source of surveillance is provided by the local bosses, many of them in drug and crime cartels, from the *favela* itself. Given the known corruption in urban police forces, however, one could not say there would be a discernible difference between policing provided by the local *favela* boss and that of the police. Brazil's police are known to draw a steady income from payoffs from crime syndicates.

Benedita da Silva, who grew up in one of Rio's largest slums and serves in the senate, offers an optimistic appraisal of the funk phenomenon. Commenting on the parties that dominate the square in her *favela,* she estimated that 80 percent of those who frequent the dances are "kids slumming in the *favelas.* You see them come here in their cars or fancy motorcycles. Some people think that funk is associated with delinquency and encourage the police to ban funk dances. A lot of the better-off parents don't like their kids going to the *favelas.*" Da Silva offered an interesting contrast to the complaints expressed in the newspaper regarding the mixing of social classes at the parties. "I remember a letter a mother wrote to the newspaper complaining that thanks to funk, 'my children now think that poverty is beautiful and that the *favelas* are wonderful places.' But I think it's really healthy to bring the youth of different classes together. The more we understand each other's realities, the better." (Benjamin and Mendonça 1997: 39–40).

As reported frequently in newspaper accounts, the attraction of middle-class youths to the funk dances provided a steady source of income to *favelados* employed to watch over the sleek automobiles and motorcycles during the course of the evening. Along with providing drinks, collecting admissions at the door, and employing bouncers and others to maintain order and, commonly, to enforce a prohibition against overt sexual acts on the dance floor, the funk parties bring revenue to the poorest part of Rio society. Nonetheless, the funk parties are under the control of the crime syndicates that operate freely in the *favelas.* In 2002, a well-known journalist was executed, reputedly by drug gangs, for his role in uncovering the links between drug traffickers, the managers of the funk parties, and the police.

Soccer, a Brazilian Mania

Writing in 1949 in *A Gazetta* newspaper, a Brazilian journalist compared the British and Brazilian approaches to soccer, or *futebol:* "English football requires that the ball move faster than the player; Brazilian football requires that the player be faster than the ball." Regarding the mania to win, he noted that the "Englishman goes on the field disposed either to win or to lose; the Brazilian either to win, or to blame the referee." (Mazzoni, quoted in Mason 1995:119)

Soccer is the most popular sport in the world and the long-standing favorite in most Latin American countries. The reason soccer holds such a dominant place in Brazilian culture, at least among men, is probably because it has so few rivals. Soccer is Brazil's most popular national sport, but it is also just about the only one. It is the game nearly every Brazilian boy plays from the time he can run and kick. In later years it is the game most Brazilian males will watch, dissect, and follow with almost religious fervor for most of their lives.

Origins of Soccer in Brazil

The game of soccer was brought to many South American countries in the latter half of the 19th century by British sailors who played pick-up games while on shore leave. Buenos Aires in Argentina, Montevideo in Uruguay, and Santos in Brazil were some of the port cities where soccer began to be played. An Englishman named Charles Miller is thought to have introduced organized soccer to Brazil. The son of Paulista merchants, Miller had been sent to England for his education and returned to São Paulo in 1894. He brought back two soccer balls with him. Miller organized a couple of teams made up of young British employees of the Gas Company, the London and Brazilian bank, and the São Paulo Railway Company. They played their first game in 1895. Shortly after this, the São Paulo Athletic Club, formed in 1888 as a British cricket club, added *futebol* to its sports.

In subsequent years, *futebol* spread to members of the elite Brazilian society. One tale has it that American Methodist missionaries brought basketballs to their school, but the young men, having been exposed to soccer, used the ball as a soccer ball. In addition, a German immigrant to Brazil in 1897 brought with him not only soccer balls but also the rules to the game, as played in Germany at that time. Soccer began to be played in the German gymnastic club and from there spread to members of the immigrant community. By 1910, soccer had been picked up by many members of the Brazilian elite and was being played in nearly all the private academies in the European expatriate community.

Competition became more commonplace, and soon enough clubs had emerged in Rio de Janeiro and São Paulo to establish intense rivalries among themselves. Some of the most respected soccer clubs, Fluminense, Botafogo, America, International, and AC São Paulo, began to compete publicly. For the most part, the clubs were elite organizations: Players were known to travel to matches in dinner jackets and to celebrate afterwards with fine banquets, indulgences that the vast majority of Brazilians could never afford. A history of Brazilian soccer by Tony Mason notes that in the early years *futebol* matches were social occasions where young men from the best families came together to display their masculine qualities, generally in front of the admiring eyes of young women.

One of the few non-elite clubs, Bangu, formed in 1904. It was organized by the British owner of the Bangu textile mill, located in a working-class district in the north of Rio de Janeiro. The sport was intended to be a diversion for the British managers, who were soon joined by the mill workers, who proved to be superior practitioners. Before long, the club was far more important an enterprise than was the factory. Similar clubs for railway workers, mill workers, and other workers developed. Although the elite clubs shunned these new organizations, and even refused to play them, the sport had wrested loose from the confines of the European expatriates and had begun to germinate among Brazilian society as a whole.

Because *futebol* is organized around clubs, and a city such as Rio de Janeiro or São Paulo can have dozens of clubs, fans' loyalties are tied to clubs, many of which have grown out of specific communities and reflect the class and social status of those communities. In São Paulo, for example, Palmeiras was founded by Italian immigrants, the descendants of whom still run it. Palmeiras is thought to hold the loyalties of the large Italian community. The São Paulo club holds the allegiance of middle-class Paulistas, while Corinthians is known for the loyalty of the lower class. In Rio de Janeiro, Fluminense still is seen as the club of the high-status white families, while Flamengo is the team of the poor blacks and mulattos, and Botafogo has the following of the Rio middle class. Obviously these are not firm lines of demarcation, since fans switch their loyalties depending often on the success or failure of the teams. But as with Mets and Yankees baseball fans in New York, or Cubs and White Sox fans in Chicago, long-standing affections tend to persist.

From time to time various political entities have exploited this link between diverse social groups and *futebol*. This was possible because *futebol* established itself in Brazil, as well as in other places in South America, as a rivalry not between cities but between clubs, often within a city. As a result politicians used the *futebol* club as a local base, in much the same way machine politicians have always drawn on local neighborhood institutions such as churches, union halls, and ethnic meeting halls. The *futebol* club, and support for it, was a base on which politicians could build their popularity and eventually their careers.

For decades, many of the clubs assumed that their close ties to politicians protected them from scrutiny. That may no longer be the case. In 2001 President Cardoso changed the clubs' status from social organizations to "commercial enterprises," thereby subjecting them to fiscal and legal oversight. Subsequently the government and sports federation began uncovering widespread incidences of money laundering, tax evasion, fraud, and multiple financial abuses in the soccer clubs.

Politicians and Futebol

No politician exploited the link between soccer and the national psyche as well as did Getúlio Vargas. Under Vargas in the 1930s, *futebol* began to achieve its standing as a national pastime. Similar to what he had done with samba and Carnival, Vargas sought to use soccer as a way of unifying the nation, creating a common source of identity, and developing a single national culture. And as had happened with samba, this meant discrediting the racist notions that kept black and mulatto Brazilian players from competing widely. In 1941, he established the National Council of Sports as a part of the Ministry of Education and Culture. His goal was not only to solidify soccer as a key component of popular culture, but also to establish the nation's reputation abroad as a leading contender in South American soccer play. In the last years of his presidency Vargas arranged for the prestigious Rio club, Flamengo, to build a 24-story-high office building overlooking the bay.

The military dictatorship that came to power in 1964 sought to gain legitimacy by supporting soccer clubs and backing the construction of soccer stadiums throughout the country. New stadiums dotted the urban landscape from Belém in the North, Recife and Salvador in the impoverished Northeast, Fortaleza and Pôrto Alegre in the South, as well as in large and small cities in between. The generals, unpopular with the Brazilian citizenry, tried to use *futebol* as a link with the masses by proclaiming their allegiance to various soccer teams and making regular appearances at games. From 1969 until 1975 13 new stadiums were built in cities throughout the country; by 1978 seven of the world's largest stadiums were in Brazil.

Following in Vargas's footsteps, the dictators sought to tie *futebol* to the military's nationalist program. *Futebol* was used as a way of swaying the electorate. Critics claimed that the military's ARENA party candidates finagled places for teams in the national championship playoffs in locales where the party was not doing well. As Mason's study notes, "leading football personalities know that being a football person helps if you want to go into politics in Brazil and if you are a politician an interest in football is a real advantage." (Mason 1995:62)

Observers in the early 1970s argued that the generals gained four years of peace after Brazil won the World Cup in 1970, and maybe lost it when the team was eliminated in 1974 in the competition in Rome. Beginning in 1974 the presidency of the ARENA party and the presidency of the Brazilian Sports Council (CBD) were both in the hands of Admiral Hélio Nunes, a man who spent considerable energy trying to convince soccer superstar Pelé to play for Brazil in the 1974 Cup. Pelé refused, presumably for no more political reason than that he had signed a multimillion-dollar contract with Pepsi to promote soccer in the United States.

Ironically, in the 1980s the powerful trade unions in São Paulo and other industrial cities began to draw such huge crowds of demonstrators in opposition to the military government's labor policies that they had nowhere large enough to meet except in the gigantic soccer stadiums. In the 1989 presidential campaign, the Workers Party rallied its supporters in packed soccer stadiums where Lula and other candidates called for an end to military rule.

The four-year cycle of World Cup matches has coincided frequently with Brazil's national elections. David Fleischer of *Brazil Focus* discounts any particular connection between the events, but does note that 1950, 1994, 1998, and 2002 were all presidential election years as well as historic Cup games. In 1950, Brazil lost to tiny neighboring Uruguay in a final still referred to as a "national disaster," only worsened because it was played in Rio's Maracanã stadium. In 1998 Brazil suffered its most humiliating defeat in the Cup final against France, and then in 1994 and 2002 it won.

Pelé

Brazilian soccer achieved its greatest popularity in the 1960s, and it was very much due to the skill of one player: Pelé. Born Edson

Arantes do Nascimento on October 23, 1940, Pelé is from a small town in Minas Gerais. His father was a semiprofessional soccer player who made his living as a warehouse worker. Pelé began to play on the dirt lots in his neighborhood at a young age. It was while he was a member of a local team that played without shoes that he was given the name "Pelé." No one, including Pelé, knows precisely where the name came from, but at least in the beginning, it was not a name the young player liked.

Pelé's talent was apparent, and at the age of 15 he began playing with men on a semiprofessional team. By his mid-twenties he was recognized as one of the best players in Brazil. He played in international competitions throughout the 1960s, including three World Cups, and became known as the best player in the sport, possibly of all time. There are several reasons why Pelé was so good. In the first place, he was a natural soccer player. His coach on the Santos team, for which he played throughout his Brazilian career, stated that Pelé possessed "all the qualities of the ideal football player. He is fast on the ground and in the air, he has the physique, the kick, the ball control, the ability to play, a feeling for the manoeuvre, he is unselfish, good natured and modest." (Mason 1995:87) Commenting on Pelé's feats in the second World Championship final in Lisbon, the Italian sportswriter covering the event wrote that spectators were left "openmouthed at the complete athletic prowess of this young man." (Mason 1995:87)

Not only did Pelé have great skill, his body seemed impervious to the punishing blows and kicks of the fiercest competitors. And he was tireless. For 14 years he played 60 to 100 matches a year. By the time he left for the United States in 1975 to play with the newly formed Cosmos soccer team, he had played 1,254 games. The hard work did have its rewards. In 1963 he was the highest-paid professional athlete in the world, drawing more than $200,000. Some 10 years later he was paid $7 million when he signed for the Cosmos in the United States.

Pelé's importance to Brazilian history is far beyond the personal success he achieved. His rise to international fame and riches from the poverty of a small town in an interior state was more of a "Brazilian miracle" than any of the successes touted by the military government during the same period. Possibly the greatest player in a game that captures the attention of most sports spectators in the world, Pelé's international celebrity ranks with Muhammed Ali's and outstrips that of many of history's world-famous sports figures.

By the time Pelé retired in 1977, he had been declared a national treasure of the Brazilian government. He had been the first black man

On May 18, 1967, Edson Arantes do Nascimento, known to the world as Pelé, the "King" of soccer, was awarded the medal of the Rio Branco order, the highest Brazilian decoration awarded by the Foreign Ministry. Pelé received the decoration from Foreign Minister José de Magalhães Pinto during a formal lunch at the ministry, where he was guest of honor. (AP Photo)

to appear on the cover of *Life* magazine. He had played in Brazil for the queen of England in a special match, and while in England the duke of Edinburgh broke with royal tradition by going to Pelé and extending his greeting first instead of waiting for the latter to approach him, as called for by royal protocol. When Pelé played in France in 1971, a minister of the government met him at the airport and shepherded him through Paris in an open motorcade through streets lined with thousands of cheering fans. It was a welcome France usually reserved for visiting heads of state. In the mid-1970s, competing sides in the Nigerian civil war negotiated a cease-fire when the Santos team played there, so that everyone could watch this genius of soccer play. In 1977, Pelé was given a special reception at the United Nations for his work in helping the children of the world, and President Jimmy Carter paid tribute to Pelé for the "thrills he gave the fans of this nation and the dimension he added to American sports." (Carter quoted in Mason 1995:93)

Finally, in June 2008, at the age of 67, Pelé headlined the Goal 4 Africa international soccer match in honor of South African Nobel Prize winner and former president Nelson Mandela, on the occasion of the latter's 90th birthday. The match was one of many held around the world to raise funds for African education. Pelé broke barriers as a both a black man and as an individual from a poor Latin American country. He put not only soccer on the world map but Brazil as well.

Twenty-First Century Soccer

A recent contribution to international soccer fame is Ronaldo Luís Nazario da Lima (born 1976). Similar to Pelé, Ronaldo is considered one of the best players in the sport's history, having been named best world player in 1996 and 1997. In 2002 Cup competition he tied Pelé's record of 12 goals in 14 games.

Despite a lackluster performance in 2006 when he was booed for showing up overweight at the run-up to the Cup competition, Ronaldo set a new world record of 15 goals in World Cup play. Ronaldo paid tribute to Pelé as he basked in the glory of the 2002 World Cup victory, crediting Pelé with offering advice and encouragement when the younger player was plagued with repeated injuries over the previous two years.

A key difference in Ronaldo's career from Pelé's is that Ronaldo does not play for a Brazilian club. Like Pelé, Ronaldo attracted the attention of scouts as a young player, but unlike his predecessor, Ronaldo did not continue to play for his club in Belo Horizonte. Ronaldo moved to Europe, where he has competed mainly in Italy and Spain. Pelé, by contrast, played for Santos his entire career, until he left to join the Cosmos. Indeed, almost no member of Brazil's victorious 2002 World Cup team lived and competed in Brazil. This pattern is repeated throughout Latin America and Africa, where many local teams cannot compete with the salaries and advertising deals offered to players in Europe and the United States. The best players return to their homelands simply to play on their nation's World Cup team every four years.

Brazil's latest star in the world soccer pantheon is Marta Vieira da Silva, considered the best and most electrifying player in the game. Marta's rise to fame has paralleled other soccer sensations in breaking through economic and national barriers, while adding gender to the mix. From a modest single-parent family in a small interior town that lacked any soccer teams, much less one for girls, Marta learned to play with boys on the street. At the age of 14, she traveled on a bus for three days to Rio de Janeiro, where, through a tenuous family connection, she won a tryout for the national team. She never returned to her distant hometown. Dubbed the best female player in the world for three years running (2006–2009), Marta plays for Sol, the Los Angeles–based women's soccer team. Marta's Brazil-based agent, Fabiano Farah, also represents Ronaldo, as well as other leading male players, but the young woman is most often compared to Pelé for her dazzling footwork, speed, and unbridled enthusiasm for the game.

Television and *Telenovelas*

The *telenovela* is one of the most widespread expressions of popular culture in Latin America. Similar to the soap opera, which some consider its North American distant cousin, the *telenovela*, examines personal and familial themes. Plots revolve around power relations in work and domestic settings, bad women and competition between women for the attentions of men, or rivalries between two men for the favor of a woman. They include sacrifice combined with either success or failure, mercenary marriages, and controversies over paternity. According to sociologist José Antonio Guevara, the typical theme of the *telenovela* is the struggle to found a traditional family: falling in love, marrying, having children. It pursues this theme by showing the contrasting lives of rich and poor, good and evil. From this tension the melodrama develops its plot, which is based on a projection of reality.

By contrast, the North American soap opera takes place in an artificial upper-class and upper-middle-class society. The central tension of the soap opera generally involves money and sex, and the complications endured in holding on to both in the face of competitors. Structurally, the soap opera and *telenovela* also differ. There is no final episode to the soap opera (unless it goes off the air), since the events with which its characters struggle never end and cannot be solved. For the *telenovela*, on the other hand, the goal is to solve the problems of society, to even teach a way to resolve the contradictions and tensions inherent in the progress of human events. The plot reaches its culmination in three to four months of daily episodes. The final episode presents a happy resolution to the problems faced in the series. Finally, soap operas are shown in the daytime and largely attract a female audience. The *telenovela* shows at night, and is the main source of entertainment for many men, women, and the whole family.

According to most studies of TV viewing in Latin America, the *telenovela* is the main source of support for many television channels and the basic staple of both daytime and evening programming. The modern *telenovela* traces its origins to Cuban *radionovelas* in the 1930s, which soon became the standard for all of Latin America. The serial radio programs were inexpensive to produce because they repeated (and perfected) the same broad plotline, generally involving two main characters and three or four secondary figures. The *radionovela* gave way to the *telenovela,* first in Mexico and then throughout the continent, as television became more available in the 1960s.

The Brazilian *Novela*

For a couple of reasons, the popularity of the *telenovela* grew during the era of the military dictatorship after 1964. In the first place, the repressive nighttime curfew drove underground many public forms of entertainment. The regime governed through decrees, prohibited the assembly of more than 10 people in a public place, and policed the streets at night to ensure that potential dissidents could not make contact with one other. In this vacuum Brazilians developed the routine of watching the *telenovelas* that dominated the airwaves from 6 to 10 P.M. There is still a tendency to refer to specific shows according to their time slot rather than by names, a practice that emerged during the military government. People will speak of "the 6:00 *novela*" or the "the 8:00 *novela.*"

Second, the state supported the development of a national TV network, Rede Globo, and conferred many financial favors on the private owners. Under the leadership of the archconservative Roberto Marinho, a strong supporter of the military dictatorship, TVs were made accessible to even the poorest Brazilians. The formula was quite simple. There was little competition, thus advertising rates were held to a minimum. In addition, a black-and-white TV was available to most Brazilian families individually or in a neighborhood, while TV Globo and its closest competitor, TV Manchete, filled the airwaves with a steady stream of fantasy.

TV Globo is Brazil's most important media monopoly, with 32 affiliates. The network garners an estimated 70 percent of the advertising and about 35 percent of the audience in the prime-time slot. Every night it broadcasts three different *novelas* to an estimated 40–50 million viewers, out of a possible audience of around 85 million. Nighttime programs appear as well on three other competing networks, but they trail far behind TV Globo in both the quality and expense of their programs, and their share of the audience.

While TV Globo continues to dominate the *novela* market, Sistema Brasileiro de Televisão (SBT) has begun to carve inroads. SBT's founder

Sílvio Santos is a rags-to-riches media mogul who started out selling on the streets of Rio. He turned a street hawking enterprise into a network of retail stores that sold lottery prizes on the installment plan. With occasional forays into national politics, including a brief flirtation with the 2002 presidential campaign, Sílvio Santos is proving to be an important figure in the Brazilian political spotlight. As a result of his aggressive business tactics, SBT has captured a share of the television-viewing audience by showing game shows imported from the United States and Europe. SBT also features dubbed Mexican *telenovelas* which, while not as original as those broadcast on TV Globo, are much less expensive to produce. Moreover, the *novela* audience is so vast that even Mexican knockoffs can find an audience.

Although *telenovelas* are wildly popular throughout Latin America, the Brazilian variant is the most original, is considered the most risqué, even lurid, and holds the greatest market share of its respective audience. Brazil's *novelas* are lavishly produced melodramas, written exclusively for the TV audience by some of the nation's major writers. In addition to melodramas, the shows are sometimes comedies, raise social criticism, and retell major works of fiction or history. They feature Brazil's best actors, including top movie actors in starring roles and guest appearances. Whereas Mexican or Colombian *telenovelas* might last for around four to six weeks, the Brazilian drama routinely extends to six months or more. Finally, the Brazilian shows are an important cultural export to the rest of Latin America, where the Spanish translation from the original Portuguese is shown to audiences throughout the continent.

Reasons for the *Novela's* Popularity

There are many reasons why the *novelas* capture the imagination of so many Brazilians on a nightly basis. In the first place, this is a TV viewing nation. More households in Brazil have televisions than have refrigerators. The two leading newspapers in the country, the *Folha de São Paulo* and Rio de Janeiro's *Jornal do Brasil*, have a combined readership of about 300,000 people. Along with the other major newspapers, it is estimated that less than a million readers follow newspapers on a daily basis, while 50 million watch *Jornal Nacional*, the nightly news program aired on TV *Globo*. In a country where an estimated 70 percent of the population has no more than a sixth-grade education, where millions are illiterate, and more than half the population lives in poverty and goes hungry, the television is the single form of entertainment. As the Mexican commentator and journalist Alma Guillermoprieto has observed, "*Telenovelas* substitute for all the pleasures that most

211

Brazilians cannot afford: the movies, the theatre, the circus, or, for that matter, the carnival parade or a soccer game, since the tickets are priced for tourists." (Guillermoprieto 1987: 45)

In addition, the moral trajectory of the *novela* never changes. Guillermoprieto argues that the 50 million viewers of the daily news shows find in Brazil a world filled with crime, corruption, drug lords, wars in the *favelas,* a plummeting economy, and a total breakdown in public services. In Brazil, little changes, at least for the better. By contrast, in the TV version "executives are kidnapped and drug lords wage war in the *favelas,* but then the kidnapper is caught, the drug lord meets a nice girl and goes straight, the crooked executive's righteous son inherits the family business, and moral order is restored to the world." (Guillermoprieto 1987:45–46)

Finally, the Brazilian *novela* is famous for its treatment of lurid, incestuous, gender-bending and sexual themes. One plot involved the search for a lost gold mine, the map for which had been tattooed on the buttocks of a shapely young woman, which were frequently plastered across the screen. Other plots have featured such stories as a torrid love affair between a 50-year old matron and a male stripper, or a gay and transvestite lovers' tryst, or a serendipitous romantic encounter between the recipient of a heart transplant and the donor's former lover, and so on.

This routine projection of circumstances related to sex, nudity, illegitimacy, racial barriers, betrayal, adultery, incest, and violence differentiates Brazilian *telenovelas* from those in other Latin American countries. Since the Latin American–produced *telenovelas* appear on Spanish-language TV in the United States, the U.S. Latino population keeps up with the same cultural obsessions as their relatives and friends abroad. In 2001 a Brazilian *telenovela,* translated into Spanish, showed on a New York TV station but the producers pulled it when they thought it too sexually explicit for the U.S. Latino audience, who are mainly from the Spanish-speaking countries of Latin America and the Caribbean.

Cinema

Although Brazilian cinema has a history stretching back to the early 20th century, its most famous film was, and possibly still is, *Black Orpheus (Orfeu Negro)*, made in 1959 by a Frenchman, Marcel Camus. Drawn from Vinicius de Moraes's play *Orfeu da Conceição*, adapted from the mythical Greek drama of Orpheus and Eurydice, the film introduced a world audience to Carnival, the beauty of Rio de Janeiro, the centrality of African ritual and belief in Brazil's culture, and the bossa nova music of one of the nation's most important artists, Antonio Carlos Jobim. The movie won the 1959 Palme d'Or at Cannes and the 1960 Academy Award for Best Foreign-Language Film. The film was a collaborative effort with Brazilian filmmakers, but the honors all went to France.

Carmen Miranda's popularity in Hollywood films brought Brazil a minor degree of fame on the international stage during the 1930s and 1940s, along with a steady stream of domestic releases. At the end of the 20th century, and in the early decades of the 21st, several major Brazilian film directors won widespread acclaim both among domestic and international audiences for such films as *Dona Flor and Her Two Husbands* (Bruno Barreto, 1976), *Bye Bye Brasil* (Caca Diegues, 1979), *Pixote* (Hector Babenco, 1981), *O Quatrilho* (Fabio Barreto, 1995), and *Central Station* (Walter Salles, 1998). *Pixote*, starring an actual boy from the *favela*, depicted the sordid underworld life of poverty. The movie won a number of international awards and established a kind of cinema verité trend that is apparent in recent, highly acclaimed releases such as *City of God* (Fernando Meirelles, Katia Lund, 2002), *Bus 174* (José Padilha, 2002), *Carandiru* (Héctor Babenco, 2003), *Favela Rising* (Jeff Zimbalist and Matt Mochary, 2005), *The Elite Squad* (José Padilha, 2007), *Blindness* (Fernando Meirelles, 2008) and *Manda Bala*, 2007, the Documentary Grand Jury Prize winner at the 2007 Sundance Film Festival. While the films are all skillfully made, the fact that they all rely on graphic depictions of violence, in either documentary or documentary-like format, and show either a callous disregard for human life or the failure of the Brazilian state to control violence, has made them all controversial. Nonetheless, the films have earned Brazilians a place among the growing coterie of internationally acclaimed Latin American directors and actors.

It is samba, soccer, the nighttime melodramas, and movies, in addition to several million Orkut (Brazil's counterpart to Facebook) users who troll the Internet to remain in touch with popular culture, that connect Brazilians with one another. These are cultural products that cut across class, race, and region to bind people together in a common nationality. They are the substance of Brazilian daily life, that which is debated in bars, listened to on the radio, discussed at the office water cooler. Moreover, a great share of the Brazilian economy revolves around the production, distribution, and consumption of these cultural entities. In all four cases, their popularity owes a great deal to the intervention of government and political figures, especially Getúlio Vargas. Official recognition, promotion, subsidies, and corporate sponsorships have brought these aspects of popular culture into the day-to-day lives of nearly all Brazilians.

10

BRAZIL IN THE TWENTY-FIRST CENTURY

These days there is no shortage of news and information on Brazil In contrast to stories of beaches, Carnival, and Amazon adventures, or glum tales of crime, street children, and poverty, the news today has a more positive bent. A story on petroleum reserves and the haves and have-nots in the world of energy resources will invariably mention the Tupi oil fields, a huge discovery off the coast of Santos announced in November 2007. In January, 2008, Petrobras, the state-owned oil company, reported the discovery of Jupiter, a gigantic natural gas and light oil field, about 20 miles to the east of Tupi, with more discoveries to follow. The combination of Jupiter, Tupi, and other oil fields nearby has catapulted Brazil from a net oil importer to energy self-sufficiency, just as oil and gas prices skyrocketed. With an invitation to join the Oil Petroleum Exporting Countries (OPEC) a distinct possibility, Brazil is looking toward a future as energy self-sufficient and even as an exporter. Among Latin American countries, only Venezuela has membership in OPEC. An estimated yield of 5,000 to 8,000 barrels of oil a day adds to Brazil's already ample supply of biofuels. As the second-largest producer of biofuel in the world, Brazil has since the late 1990s transformed the face of energy consumption, today managing almost half of internal transport on biofuel. As opposed to the expensive and inefficient corn ethanol produced in the United States, Brazil's sugar-based ethanol can be grown widely and produced and refined more cheaply.

The International Monetary Fund (IMF) has tracked Brazil's growth at above 5 percent for the last few years and projects modest prosperity and a $40 billion trade surplus in 2008. Nearly as fast as the United States moved from creditor to debtor status, Brazil moved in the other direction, chalking up respectable foreign reserves. Verification of Brazil's move from "developing" to the status of major player came in

April 2008 when Standard & Poor's upgraded Brazil's long-term foreign currency sovereign debt to investment grade. The move instantly drove stock prices for Brazilian companies to record highs, and São Paulo's BOVESPA (Bolsa de Valores de São Paulo) Brazil's major stock exchange, became one of the world's top performing equity markets.

According to Zachary Levey of the Inter-American Development Bank in Washington D.C., Brazil's elevation to investment grade indicates international confidence in the economy's performance and the country's ability to meet debt payments. Moreover, not only is Brazil itself investment grade, but Petrobras, likewise, has an investment-grade rating, and given the extensive oil and gas reserves, it promises to be an attractive investment option. Brazil now joins Chile, Mexico and, recently Peru, as good risks for international investments, which, combined with other positive indicators, have signaled a turnaround from a few years ago.

In the first four months of 2009, China surpassed the United States as Brazil's largest trading partner. In a move indicative of the increasing commercial ties between the two nations, Beijing announced that China's state-owned oil company, Sinopec, would provide up to $10 billion of financing to Petrobras over the next 10 years in exchange for 200,000 barrels of oil a day. The researcher Lilly Briger wrote on the Council on Hemispheric Affairs Web site that this agreement was all the more remarkable since it occurred during a period in which liquidity has all but evaporated from the global financial system. China's move to finance the excavation of Brazil's huge crude oil reserves signals a new cooperation between two emerging powerhouses, which Washington may find discomforting. On the other hand, Brazil experienced a significant downturn in late 2008 as the worldwide recession that began in the United States and Europe reached Asia and Latin America. A shortage of credit and contraction in both industrial and consumer spending has slowed both production and trade in Brazil.

Ongoing social problems will no doubt get worse before they get better as economic growth stagnates. High crime rates, violence, corruption, pollution, and other effects of rapid industrialization and persistent poverty seem to drag the country from one crisis to another. More than 30 percent of the population lives in poverty, and the country's per capita GDP is just $9,700. By comparison, Chile's is $13,900 (18 percent in poverty), Argentina's is $13,300 (24 percent in poverty), and Mexico's is $12,800 (14 percent in poverty). On the other hand, it is also a nation of very vibrant, artistic, active, creative, and combative people who have forged one of the most interesting cultures in the Americas. Many tourists and scholars from outside the country who spend time in Brazil come away with memories of a warm and generous people who enjoy life despite the many hardships they face and who have made extraordinarily creative contributions to the world of literature, music, dance, art, movies, television, and more. It seems at times that Brazilians are a people who play hard on the soccer field and dance floor, as they do also in the political arena and in the struggle to make a better life. Furthermore, they always seem immensely proud of being Brazilian, even if there are things about their homeland they would like to see changed.

The People Make the Country

Brazilian pride derives from the knowledge that theirs is a place of tenacious people and indefatigable heroes and heroines. Benedita da Silva (1943–), an illiterate black woman from one of the poorest neighborhoods of Rio de Janeiro, learned as an adult to read and write and was elected to the national Senate. Da Silva's is a story similar to that of Lula, who rose from a metalworker and union leader to two-term president. Another hero, Francisco "Chico" Alves Mendes Filho (1944–88), a rubber tapper from remote Acré, achieved worldwide prominence as an articulate spokesman for the rubber tappers union and for a policy of sustainable development of the jungle. For his success, and the international attention he drew to the environmental cause in Brazil, he was slain in 1988 by the mercenaries of local landlords. Another notable case is that of Archbishop Hélder Câmara (1909–99) from the distant state of Ceará. His life trajectory moved from a youth member of the fascist Ação Integralista Brasileira to being ordained a priest and establishing himself in Rio de Janeiro as one of the foremost proponents of Catholic Action and liberation theology. When he was named archbishop of Olinda and Recife in Pernambuco, he used his office to criticize the military government after the 1964 coup. While in Paris in 1969, the archbishop publicly condemned the practice of torture in Brazil. In response, the military government prohibited any mention of Dom Hélder or his work in the media. As a highly public advocate of benefits to the poor, restraints on the military, and democratic rights for all citizens, Dom Hélder inspired many Brazilians. He was a man of privilege who became the champion of the less fortunate.

From the life histories of Benedita da Silva, Chico Mendes, Dom Hélder Câmara, and President da Silva, one can draw a picture of a society in which rigidity no longer prevails. Brazilian history is one of many twists and turns, many contradictions and conflicts.

The Workers Party in Power

Consideration of Brazil's position at the start of the 21st century begins with a look back at the road the nation has traveled in the last decade. On the political front, Lula's victories in the presidential races of 2002 and 2006 strengthened the reform agenda, although the PT lost some of its moral high ground because of corruption scandals. In the presidential election of 2002, the first round, held on October 6, winnowed the field of eight candidates to a run-off between Lula and the Social Democrat candidate, José Serra, President Cardoso's designated heir. In the second round, Lula defeated Serra by a margin of more than 20 percent and brought with him a majority in the Chamber of Deputies, which holds 513 seats elected proportionally from the 26 states and federal district. In the Senate, the PT garnered 14 of the 81 seats (three senators represent each state and the federal district), making it not the largest party, but one of the top three, and in a position to broker alliances with smaller leftist and progressive parties.

The PT victory in 2002 indicated that Brazilian voters were unmoved by a storm of unfavorable publicity that a potential left-wing triumph generated in the U.S. press. When in April 2002 Lula polled a favorable rating of greater than 40 percent, the reaction from Wall Street bankers and investors was swift. Several investment houses issued warnings that a Lula victory would be harmful to Brazil's "risk rating" and could increase the interest rate the big banks charge on loans. (As shown in the current investment-grade rating, discussed at the start of this chapter, the gloomy forecast was completely false.) Actually, the warning may have produced the opposite effect in Brazil. A member of the Chamber of Deputies sharply rebuked the Morgan Stanley investment house for its gloomy prognosis, and comments from both Morgan Stanley and Merrill Lynch investors came under immediate fire from the Cardoso government. Such interference from foreign creditors may have backfired and served only to galvanize Lula's supporters. The memory of overt foreign intervention in Brazilian affairs lingered in the minds of many voters, and even Lula's opponents did not want to appear as though they were beholden to Washington's financial interests. In the months prior to the election, Lula worked to moderate his message. Much to the dismay of many PT activists, he chose José Alencar, a textile manufacturer and well-known conservative with ties to the evangelical Christian right, as his running mate.

In his first year in office, Lula devoted himself to reformulating the complex and unequal tax code, streamlining the civil service pension system (unsettling PT supporters among public employees and university professors who had benefited from the government's generous pension

217

plan), and continuing to hold down inflation. While maintaining a solid approval rating throughout his first year, Lula ran into difficulties with his left-wing base. Some environmentalists accused the government of reneging on promises to ban genetically modified seeds, which Brazil accepted in hopes of better competing with the United States in soybean sales abroad, as well as improving the environment and fighting poverty.

Early in the first term, Lula moved to settle 400,000 poor families on land in the biggest land distribution under a single Brazilian government. Critics argue, however, that thousands more landless workers remain dispossessed of holdings that were taken illegally from them in years past and disagreed with a government plan to require the landless to buy back lands that should be rightfully theirs. Finally, Lula scored well with investors in the first term by pulling out of recession and posting 0.4 percent growth in the third quarter of 2003. While a far cry from the "spectacular growth" Lula had predicted at the start of the year, the economy stabilized and improved moderately. Central to the government's stimulus package was Lula's move to form a closer trade alliance with China, India, Russia, South Africa, and other emerging markets, as a way of diversifying Brazil's foreign markets and offsetting the nation's dependence on the U.S. consumer market. This effort met with displeasure in the United States, as well as in Belgium and Japan, because closer links between China and Brazil, in particular, cuts against the flexibility the dominant nations like to protect.

The primary problem Lula faced in the first term stemmed from within his own party. Accusations of vote tampering, corruption, and graft brought down much of the top leadership of the PT and Lula's own close advisers but managed to leave the president in office, if badly scarred. A much weakened PT entered the 2006 elections poised to lose seats but hopeful of holding the executive. Again forced into a runoff, Lula still managed to carry 20 of 26 states and the federal district, drawing his support from the poorest districts of the North, while losing or splitting the prosperous South. No doubt his reputation as a poor worker who made it to the top resonated with the traditional PT supporters in the countryside and with unions, but the key issue was fear of a return to the domination of big business. Geraldo Alckmin ran on a program intent on restoring the pro-business agenda and rolling back the social gains of the PT first term. Lula won with nearly the same margin as he had in 2002. He had not delivered the workers' paradise promised in the first term, but he was viewed as far better than the alternative.

The picture since 2006 has been free of scandal, major corruption, and the debilitating bickering that characterized Lula's first term. A more mature government has demonstrated an ability to forge a consensus among neighboring governments in Argentina, Bolivia, and Venezuela that have been racked with conflict and to begin to enact a series of reforms at home. Stable growth has been a political advantage, but it remains to be seen whether the many who endure lives of desperate poverty will be willing to wait until (if ever) the rising tide of prosperity lifts all boats.

Economic Growth

Any quick summary of Brazil's economic prospects seems to be remarkably uniform. Most say that is it a country of vast natural resources, an immense pool of labor, and the leading economic power and potentially the most important political power in South America. A Goldman Sachs economist, Jim O'Neill, coined the term *BRIC* for the nations he predicted to become the economic powerhouses in the year 2050: Brazil, Russia, India, and China. Brazil's place in this group of emerging powers is owing to its large and well-developed agricultural, mining, manufacturing, extractive, and service sectors. The exploitation of the huge Tupi petroleum field, combined with the widespread use of renewable sugar-based ethanol for most ground transportation, would seem to ensure a very bright future. Nonetheless, this bright economic picture dims in the face of such problems as highly unequal income distribution, persistent poverty, numerous educational challenges—especially in the vast rural areas—and high crime rates. Brazil escaped the severe economic crisis that gripped neighboring Argentina in 2001–03, with only minor financial turmoil; however, the deep financial crisis beginning in late 2008 cut into growth projections.

In essence, the financial and economic picture is generally ambiguous, and Brazil's outlook varies according to the point of view of the economic analyst. International market sources herald the fact that Brazil's growth has yielded increases in employment and real wages, particularly applauding the responsible payment of the tremendous debt inherited from the years of mismanagement under the military government. The *CIA World Factbook* applauded the PT government, noting that "Lula da Silva restated his commitment to fiscal responsibility by maintaining the country's primary surplus during the 2006 election. Following his second inauguration, Lula [da Silva] announced a package of further economic reforms to reduce taxes and increase investment in infrastructure" (*CIA Factbook,* 2008). On the other hand, Duncan Green in the *Financial Times* remarks that the World Bank, not the usual source of radical pronouncements, contends that all the poor in Latin America could be raised above the poverty line by enacting as little as a 2 percent income tax increase on

Vendors such as this woman in Belém sell herbs for cooking and as cures for a wide range of ailments. Too poor to go to a doctor, many people rely on herbal cures. (Photograph by Erich Goode)

the wealthiest fifth of the population (CLAH, 503). Brazil's path to social equality and a better standard of living for the majority of its people is a matter of political will more than just economic prosperity.

Poverty

The neglect of the welfare of the Brazilian majority has been a long-standing phenomenon that accelerated during the military dictatorship and persists today. At the end of the 1980s, 17.2 million people above the age of 15, about 15 percent, concentrated mainly in the Northeast, were illiterate. After more than two decades of democracy and increased social spending, 89 percent of the total population can read and write, a gain of 4 percent. As the population has increased, from about 120 million in 1980 to 198 million today, so has the number of adult illiterates. In contrast to Brazil, literacy in neighboring Argentina stands at 95 percent. Only 3.5 percent of Brazil's population attended college in the 1980s, a figure that has increased only slightly by century's end. An adequate homegrown technological stratum of workers seems far off. Poor education levels are a severe impediment to a nation that expects to compete in a world that increasingly relies on an educated, technologically savvy workforce. Moreover, dire economic problems have skimmed off the top layer of educated and skilled members of society, who recently have immigrated

SENATOR FOR SOCIAL JUSTICE

The reality of improved opportunities for some Brazilians, even if only a few, is exemplified in the life history of Senator Benedita da Silva. Known as "Bené," she is from a family of 13 children born and raised in a Rio de Janeiro shantytown, Chapéu Mangueira. She worked as a maid, earning so little money that she was unable to buy medical care for her children. Two of her four children died of curable diseases. She was exploited, raped, humiliated, and nearly died of an illegal abortion. Despite this history of depravation, da Silva emerged as a leader in her neighborhood when she organized community members to demand water, sewers, and electricity for their poorly serviced *favela*. As an adult, she learned to read and write and has instructed others. In the waning days of the military dictatorship, she became involved in politics, ran for office, and was elected to the Rio de Janeiro city council on the Workers Party ticket. In subsequent elections, she ran for, and won, office as a federal deputy and later as a senator.

A well-known figure in the halls of the Brazilian Congress, Senator da Silva was an active proponent of benefits for poor, working people, a supporter of policies to help the many street children in Brazil's cities, and an advocate of rights for the indigenous population and for environmental protection. In 2006, she was Lula's campaign coordinator in the state of Rio de Janeiro in his successful reelection bid. Da Silva continues to live in Chapéu Mangueira, from which she maintains an active role in local, regional, and national politics.

by the thousands to the United States, Canada, and Europe. Large numbers of people make a subsistence living selling whatever they can on the streets of Brazil's cities and taking jobs at lower skill levels abroad.

Highly unequal income distribution remains a pressing problem. Whereas the richest 10 percent of households in 2007 earned 46 percent of the nation's total income, the poorest 10 percent had less than 1 percent, figures that have changed little over the last five years. Poverty and the government's lack of attention to public health have resulted in the spread of epidemic diseases such as malaria and tuberculosis. In 1989, a cholera epidemic struck 1.1 million people. On the other hand, the average life expectancy was 63 years in 2000 and has now increased to 73 years, with a corresponding drop in the percentage of the population over the age of 65 from 8 to 6.4 percent. The average life span for men at the turn of the 21st century stood at 59 and is now 69; for women the average of 68 years has increased to 77. Dire predictions of increased mortality rates have proven untrue, mainly because Brazil has done remarkably well in combating the spread of HIV/AIDS.

The Effects of Persistent Inequality

If Benedita da Silva is the face of possibility and change that has marked the democratic transition in Brazilian life, urban crime is the real evidence of persistent poverty. Impersonal statistics of low rates of literacy, inadequate education, entrenched poverty, and high unemployment come alive on the streets of Brazil's major cities in all too visible criminal activity. Note for example that with 198 million inhabitants, Brazil is South America's most populous country, and São Paulo, with 18 million residents, is the continent's largest city and the world's fourth largest. Another dubious honor, however, is that Brazil ranks near the top in worldwide calculations of crime statistics. In 1997, 1,335 Brazilians were killed during robberies. By the end of 1999, that number had tripled. According to statistics from the Center for the Study of Violence, in São Paulo, Brazil has an annual homicide rate of 25 per 100,000 inhabitants. By comparison, in the United States, the country with the highest per capita crime rate of the industrialized world, there are 11 homicides per 100,000 people. The perpetrators of robberies are often young drug addicts, while the victims are often young women. Murders are committed most often by men, a large number of whom appear to be in uniform. In 1999, in São Paulo alone, the police killed 380 civilians, most in execution style.

Crime is a frequent subject of discussion in the Brazilian media, where the methods of attack on victims and the crime scenes are publicized in gory detail. Several common scenarios are for thieves in

With 18 million inhabitants in the greater metropolitan area, São Paulo is the largest city of Brazil, as well as the most prosperous and the center of industry, commerce, finance, arts and culture. It is the fourth-largest metropolis in the world. (Shutterstock/Vinicius Tupinamba)

suburban utility vehicles to sandwich a car against the curb at a stoplight and demand money from the driver by holding a gun to his or her head. Other armed robbers pounce at condominium entrances, outside banks, and even on downtown streets. A recent feature on the crime scene, which affects a broad section of the middle and working-class population, is the *sequestro relampago,* or "lightning kidnap." A person is grabbed at random off a downtown street and forced at gunpoint to make a withdrawal at an automated teller machine. In some cases, if the person does not have enough money in his or her account to satisfy the thief, the victim is simply executed. As a precaution, Paulistas usually carry a wad of cash and an ATM card with them at all times, so that they can appease a robber in case they are mugged.

Even the very rich, or visiting celebrities and sports teams, have not been spared. In one well-publicized case, three international teams in Brazil for the 2001 Formula One Grand Prix were victims of violence. The British manager of the Minardi team was cornered after he left the bank with $8,000 to cover the team's weekend expenses, pistol whipped, and robbed. Other teams lost tires, auto equipment, and laptop computers. Another high-profile incident occurred in June 2008 when Pelé, a "national treasure," was robbed at gunpoint in Santos

223

shortly before leaving for South Africa to appear in the soccer benefit match to honor Nelson Mandela's 90th birthday.

The Brazilian rich, who have garnered a disproportionately high share of the national wealth, have been able to pay for ways to inure themselves of crime. "Brazil is the biggest market in the world for armored cars," according to Joe McCullough, president and CEO of Pilkington Aerospeace of Garden Grove, California (*The Daily Yomiuri,* November 30, 2000). McCullough's company opened a $3 million bulletproof glass factory in São Paulo in December 2000. He notes that every month about 850 cars are equipped with armor throughout the world, and from 250 to 300 of them are sold in Brazil. Armored cars are the wealthy's answer to the escalating crime rate in Brazil's cities. At the 2000 Exposec, an annual security fair showcasing the latest in anticrime technology, the São Paulo organizers reported $120 million in sales, in just three days, of alarms, surveillance gear, and protective equipment such as electric fences. Firms selling security devices reported a 44 percent increase in sales from 1998 to early 2001.

To avoid the pollution and chaos on the street, the wealthy fly to work in helicopters, a method of transportation that adds even more pollutants to the atmosphere. From 1994 to 2001, nearly 500 helicopters were added to commercial fleets that service wealthy Paulistas who commute to their offices over the city and not on its streets. São Paulo has the world's third-largest urban fleet of helicopters after New York and Tokyo, with thousands of helipads atop private mansions, hotels, banks, shopping malls, and government and apartment buildings. A major private university in São Paulo installed a helipad for the use of students, who are transported from their homes to classes at the inner-city campus. Helicopters are one more sign of the division between wealthy and middle-class urbanites and the growing number of urban poor. In the 10 years before the end of the 20th century, the cities and suburbs saw a proliferation of fortified communities, where residents lived protected by armed security guards. Those able to afford such protected residences travel to shopping malls in helicopters and armored vehicles, patronizing at stores and malls that have been declared off limits to poor and working-class, mainly black, Brazilians.

Whereas international tycoons and corporate CEOs who fall victim to crime have their stories spread across the pages of the tabloids and reported in vivid detail on television, they are not the most common victims. The most frequent victims are middle- and working-class Brazilians, who are unable to afford expensive protection services, live in ordinary and low-income apartments and houses, and use public transportation or walk to work. The cities of Brazil sport woefully inadequate public transportation systems. Commuters routinely spend one to three hours on busses slogging through streets choked in exhaust fumes in the heat and flooded when it rains, exposed to marauding criminals. Buses in Rio or São Paulo frequently travel less than 10 MPH because the streets are so packed with vehicles. If it were safe enough, many commuters report that they would walk or ride bicycles. Although both Rio de Janeiro and São Paulo have limited subway systems, they in no way service the majority of commuters. In comparison, Mexico City, a city of comparable size and level of development, moves its vast population on far-reaching subway lines, while cities such as Tokyo, London, and Paris move nearly twice as many commuters on public bus, rail and subway lines than does São Paulo.

The statistics on crime, inadequate public transportation, and horrendous levels of pollution signal the needs any government concerned with improving the welfare of the majority should be addressing. According to Jorge Wilhelm, a professor of urban affairs and former planner for the state of São Paulo, cities in Brazil have become places abandoned to poor people and bandits, avoided by the rich and the middle class. "This organization of society could get worse, and we shall go through life as some of the worst science fiction films." In the words of Luis Antonio de Sousa of the São Paulo Center for the Study of Violence, "Brazilian citizens are prisoners of their own fear" (*Los Angeles Times,* March 26, 2001).

The Environment

Many feel that the intersection between social woes and the overall quality of life is represented by concern over the environment. The Rio de Janeiro–based Economy and Energy Institute published a study in 2007 noting that between 1994 and 2005, carbon dioxide output grew by 45 percent, with annual greenhouse gas production outstripping economic growth. "The country is polluting more than the wealth it is creating," according to the newspaper account of the study. Moreover, these figures did not include emissions from the deforestation of the Amazon, which, if included, would make Brazil "the fifth-biggest polluter in the world".

As with so many things, Brazil has a mixed reputation with regard to concern for the environment. In June 1992, Rio de Janeiro hosted the second international conference on the environment and development. (The first had been in Stockholm 10 years earlier.) By choosing a Latin American country, and Brazil in particular, as the site for the conference, the United Nations sought to draw attention to the well-known environmental issues on the continent and in Brazil. While many Brazilians decry pollution, much of the world's attention has focused on preservation of the Amazon. The human quest to tame the Amazon forest and extract its wealth, a part of Brazil's development scheme to provide the resources to raise the standard of living, has victimized biological diversity. As with many other emerging economies, Brazil toes a line between environmental degradation and industrial development.

Since the early 16th century, adventurers and explorers have exploited the region for minerals, animal skins, gold, emeralds, oil, rubber, and a host of precious stones. Gold miners have polluted the river and its tributaries with mercury and other chemicals; lumber companies and industries searching for iron, aluminum, petroleum, and other raw materials have contributed to the ongoing destruction of the forest. In less than 500 years, one of the richest ecosystems on the planet that sustained millions of inhabitants for millennia has fallen on the list of severely endangered environments. After years of lobbying by environmental groups, in September 1999 President Cardoso signed an environmental crime bill that for the first time defined pollution and deforestation as crimes punishable by stiff fines and jail sentences. Unfortunately, many large corporate polluters, ranchers, and mining companies have been able to avoid prosecution and conviction. Many have openly shunned the government's attempts to impose legal restraints or, more often, been able to protect themselves by buying off the local law enforcement officials.

Industrialists and developers have continued to search the Amazon for resources. In fact, the 20th century has seen the greatest exploitation of the rain forest basin, bringing with it threats to the continued existence of this major reservoir of the world's natural resources. The changes have been threefold: destruction of the indigenous community, exploitation of land and mineral resources by multinational and national enterprises, and migration to the region of large numbers of non-natives.

Despite earlier interaction between outsiders and the indigenous population dating back to the 16th century, the first sustained contact with native Amazonian people began in 1947. It has not been an encounter that has benefited the Indians. Overall, the indigenous population has decreased dramatically in the 20th century as a result of disease, loss of land to ranchers and squatters from other parts of Brazil, usurpation of Indian lands by miners and gold prospectors, and the Indians' inability to maintain their traditional lifestyle in the face of encroachment from the outside.

Brazil's 20th-century Indian policy has been fraught with contradictions. Since the 1940s, the Brazilian Indians concentrated in the

Ataulo "Cotia" Kamayura, a skilled fisherman from the Kamayura tribe, is shown here catching fish near the lakeside Kamayura Village. (Shutterstock/Frontpage)

regions of Mato Grosso and Amazonia have attempted to bring their situation to the attention of the world, without suffering great loss. One group of Indian activists was the Villas Bôas brothers, who were members of the survey expedition sent into unexplored territory in 1943. When they arrived in the Upper Xingu River Basin, the three brothers, Caludio, Orlando, and Leonardo, determined to stay and protect the endangered Indians. They were successful in 1961 in persuading the Brazilian government to set aside most of the Upper Xingu region as a reserve (8,800 square miles). This park remained a reserve and has been kept off limits from encroachers, a success that has not been achieved in other areas.

Like other Latin American governments, Brazil's has not been anxious to negotiate with the many Indian tribes. The weak administrative structures of the Indian communities, worn down by centuries of disruption, have found it difficult to reach agreement with the centralized modern political administrations of Brazil, Colombia, Venezuela, and Guyana. Finally, after years of negotiations, in 1991–92, both Brazil and Venezuela set aside 45 million acres of land as designated indigenous territory. For the native peoples of the Amazon, this may be too little too late. A population estimated between 4 million and 6 million Indians in 1500 stands today at about 350,000, divided among 215 ethnic groups, or 0.2 percent of Brazil's current population.

Exploitation of Amazonia's resources continued apace throughout the second half of the 20th century. The federal government launched programs to attract homesteaders, as well as offered tax incentives and subsidies to businesses willing to exploit the region's resources and promote the integration of the Amazon region into the national economy. One of the primary means of integrating the region was the construction of a series of roads and highways linking the area to the capital in Brasilia. Highways have facilitated the movement of people and goods

Water buffalo herd on Marajó Island in Pará. (Photograph by Erich Goode)

CUBATÃO: THE CLEANUP CONTINUES

The situation in Amazonia frequently captures world headlines, but many other areas are of equal or greater significance. One site that has attracted considerable attention since the 1970s is the city of Cubatão, south of São Paulo. Once considered one of the most polluted places on the planet, rivaling Bhopal, India, as an environmental disaster site, or city awaiting disaster, Cubatão's water, soil, and air were saturated with deadly contaminants, including high levels of DDT. It registered cancer and infant mortality rates hundreds of times above even the Brazilian average. In the 1980s, a report detailed that there were so many miscarriages in the city, women faced pregnancy with horror, and the town was running out of places to bury stillborn children. In the 1990s, with the assistance of a loan from the World Bank, the local government was able to launch a cleanup effort that significantly reduced pollution by forcing the close of some of the worst factories and promoting better standards for others that remained.

Although Brazil has declared Cubatão clean, Greenpeace has criticized the continuing level of pollution in its *International Report.* In January 1999, activists fenced off a contaminated area containing waste from a Rhône-Poulenc plant, noting that persistent pollutants such as hexachlorobenzene (HCB) and HCBD (hexachlorobutadiene), by-products from chemical processes using chlorine, remain in the ground. For example, the Rhône-Poulanc plant was ordered closed in 1993, but activists contend that toxic elements continue to be released into the environment.

The Cubatão case is often pointed to as the long-term problem with environmental pollution. Although the government has been able to reduce significantly the level of current and future contamination, the effects from saturation of the soil in particular remain long-term ones. Marcelo Furtado of Greenpeace International argues that the site will only be clean when the toxic substances in the ground and water are eliminated. According to research by United Nations environmental agencies and the International Association for Research on Cancer (IARC), HCB and HCBD are possible human carcinogens. Since they collect in the fatty tissue of animals, they enter the food chain, and contaminants pass from mother to child in the womb and through breast-feeding.

into the formerly sparsely settled region, promoted the founding of towns along the roads, and augmented the settlement of urban areas. Agricultural homesteads, however, have proven unsuccessful, owing to the infertility of the soil. By contrast, lumber companies, large-scale cattle ranching, and extractive mining of gold, manganese, iron, and copper have been profitable. Needless to say, these are all enterprises that rely on large-scale production and are highly capital intensive. In that regard, the Amazon has developed, not as a level frontier where upstarts can earn a good living by working hard and tilling the soil, but it has mirrored the rest of Brazil's class structure of a few rich at the top and many poor at the bottom.

The environmental consequences of this development pattern in Brazil have been widely reported. Protection of the Amazon, as well as of the indigenous people who inhabit it, has become an international concern, attracting the attention of environmental and human-rights advocates, rock stars and celebrities, nongovernmental organizations (NGOs), the United Nations, and other international government agencies. In fact, it is during the recent period that questions have been raised about who should have jurisdiction over the Amazon region: Brazil or the world at large? Many environmentalists and scientific researchers argue the Amazon rain forest is too precious a resource to be held by one nation. Moreover, the endless search for the modern-day El Dorado has turned millions of acres of rain forest into wasteland. In so doing, environmental advocates and scientists contend, the keys to the future of life on the planet, both in terms of oxygen supplies from plant life and the medicinal qualities available from thousands of plant species, are being lost. Regardless of formal ownership, the protection of the Amazon's resources remains, or should remain, closely watched by international bodies.

Environmental Activism

Many activists in Brazil are working hard to show that protection of the environment is a priority. Since the return of democratic government, environmental activism has increased decidedly both on a local and national level. Brazil is one of the few countries of Latin America, or the world for that matter, to have an entire ministry devoted exclusively to environmental policies and oversight. Many "green" activists argue that with proper oversight, the fate of the Amazon will not go the way of the Atlantic forest in centuries past. Whereas less than 7 percent of the original growth that forested the coastline remains, almost 90 percent of the Amazon rain forest is intact. Bringing back the forest to the

Children sell handicrafts and show off animals to tourists on the Amazon River in exchange for money. Here a girl holds a monkey in her lap. (Claire Skotnes photo)

coastline and preserving the jungle of the Amazon basin are, therefore, two key aspects of current conservation efforts.

There are, nonetheless, those who have little interest in preservation who have shown they will go to any length to undermine the environmental cause. Environmental activists have been threatened, physically assaulted, repeatedly ridiculed, and even killed. In December 1988, a well-known activist and leader of the rubber tapper trade union, Francisco "Chico" Mendes Filho (1944–88) was killed in front of his home in Xapuri, Acre.

Chico Mendes had gained international acclaim for his work in founding the Xapuri Rural Workers Union in 1977. Under Mendes's leadership, the union organized health clinics, set up education classes for members and their children, and disseminated information on environmental issues to residents in the area. With the assistance of an anthropologist working in the area, Mendes formed the National Council of Rubber Tappers (CNS) as a kind of mutual-aid society. Residents of this most remote of all areas of Brazil for the first time learned of their rights as citizens, formed into cooperatives, and learned the benefits of collective bargaining.

One of the most important ecological innovations of the CNS was the promotion of "extractive reserves." This was a method whereby rubber tappers and their families could live off designated reserves by extracting only the rubber and other resources necessary for their subsistence without bringing harm to the forest. Mendes brought his program to the United Nations, presented it to members of the U.S. Congress, and argued for the designation of extractive reserves before the Brazilian Congress. His efforts paid off. In 1988, the Brazilian government expropriated land from landowners in Acre to provide for the first extractive reserve program.

The landowners immediately retaliated. Chico Mendes received death threats, members of the rubber tappers' union and their families were harassed, and at least one tapper was killed. On December 22, 1988, Chico Mendes himself was murdered in front of his house. Indicative of the impunity with which the landowners in the area operated, the crime took place at midday in full view of Mendes's neighbors. The police ordered to protect Mendes and his family "mysteriously" disappeared from the front of the house when the assassins approached.

Because of the national and international reputation Chico Mendes had achieved, and because of the attention that had been drawn to the rubber tappers' campaign, the local government was forced to investigate the death. In December 1990, two local landowners were convicted of committing the murder. Despite allegations of a wider involvement—Mendes had named his assassins in a letter to the governor earlier in the year—including a network of at least 30 landowners, the investigation was not broadened.

Chico Mendes had often declared that the most powerful ally to the Brazilian rubber tappers was the international environmental movement. Indeed, it was owing to international pressure that Mendes's killers were brought to trial. By 1990, Brazil was attracting a great deal of attention. Media throughout the world reported on the killing of street children, human-rights violations, and harassment of environmental activists. Embarrassed by the spotlight on corruption in the environmental agencies, President Collor fired the minister of the environment and initiated an investigation of corruption in the ministry. Collor's own impeachment on corruption charges truncated the cleanup however.

Challenges to Environmental Activism

A case that galvanized the human-rights and environmental movement was the murder of Ademir Federici (1959–2001) in August 2001. Both the boldness of the attack and the impunity with which local landowners and loggers threatened Federicci drew international attention to the case. Reportedly 18 months before his death, Dema, as the popular peasant and environmental leader was known, was told by a wealthy logger "to buy some wood for his coffin" (*New York Times*, October 12, 2001).

Federicci was the director of the Movement for the Development of the Trans-Amazon and the Xingu. He had reported on illegal deforestation on Indian reserves, opposed a government dam project that would benefit only the big landowners and drive out the small holders, and had attempted to stop car thieves and hijackers from terrorizing users of the Trans-Amazon Highway. Similar to Chico Mendes, Federicci was a man from a poor background, having little formal education but enormous charisma. In addition to religious, environmental, and labor leaders, he had provided effective leadership to the grassroots movement to preserve the land, protect the indigenous and peasant population of northern Pará, and pressure the government to enforce laws. He was the seventh in a continuing line of local leaders to be killed for his efforts.

The cases of Dema Federicci and Chico Mendes expose the ineffectiveness of the government policing, regulatory, and administrative apparatus, especially in the distant Amazon regions. If deaths of activists are frequent, threats against anyone who stands in the way of the loggers are practically commonplace. The representative from Pará to the national Chamber of Deputies, José Geraldo Torres, a member of the Workers Party, has been pressured to protect land titles for wealthy loggers. One logger, traveling on a plane with a friend of Deputy Torres, loudly proclaimed in front of all the passengers, "You tell José Geraldo that if my land title gets canceled, I will cancel him" (*New York Times*, October 12, 2001).

The Catholic Church: Advocate for Social Reform

The Catholic Church and priests in many rural areas have taken stands against corrupt government officials and local landowners. The pattern of church activism stretches back to the 1960s when members of the Catholic clergy began to speak out against human-rights abuses. The doctrine of liberation theology that swept much of Latin America found a particularly strong set of advocates in Brazil. Organized through Christian base communities (*communidades ecclesiasticas da base*, or CEBs), radical clergy and nuns organized in the backlands, in urban *favelas*, and among progressive students and activists in support of rights for peasants, Indians, protection of the environment, and labor unions. For their efforts, some have been killed, and a number has endured the censure of the Vatican. Leonardo Boff, one of the movement's foremost theologians, resigned the priesthood in 1992 after many years of conflict with Rome, while others, such as Archbishops Paulo Evaristo Arns of São Paulo and Hélder Câmara in Recife, were replaced by more conservative clerics after their retirement. On most issues the liberal voice of the church remains strong. However, consistent with Vatican doctrine, the Brazilian Church has blocked legislation to decriminalize abortion. Reproductive rights advocates were distressed in 2005 when Lula promised the church hierarchy that he would not support abortion rights.

Probably the single greatest threat to Catholic hegemony has come from Pentecostal and evangelical Protestant sects. Advocating individual salvation in the place of social reform, these rapidly expanding religious groups place fewer demands for social action on their followers. The devout do not have to learn to read or to protest bad government. At the same time, many evangelicals rejoice in the stability these movements advocate, including sobriety, honesty, and hard work. Many women, for example, find the pressure from the evangelical churches on men to stay sober, tend their families, and eschew violence has brought more tranquility to the domestic sphere.

Social Reforms on a Local Level

Church organizations, environmentalists, and labor leaders at century's end began coalescing around a critique of neoliberalism. In 2001, 2002, 2003, and 2005, thousands of activists met in Pôrto Alegre to declare their opposition to the global agenda promoted by the World Bank, IMF, and other international bodies. The conference, dubbed the World Social Forum (WSF), first met in 2001 at the same time as the World Economic Forum, a meeting of leading economic advisers to the world's wealthiest nations, was being held in Davos, Switzerland. At its first meeting in 2001, Pôrto Alegre drew together a core of international trade union, feminist, environmental, and human-rights workers. Although more heavily represented by members from Latin America, this is a group that overlaps with antiglobalization activists who have demonstrated at meetings of the IMF and World Bank in Genoa, Italy, Seattle, and other places. The Pôrto Alegre meetings in 2002 and 2003 attracted a wider range of participants, including a large number of politicians from Europe and other parts of the world. Politicians campaigning for office in France took time out to travel to the WSF, as a way of demonstrating their concerns for ecological and social justice issues. The meetings have moved to sites outside Brazil over the last decade, including Mumbai (2004), Caracas (2006), Nairobi (2007), and returned to the Amazonian city of Belem in January 2009, after a year when the forum did not meet anywhere. The meetings have grown in size and influence since 2001, issuing calls for debt cancellation for poorer countries, dismantling tax havens, universal employment and social welfare, environmental protection, demands for food, peace, security, human rights, and social justice for the world's people. The list of WSF speakers, and signatories to statements, such as the 2005 Pôrto Alegre Manifesto enumerating the organization's demands, include Nobel Prize winners, major authors, intellectuals, scientists, and social activists.

Local and Global Initiatives

Tarso Genro, the mayor of Pôrto Alegre, was the moving force behind the early World Social Forum. The citizens of Pôrto Alegre, a city of 1.3 million people and capital of Brazil's southernmost state of Rio Grande do Sul, had seen at close hand the December 2001 demise of the Argentine economic and political system, an event many blame on the neoliberal financial policy of world banks and loan institutions. Pôrto Alegre and the state of Rio Grande do Sul both have been in the hands of the PT since 1998. Experimenting with grassroots residents' democracy, the state and city have instituted a wide range of locally based initiatives to launch self-help projects and distribute public funds. Residents claim to be integrally involved in financial planning, and the reported success of Genro's initiative helped him attain appointment as Lula's minister of justice in Brasilia.

Foremost among Brazil's social activist organizations is the Landless Workers' Movement, or MST (Movimento dos Trabalhadores Rurais Sem Terra). Claiming 1.5 million members organized in 23 of the country's 26 states, the MST is often said to be the largest social movement in Latin America. Fortified by Article 186 of the 1988 constitution, which states that land must serve "a social function," the MST leads occupations of vacant and underutilized land. In a country where reportedly 1.6 percent of landowners control almost half (46.8 percent) of the land suitable for supporting a crop, the MST considers itself the guardian of productivity.

Although landowners dispute the MST claims, and violence between owners and squatters is common, the latter have registered many victories in the courts. Judges have ruled in favor of the MST when squatters have successfully shown that existing plots are not in compliance with the four constitutional requirements for all stewardship of property: (1) rational and adequate use of land; (2) adequate use of available natural resources and preservation of the environment; (3) compliance with the provisions that regulate labor relations; and (4) exploitation that favors the well-being of the owners and workers.

Drawing on the 1988 constitution has proved highly effective in pushing a reform agenda on other issues as well. Article 68 allows titles for land claimed by communities derived from those originally formed by runaway slaves, called *quilombos,* to pass into the ownership of the inhabitants. Although fewer than 100 of these have been granted to the occupants, there are estimated to be more than 2,000 *quilombos* that could fall into the hands of rural descendants of former slaves. Another area of dispute that has arisen as a result of this law is the claim that many rural dwellers, not *quilomb,* actually had title to land but lost it in land grabs by big landowners, especially during the military dictatorship. Their claims are not directly addressed in Article 68.

Redressing Racial Inequality

The most controversial issue in contemporary Brazil that has arisen from the constitution's grant of social equality is the claim for redress of grievances owing to racial discrimination. In 2003, the federal government began to implement an affirmative-action policy in university admissions, which by 2005 had expanded to a call for racial quotas. Highly controversial in a society that has long claimed no racial discrimination and in which racial categorization does not exist as a census or official category, implementation has proved problematic. By 2008, there were four state universities with specific racial and social class quotas. In a few cases, students are required to self-identify according to race, and in others, a panel of experts reviews files to determne eligibility.

Another step in redressing racial discrimination is the establishment of a university in São Paulo specifically for Afro-descendant students. The Universidade da Cidadania Zumbí Palmares de São Paulo, known as Unipalmares, is named for the hero of the 17th-century runaway slave community and its leader, Zumbí. Unipalmares graduated its first class in 2008, 90 percent of whom were self-declared as black. Indicative of the extent of official backing for this controversial program, Lula gave the commencement speech, and major dignitaries of the state and local government were all in attendance. While fraught with complications, these steps toward recognizing the legacy of slavery and the existence of racism are entirely novel in the history of Brazilians' identity.

Ipanema Beach, Rio de Janeiro. (Meade-Skotnes Photo Collection)

In other ways, an active judiciary has been forcing change that has proven more cumbersome on the political front. In July 2001, Colonel Ubiratan Guimaraes was convicted of charges stemming from the execution of more than 100 prisoners following an uprising at the notoriously overcrowded Carandirú Prison in 1992. Colonel Guimaraes was sentenced to 600 years in prison for his part in the massacre (although it would be unprecedented for a powerful military officer to serve out a sentence). Eighty-four prison officials have been indicted in the death of 111 prisoners who, according to survivors, were shot at point-blank range as they tried to surrender. The São Paulo prison, really a jail, built to hold 8,000, now houses as many as 20,000 prisoners, most of whom are awaiting trial or are being held without charge.

The government has renewed its attempts to confront the continuing issue of violence and crime, as well as the public's disgust with corrupt law enforcement. Under Cardoso, the Ministry of Justice appointed as secretary for human rights Paulo Sérgio Pinheiro, former University of São Paulo history professor and coordinator of the Nucleus of Violence Studies. As a founding member of the Center for the Study of Violence, Professor Pinheiro was a frequent and outspoken critic of police brutality and official misuse of power. He and members of the center he heads have been threatened for their tireless work to expose official corruption, denounce torture, and to bring to the public's attention violence against children. Today, Pinheiro works with the United Nations, advocating for the rights of children worldwide.

In the fall 2001, the Ministry of Justice called for tough new measures against torture, police violence, and intimidation of political activists. Skeptical observers contend that until Brazil resolves the wide gap between rich and poor, the lack of social services for the majority of the population, and widespread crime, any attempt to resolve corruption will fail. Professor Pinheiro is more optimistic. He has demonstrated that it is possible to work with government institutions to promote human rights, that many agencies are receptive to learning alternative strategies, and that the rate of police violence and civilian violence can be stemmed. Currently, President da Silva has found, as did Cardoso before him, that the only permanent guarantee for peace and human rights rests with ending the extreme social inequalities that characterize Brazilian society.

Brazil's Prospects for the Future

Brazil is a country beginning the 21st century with formidable problems. Inefficiency, corruption, crime, underemployment, and unemployment take a severe toll on resources that could go toward making real improvements in the quality of life for more of the nation's population. With that in mind, increased investment in the needs of Brazil's people would produce a more equitable society. At the same time, Brazil is a nation equipped with many resources, both human and natural, from which to build a better future. In which direction the country will move in the next decades is an open question. Many analysts fear that the economic problems, and the resultant civil disorder, that periodically have racked Argentina could erupt in Brazil. Others are more optimistic and argue that Brazil's larger economy and considerable resources may help stave off a crisis even as the world enters a severe economic recession. Brazil has an ample supply of natural resources that are in high demand on the world market and the capacity for vast industrial output. While a prolonged recession in the United States would have negative effects, Brazil's large and widely diverse trading partners might provide some protection from the worst effects of economic crises

Most important, one cannot fail to be impressed with the indomitable spirit of Brazil's citizens. The amazing ingenuity of its literary, artistic, and cultural community, in addition to the work of tireless social reformers, promises to carve out a place for Brazil among nations as a vital, innovative, and constantly renewing country. Despite its many problems, Brazil's greatest resource remains its remarkable people.

APPENDIX 1

BASIC FACTS ABOUT BRAZIL

Official Name
Federative Republic of Brazil

Government
Under the Constitution of 1988, Brazil is a federal republic with a centralized government under an elected president. The president and vice president serve a four-year term and, under a 1997 amendment to the Constitution, may serve a second consecutive term. The bicameral national congress is made up of a chamber of deputies and a senate. The third branch of the government is the judiciary, headed by an 11-member supreme court.

As of 2008 there are 20 main political parties, and no one has been dominant since the country emerged from military rule in 1988. In recent elections the four parties that garnered the most votes nationally were: the Brazilian Democratic Movement Party (PMDB), the Democrats (DEM), formerly the Liberal Front Party (PFL), the Liberal Front Party (PFL), the Workers Party (PT), and the Brazilian Social Democratic Party (PSDB).

Political Divisions
States	Twenty-six plus the federal district, which includes the capital.
Capital	Brasilia

Geography
Area	Brazil covers an area of 3,286,488 square miles and is larger than all of western Europe combined. It is the largest country of Latin America and fifth largest in the

world after the Russian Federation, Canada, China, and the United States.

Boundaries
Brazil borders on every country of South America except Chile and Ecuador. To the north are French Guiana, Surinam, Guyana, Venezuela, and Colombia. The western border is with Paraguay, Bolivia, and Peru. Argentina and Uruguay are to the south.

Topography
Brazil's landscape is dominated by the Amazon River and its basin in the north and the Central Highlands which extend south from the river basin. The Central Highlands reaches an altitude of 1,640 feet above sea level, but the plateau table mainly stands at 1,000 feet above sea level. A chain of mountain ranges extends along the eastern edge of the country, dividing the interior from the coastal plain along the Atlantic Ocean.

The Amazon River is the world's largest in volume and second only to the Nile River of Africa in length. The 4,087-mile-long river is navigable by ocean steamers for 2,246 miles from its mouth in the Atlantic Ocean. A system that combines the Paraná River and the Paraguay River drains the area from the Minas Gerais southward to the River Plate (Rio de la Plata) in Argentina. The São Francisco River flows more than 1,000 miles northward from Central Highlands and drains eventually into the Atlantic Ocean. Many small crafts and steam-powered paddle-wheelers navigate the river and serve as a main trading and communication system to areas of the interior.

Climate
Ninety percent of Brazil is in the tropical zone, but the most populous centers are in areas where the altitude and ocean winds moderate the temperature. The country's five climates are equatorial, tropical, semi-arid, highland tropical, and subtropical. The Amazon region has an annual average temperature of 72–79 degrees Fahrenheit with a small seasonal variation. The coastal Northeast and the more arid northeastern interior experience the hottest temperatures, especially during the dry season, from May through November. Frequent prolonged droughts in the Northeast push temperatures frequently to 100 degrees Fahrenheit and above.

The northeastern coastal cities of Recife and Salvador have very warm climates, however the temperature is moderated by coastal winds, as is also the case with the center-south coastal city of Rio de Janeiro. The most moderate temperatures of any major population center are in the plateau cities of São Paulo, Belo Horizonte, and Brasilia, where the average yearly temperature is around 66 degrees Fahrenheit. In Pôrto Alegre and Curitiba, in the far south bordering Argentina, the temperatures are more similar to those in parts of the United States or Europe. The southern areas experience frost and sometimes freezing temperatures in the winter months, from June through September.

Highest Elevation | The highest peak is Pico da Neblina at 9,888 feet, located in the Atlantic coastal range.

Demographics

Population | The population of Brazil is 198,739,269 (2009 est.), making it the fifth largest in the world after China, India, the United States, and Indonesia. Approximately 27 percent of the population is under the age of 14. The population has declined quite dramatically in the last decades of the 20th century, falling from a growth rate of 3 percent in 1960 to a 1.199 percent rate of increase in 2009. The decline is attributed to modernization, a very rapid rate of urbanization, and persistently high infant mortality rates (there are 23 death for every 1,000 live births).

Major Cities | São Paulo is the largest city, with a population of 10.9 million and more than 18 million in the metropolitan area. Rio de Janeiro is second, with 6 million, and Salvador is a distant third at 2.9 million. It is generally accepted that the census underestimates the total population. The number of city dwellers, as well as the number in the overall population, is considerably higher.

Language | Portuguese is spoken by everyone in Brazil with the exception of a tiny minority of indigenous people who live on remote reserves. Brazil is the only Portuguese-speaking country of Latin America.

Ethnicity The population divides ethnically and racially as 53.7 percent white, 38.5 percent mixed white/black (Afro-descendant), 6.2 percent black, 0.9 percent other (Asian, Arab, Middle Eastern, and Amerindian.

Religion Approximately 75 percent of Brazilians declare themselves as Roman Catholic, although a very large number of people from every social group throughout the country also practice one of the African-based religions. The most widespread of these is *candomblé,* a religion that traces back to Nigeria and Benin. A Brazilian variation, *umbanda,* developed in the 1920s and commands a broad following. Catholics declined 5 percent since 2003.

  Possibly the fastest-growing religion in Brazil is evangelical Protestantism. There are also mainstream Protestant denominations, Mormons, Jews, Muslims, Buddhists, and more than 1.5 million Spiritists or Kardecists, followers of the French mystic Allan Kardec.

Economy

Gross Domestic Product (2008) $1,836 trillion; the ninth largest in the world and the largest in Latin America.

Currency Since 1994 the currency has been the *real* (pronounced rey-al).

Agricultural Products Brazil produces for export and internal consumption a wide variety of goods including coffee sugarcane, soybeans and kidney beans, corn, cocoa, wheat, rice, rubber, brazil nuts, cashews, waxes, tropical fruits, citrus fruits, grapes, and nearly every type of fruit. In 1997 it was the largest producer of coffee, sugar (from sugarcane), and oranges, and the second-largest producer of beef.

Minerals Iron ore, manganese, bauxite, uranium, petroleum, natural gas, potassium, phosphate, tungsten, tin, lead, graphite, chrome, gold, zirconium, and thorium. Brazil produces 90 percent of the world's gems: diamonds, aquamarines, topazes, amethysts, emeralds, and tourmalines.

Industrial Products	Four key sectors of industrial output are steel, auto and truck, petrochemicals, and utilities. Other sectors include pharmaceuticals, clothing and shoes, textiles, mining, and many consumer durables. The National Alcohol Program (PROALCOOL) began in 1975 to produce the anhydrous fuel ethanol from sugarcane, which is combined with gasoline to produce a fuel for internal combustion engines. Brazil is the second-largest producer of ethanol, and 75 percent of all autos and light vehicles run on ethanol or "flex" fuel. Unlike oil, sugarcane is a renewable nonpolluting source of energy. Consumption has fluctuated between a high of 95 percent in 1986 to 24 percent in 2000.
Trade	China surpassed the United States as the chief trading partner, followed by the Southern Common Market (Mercosul, usually written in the Spanish, Mercosur, when adapted to English) composed of Brazil, Argentina, Paraguay, and Uruguay. The European Union is fourth in importance. In 2003 Lula persuaded South Africa and India to join Brazil in a triangular dialogue focusing on technological cooperation and efforts to promote the social interests of the Southern Hemisphere.

APPENDIX 2

CHRONOLOGY

Precolonial Brazil

Pre-10000 B.C.	Peopling of the Americas from Asia
ca. 7000 B.C.	First humans reach southern tip of South American continent
ca. 7000–1500 B.C.	Settlement of areas of Brazil by the Ge in the Central Highlands and spread from north to south many groups of Tupi speakers, including Mundurucú, Tupinambá, Siriono, and Guaraní
ca. 2000 B.C.	Yanomami, Waika, Shamatari, Shirishana, and Guajaribo groups in the Amazon Basin

European Exploration

June 4, 1494	Treaty of Tordesillas. Pope Alexander VI divides world between Spain and Portugal
1500	Spaniard Vicente Yañez Pinzón explores Amazon region
April 22, 1500	Pedro Álvares Cabral makes landfall at Porto Seguro, south of Bahia
1502	King Manoel of Portugal licenses merchants to trade brazilwood
1530	Martim Alfonso de Sousa explores southern coast and Guanabara Bay
1532	Founding of São Vicente. Sugar mills built
1534–36	King grants first 12 captaincies to courtiers (*donatarios*)
1538	First known shipment of slaves arrives in Brazil
1549	Royal governor arrives in Salvador da Bahia to establish capital

1549–1769	Jesuits establish missions
1565	Founding of Rio de Janeiro
1580	Portugal and Spain united in single Crown
ca. 1600–97	Palmares *quilombo*. The colonial army destroys the settlement of runaway slaves in 1697
1616	Missionaries establish settlement at Belém, at the mouth of the Amazon River
1628	Antonio Rapôso Tavares attacks and burns to the ground several Jesuit missions in interior São Paulo
1624–30	Dutch capture Salvador and Recife and occupy Northeast
1640	Portugal independent from Spain
1650–1715	Sugar production in Northeast declines by two-thirds
1654	Dutch withdraw from Brazil
1693	Crown divides the Amazon among four missionary orders: Jesuits, Mercedarians, Franciscans, and the Carmelites
1700–60	Gold mining boom in Minas Gerais
1703	Portugal signs Treaty of Methuen with England ensuring market for Portuguese goods and ceding commercial dominance to the British
1750	Treaty of Madrid sets new boundaries for Spain and Portugal
1755	Marquês de Pombal outlaws Indian slavery in Brazil
1759	Pombal expels Jesuits from the Portuguese empire
1763	Colonial capital moved from Salvador da Bahia to Rio de Janeiro
1789	The Inconfidencia conspiracy in Minas Gerais discovered
1792	Execution of Tiradentes, leader of the Inconfidencia
1808	House of Braganza Court arrives in Rio de Janeiro. Ports opened to world trade, restrictions on manufacturing lifted, first printing press in Brazil established
1810	Brazil grants commercial dominance to Great Britain

Kingdom

1815	Brazil raised to status of kingdom
1821	Dom João VI returns to Lisbon

Empire

September 7, 1822	Cry of Ipiranga. Prince Pedro declares Brazil independent from Portugal
December 1, 1822	Pedro I declares himself emperor
1824	Pedro I dictates a constitution
1825–28	War between Argentina and Brazil. In peace treaty, Uruguay created to serve as buffer separating the two states
1830	Brazil agrees to end the external slave trade
1831	Pedro I abdicates and returns to Portugal. A Regency rules in the place of the five-year-old heir to the throne
1835–40	War of the Cabanagem in Belém
1843	First Brazilian novel, *The Fisherman's Son,* by Antônio Gonçalves Teixeira e Sousa, is published
1850	External slave trade finally abolished with the Queiroz Law
1865–70	War of the Triple Alliance (Argentina, Uruguay, and Brazil) against Paraguay. Ends with near destruction of Paraguay
September 28, 1871	Passage of the Rio Branco or Free Birth Law, freeing children born of slave mothers
May 13, 1888	Assembly passes Golden Law abolishing slavery with no compensation to slaveholders. Signed by Princess Isabel in the absence of Emperor Pedro II

First Republic (often called Old Republic)

November 15, 1889	Republic declared, ending the monarchy. Marshal Floriano Peixoto is first president
1889–1930s	"Miracle" in Juazeiro do Norte and subsequent movement led by Padre Cícero Romão
1889–1949	Major waves (with intermittent interruptions) of immigration from Europe, Japan, and the Middle East

1890	Machado de Assis publishes *Dom Casmurro* and gains a reputation as one of Latin America's foremost novelists
	Beginning of the "coffee and cream" (*café com leite*) alliance in which São Paulo and Minas Gerais alternated control of the federal government
1891	Republican Constitution
1895	First competitive soccer game played in Brazil
1897	Canudos destroyed and its leader, Antônio Conselheiro, dies
1900–10	Urban renovation of Rio de Janeiro, São Paulo, and other cities
1912	Contestado rebellion in Santa Catarina and Paraná
1917	General strikes in São Paulo and Rio de Janeiro initiated by Paulista women in needle trades
	Brazil enters World War I on the side of the Allied powers
1922	Week of Modern Art initiates a cultural trend that values Brazilian over European art and literature
	Tenente uprising in Rio de Janeiro. Junior officers take over garrison in Copacabana, demanding fair elections
	Brazilian Communist Party founded
	Bertha Lutz forms Brazilian Federation for Feminine Progress
1924	*Tenente* uprising in São Paulo. Militant workers and junior officers hold the city from July 5–28
1925–27	March of Prestes Column through the backlands
1930	Getúlio Vargas leads a military rebellion. End of the First Republic. Frente Negra Brasileira (Negro Front) founded in São Paulo
1932	Integralist Action Party formed and led by Plinio Salgado in support of fascism in Europe and Brazil
1931	Civil code grants suffrage for literate women over age of 21
1934	New Constitution adopted
1937	Estado Nôvo formed. Vargas rules by decree

1941	Vargas forms the National Council of Sports as a division of the Ministry of Education and Culture, incorporating soccer as the national pastime
1942	Brazil enters World War II on side of Allies
1945	Brazilian Labor Party formed as political tool for Vargas
October 29, 1945	Vargas deposed in military coup
1946	New Constitution adopted
1950	Vargas reelected to the presidency
1952	National Conference of Brazilian Bishops (CNBB) formed by Dom Hélder Câmara. In the early 1960s the CNBB will be an important voice for pushing social reforms. In the 1970s it was the chief critic of the government's human rights record
August 24, 1954	Vargas deposed and commits suicide leaving a note blaming "outside powers" for undermining his authority
1955	Juscelino Kubitschek elected president
1960	Federal capital moved to Brasília. The modernist city was designed to both open the Brazilian interior and to showcase Brazil as an emerging modern power
1960	Peasant Leagues (ligas) organized by Francisco Julião to win rights for backlands peasants
1961	Election and resignation of Jânio Quadros to the presidency
1962	Vice President Jõao Goulart assumes the presidency
March 31, 1964	Goulart overthrown by military dictatorship. General Humberto Castello Branco assumes leadership of the military. First Institutional Act passed as governing edict
1967	New Constitution
1968	Workers and students stage demonstrations against the military government
1968–83	Increased repression and suspension of civil liberties. The government rules through a series of Institutional Acts. Dissidents leave the country; censorship, repression widespread

1969	Small urban guerrilla force active
September 4–7, 1969	Guerrillas kidnap U.S. ambassador to Brazil, Charles Burke Elbrick. He is freed when Brazilian government accedes to the kidnappers' demands
1969–74	Military government launches the "Brazilian Miracle" as a development and industrialization program
1975	São Paulo journalist Vladimir Herzog dies in São Paulo prison. The assumption that he was killed by the police leads to widespread protests
1978–79	Strike waves in industrial worker sectors of major cities
1979	A political opening, or *abertura,* is begun. This is a process of gradual restoration of political rights
1979	Workers Party (PT) is formed to oppose military government
1984	Military allows elections. Tancredo Neves from opposition party elected to the presidency, and José Sarney, candidate of the military party, elected vice president
1985	Tancredo Neves dies before taking office. José Sarney assumes the presidency
1988	New Constitution
1988	Francisco "Chico" Mendes, internationally known rubber tapper and environmentalist, assassinated
1989	Presidential elections. Fernando Collor de Mello wins against Workers Party candidate Luís Inácio Lula da Silva ("Lula") in a run-off
December 1992	Collor impeached and convicted on charges of embezzlement and corruption. Vice President Itamar Franco assumes the presidency
1991–92	Brazil and Venezuela sign an accord setting aside 45 million acres as indigenous reserves
1992	Rio de Janeiro hosts the Second International Conference on the Environment and Development
1993	Fernando Henrique Cardoso appointed Finance Minister. The *Real* Plan introduced to arrest inflation and stabilize economy
1994	Fernando Henrique Cardoso elected president and assumes office the following year.

1997	"Reelection amendment" added to Constitution, allowing for elected officials to run for a second, and final, term in office
1998	Cardoso defeats Lula for a second term as president
1999	President Cardoso signs the environmental crime bill making deforestation and pollution punishable crimes
2002	Brazil wins its fifth World Cup in soccer at Yokohama, Japan
	Lula (PT) defeats José Serra (PSDB) in a runoff election, winning more than 60 percent of the vote
2003	Lula assumes office, with José Alencar as vice president, on January 1.
	Government distributes land to 400,000 poor families in largest single land reform in nation's history
2005	Workers Party (PT) embroiled in massive corruption, vote-buying, and illicit campaign-financing scandal. Lula's top aide forced to resign.
2006	Lula defeats conservative business candidate Geraldo Alckmin (PSDB) in runoff election.
2007	Discovery of Tupi oil field in Santos Basin, offshore from state of São Paulo
	Lula announces Brazil as energy self-sufficient.
	Brazil wins bid to host 2014 FIFA World Cup.
2008	Brazil announces discovery of Jupiter natural gas and light oil field 20 miles from Tupi. Jupiter and two other oil and natural gas discoveries are largest finds on the planet in more than 20 years.
2008	Standard and Poor's financial services company elevates Brazil and Petrobras (state-owned oil company) to investment grade (rating given to countries and firms showing "stable and consistent" economic growth).
2009	China replaces the United States as Brazil's largest trading partner. In April, the sum of exports and imports with China reaches $3.2 billion, more than the $2.8 billion in trade with the United States, which had been Brazil's primary trading partner since the 1930s.

APPENDIX 3

BIBLIOGRAPHIC SOURCES

Albert, Bill. *South America and the First World War: The Impact of the War on Brazil, Argentina, Peru, and Chile.* Cambridge: Cambridge University Press, 1988.

Amado, Jorge. *The Violent Land.* Translated by Samuel Putnam. New York: Avon Books, 1945.

Balick, Michael J. "Green Treasure: The Useful Plants of the Amazon Valley." *Journey Into Amazonia: Companion to the PBS Nature Series.* Available online. URL: http://www.pbs.org/journeyintoamazonia. Downloaded on December 12, 2000.

Barickman, B. J. *A Bahian Counterpoint: Sugar, Tobacco, Cassava, and Slavery in the Recôncavo, 1780–1860.* Stanford, Calif.: Stanford University Press, 1998.

Bell, Alured Gray. *The Beautiful Rio de Janeiro.* London: William Heinemann, 1914.

Besse, Susan. *Restructuring Patriarchy: The Modernization of Gender Inequality in Brazil, 1914–1940.* Chapel Hill: University of North Carolina Press, 1996.

Burns, E. Bradford. "Cultures in Conflict: The Implication of Modernization in Nineteenth-Century Latin America." In *Elites, Masses, and Modernization in Latin America, 1850–1930,* edited by Virginia Bernhard. Austin: University of Texas Press, 1979.

———. *A History of Brazil.* New York: Columbia University Press, 1980.

Carvalho, José Murilo de. *Os Bestializados: o Rio de Janeiro e a República que Não Foi.* São Paulo: Editora Schwarcz, 1987.

Caulfield, Sueann. *In Defense of Honor: Sexual Morality, Modernity, and Nation in Early-Twentieth-Century Brazil.* Durham, N.C.: Duke University Press, 2000.

Chalhoub, Sidney. *Trabalho, lar e botequim: o cotidiano dos trabalhadores no Rio de Janeiro da belle époque.* São Paulo: Editora Brasiliense, 1986.

Conrad, Robert E. *Children of God's Fire: A Documentary History of Black Slavery in Brazil.* Princeton, N.J.: Princeton University Press, 1983.

Crosby, Alfred. *The Columbian Exchange: Biological and Cultural Consequences of 1492.* New York: Greenwood Publishing Group, Inc., 1990.

Cunha, Euclides da. *Rebellion in the Backlands.* Translated by Samuel Putnam. Chicago: University of Chicago Press, 1944.

Davis, Darien. *Avoiding the Dark: Race and the Forging of National Culture in Modern Brazil.* Brookfield, Vt.: Ashgate Publishing Co., 1999.

Dean, Warren. *With Broadax and Firebrand: The Destruction of the Brazilian Atlantic Forest.* Berkeley: University of California Press, 1995.

Diacon, Todd A. *Millenarian Vision, Capitalist Reality: Brazil's Contestado Rebellion 1912–1916.* Durham, N.C.: Duke University Press, 1991.

Dulles, John W. F. *Anarchists and Communists in Brazil, 1900–1935.* Austin: University of Texas Press, 1973.

Eakin, Marshall. *Brazil: The Once and Future Country.* New York: St. Martin's Griffin, 1997.

———. *Tropical Capitalism: The Industrialization of Belo Horizonte, Brazil.* New York: St. Martin's Press, 2001.

Eisenberg, Peter. *The Sugar Industry in Pernambuco: Modernization Without Change, 1840–1910.* Berkeley: University of California Press, 1974.

Fadul, Anamaria. *Serial Fiction in TV: The Latin American Telenovelas.* São Paulo: School of Communications and Arts, 1992.

Faron, Louis C. "A Continent on the Move." In *America in 1492: The World of the Indian Peoples Before the Arrival of Columbus,* edited by Alvin M. Josephy, Jr. New York: Vintage, 1993.

Fleischer, David. "Brazil Focus: A Weekly Report." Internet report on Brazilian Politics and Economics. E-mail: fleischer@uol.com.br.

French, John D. *The Brazilian Workers' ABC: Class Conflict and Alliances in Modern São Paulo.* Chapel Hill: University of North Carolina Press, 1992.

Freyre, Gilberto. *The Masters and the Slaves: A Study in the Development of Brazilian Civilization.* Translated by Samuel Putnam. New York: Alfred A. Knopf, 1946.

Galeano, Eduardo. *Memory of Fire: Faces and Masks.* Translated by Cedric Belfrage. New York: Pantheon Books, 1987.

Green, James N. *Beyond Carnival: Male Homosexuality in Twentieth-Century Brazil.* Chicago: University of Chicago Press, 1999.

Greenpeace International Report on the Status of the Environment. New York, 1999.

Guillermoprieto, Alma. "Obsessed in Rio." *New Yorker,* August 16, 1993, 44–55.

Hahner, June E. *Emancipating the Female Sex: The Struggle for Women's Rights in Brazil, 1850–1940.* Durham, N.C.: Duke University Press, 1990.

Lavrin, Asunción, ed. *Sexuality and Marriage in Colonial Latin America.* Lincoln: University of Nebraska Press, 1989.

Lesser, Jeffrey. *Negotiating National Identity: Immigrants, Minorities, and the Struggle for Ethnicity in Brazil.* Durham, N.C.: Duke University Press, 1999.

Levine, Robert M., and John J. Crocitti, eds. *The Brazil Reader: History, Culture, Politics.* Durham, N.C.: Duke University Press, 1999.

Lobo, Eulalia Maria Lahmeyer. *Historia do Rio de Janeiro: Do capital commercial ao capital industrial e financeiro.* 2 vols. Rio de Janeiro: Instituto Brasileiro de Mercado de Capitais, 1978.

Lobo, Eulalia Maria Lahmeyer, and Eduardo Navarro Stotz. "Flutuações cíclicas da economia, condições de vida e movimento operario, 1880–1930." *Revista Rio de Janeiro* 1 (December 1985):61–86.

Lombardi, Cathryn L., and John V. Lombardi, with K. Lynn Stoner. *Latin American History: A Teaching Atlas.* Madison: University of Wisconsin Press, 1983.

Mason, Tony. *Passion of the People? Football in South America.* New York: Verso Books, 1995.

Meade, Teresa. *"Civilizing" Rio: Reform and Resistance in a Brazilian City, 1889–1920.* University Park: Pennsylvania State University Press, 1997.

Mendes, Chico. *Fight for the Forest: Chico Mendes in His Own Words.* Additional material by Tony Gross. London: Latin America Bureau, 1989.

Nazzari, Muriel. *Disappearance of the Dowry: Women, Families, and Social Change in São Paulo, Brazil, 1600–1900.* Stanford, Calif.: Stanford University Press, 1991.

Needell, Jeffrey D. *A Tropical Belle Epoque: Elite Culture and Society in Turn-of-the-Century Rio de Janeiro.* Cambridge: Cambridge University Press, 1987.

van Roosmalen, Vasco, and Mark Plotkin, "The Status of Conservation of the Amazon Basin." *Journey into Amazonia: Companion to the PBS Nature Series* (December 12, 2000). Available online. URL: http://www.pbs.org/journeyintoamazonia/. Downloaded on December 12, 2000.

Sader, Emil, and Ken Silverstein. *Without Fear of Being Happy: Lula, the Workers Party and Brazil.* New York: Verso Books, 1991.

Schultz, Kirsten. *Tropical Versailles: Empire, Monarchy, and the Portuguese Royal Court in Rio de Janeiro, 1808–1821.* New York: Routledge, 2001.

Seed, Patricia. *Ceremonies of Possession in Europe's Conquest of the New World, 1492–1640.* New York: Cambridge University Press, 1995.

Silva, Benedita da. *Benedita da Silva: An Afro-Brazilian Woman's Story of Politics and Love.* As told to Medea Benjamin and Maisa Mendonça. Oakland, Calif.: Food First Books, 1997.

Skidmore, Thomas E. *Black into White: Race and Nationality in Brazilian Thought.* Durham, N.C.: Duke University Press, 1993.

———. *Brazil: Five Centuries of Change.* New York: Oxford University Press, 1999.

———. *The Politics of Military Rule in Brazil, 1964–85.* New York: Oxford University Press, 1988.

———. "Racial Ideas and Social Policy in Brazil, 1870–1940." In *The Idea of Race in Latin America, 1870–1940,* edited by Richard Graham. Austin: University of Texas Press, 1990.

State Department Cable, October 20, 1978, U.S. Ambassador Robert White (Paraguay) to Secretary of State Cyrus Vance. National Security Archive. Available online. URL: www.gwu.edu/~nsarchiv/news/20010306. Downloaded on April 12, 2002.

Sweet, David. "Native Resistance in Eighteenth-Century Amazonia: The 'Abominable Muras' in War and Peace," *Radical History Review* 53 (Spring 1992): 49–80.

Tenenbaum, Barbara A. *Encyclopedia of Latin American History and Culture.* Vols 1–5. New York: Charles Scribner's Sons, 1996.

Vargas Llosa, Mario. *The War of the End of the World.* Translated by Helen R. Lane. New York: Farrar, Straus and Giroux, 1981.

Vianna, Hermano. *The Mystery of Samba: Popular Music and National Identity in Brazil.* Translated and edited by John Charles Chasteen. Chapel Hill: University of North Carolina Press, 1999.

Weinstein, Barbara. *The Amazon Rubber Boom, 1850–1920.* Stanford, Calif.: Stanford University Press, 1983.

————. *For Social Peace in Brazil: Industrialists and the Remaking of the Working Class in São Paulo, 1920–1964.* Chapel Hill: University of North Carolina Press, 1996.

Wolfe, Joel. *Working Women, Working Men: São Paulo and the Rise of Brazil's Industrial Working Class, 1900–1955.* Durham, N.C.: Duke University Press, 1993.

APPENDIX 4

SUGGESTED READINGS

Introductory Surveys of Brazil

Burns, E. Bradford. *A Documentary History of Brazil*. New York: Alfred A. Knopf, 1966.

Costa, João Cruz. *A History of Ideas in Brazil*. Translated by Suzette Macedo. Berkeley: University of California Press, 1964.

Fausto, Boris. *A Concise History of Brazil*. New York: Cambridge University Press, 1999.

Galeano, Eduardo. *Memory of Fire Trilogy*, vol. 1, *Genesis*; vol. 2, *Faces and Masks*; vol. 3, *Century of the Wind*. Translated by Cedric Belfrage. New York: W. W. Norton, 1998.

Lockhart, James, and Stuart Schwartz. *Early Latin America: A History of Colonial Spanish America and Brazil*. New York: Cambridge University Press, 1983.

Levine, Robert M., and John J. Crocitti, eds. *The Brazil Reader: History, Culture, Politics*. Durham, N.C.: Duke University Press, 1999.

Matta, Roberto da. *Carnivals, Rogues and Heroes: An Interpretation of the Brazilian Dilemma*. Translated by John Drury. Notre Dame, Ind.: University of Notre Dame Press, 1991.

Page, Joseph A. *The Brazilians*. Reading, Mass.: Addison-Wesley, 1995.

Ribeiro, Darcy, and Gregory Rabassa. *The Brazilian People: The Formation and Meaning of Brazil*. Gainesville: University Press of Florida, 2000.

Roett, Riordan. *Brazil: Politics in a Patrimonial Society*. Westport, Conn.: Greenwood, 1999.

Schneider, Ronald M. *"Order and Progress": A Political History of Brazil*. Boulder, Colo.: Westview Press, 1991.

Land and People Before and After Portuguese Exploration (Prehistory to 1530)

Boxer, C. R. *The Portuguese Seaborne Empire, 1415–1825.* New York: Alfred A. Knopf, 1969.

Dorson, Mercedes, and Jeanne Wilmot. *Tales from the Rain Forest: Myths and Legends from the Amazonian Indians of Brazil.* Hopewell, N.J.: Ecco Press, 1997.

Early, John D., and John F. Peters. *The Xilixana Yanomami of the Amazon: History, Social Structure, and Population Dynamics.* Gainesville: University Press of Florida, 2000.

Hemming, John. *Amazon Frontier: The Defeat of the Brazilian Indians.* Cambridge, Mass.: Harvard University Press, 1987.

———. *Red Gold: The Conquest of the Brazilian Indians, 1500–1760.* Cambridge, Mass.: Harvard University Press, 1978.

Lévi-Strauss, Claude. *Tristes Tropiques.* Translated by John and Doreen Weightman. New York: Atheneum, 1974.

Murphy, Yolanda, and Robert F. Murphy. *Women of the Forest.* New York: Columbia University Press, 1990.

Peters, John F. *Life Among the Yanomami: The Story of Change Among the Xilixana on the Mucajai River in Brazil.* Orchard Park, N.Y.: Broadview Press, 1998.

Russell-Wood, A. J. R. *The Portuguese Empire, 1415–1808: A World on the Move.* Baltimore, Md.: Johns Hopkins University Press, 1998.

Shoumatoff, Alex. *The Rivers Amazon.* San Francisco: Sierra Club Books, 1978.

The Portuguese Colony (1530–1800)

Bethell, Leslie, ed. *Colonial Brazil.* Cambridge, England: Cambridge University Press, 1987.

Boxer, C. R. *The Dutch in Brazil, 1624–1654.* Oxford: Oxford University Press, 1957.

Cohen, Thomas. *The Fire of Tongues: António Vieira and the Missionary Church in Brazil and Portugal.* Stanford, Calif.: Stanford University Press, 1998.

Graham, Richard, ed. *Brazil and the World System.* Austin: University of Texas Press, 1991.

Maxwell, Kenneth. *Pombal: Paradox of the Enlightenment.* Cambridge, England: Cambridge University Press, 1995.

Mörner, Magnus. *The Expulsion of the Jesuits from Latin America.* New York: Alfred A. Knopf, 1965.

Schwartz, Stuart B. *Sugar Plantations in the Formation of Brazilian Society: Bahia, 1550–1835.* New York: Cambridge University Press, 1985.

Stein, Stanley, and Barbara Stein. *The Colonial Heritage of Latin America: Essays on Economic Dependence in Perspective.* New York: Oxford University Press, 1970.

Society in Early Brazil: Slavery, Patriarchy, and the Church (1530–1889)

Abreu, Martha. "Slave Mothers and Freed Children: Emancipation and Female Space in Debates on the 'Free Womb' Law, Rio de Janeiro, 1871." *Journal of Latin American Studies* 28 (1996):567–80.

Conrad, Robert E. *World of Sorrow: The African Slave Trade to Brazil.* Baton Rouge: Louisiana State University Press, 1986.

Dean, Warren. *Rio Claro: A Brazilian Plantation System, 1820–1920.* Stanford, Calif.: Stanford University Press, 1976.

Graham, Sandra Lauderdale. *House and Street: The Domestic World of Servants and Masters in Nineteenth-Century Rio de Janeiro.* New York: Cambridge University Press, 1989.

———. *Caetano Says No: Women's Stories from a Brazilian Slave Society.* New York: Cambridge University Press, 2002.

Higgins, Kathleen J. *"Licentious Liberty" in a Brazilian Gold Mining Region: Slavery, Gender, and Social Control in Eighteenth-Century Sabará, Minas Gerais.* University Park: Pennsylvania State University Press, 1999.

Karasch, Mary C. *Slave Life in Rio de Janeiro, 1808–1850.* Princeton, N.J.: Princeton University Press, 1987.

Klein, Herbert S. *African Slavery in Latin America and the Caribbean.* New York: Oxford University Press, 1986.

Kuznesof, Elizabeth Anne. *Household Economy and Urban Development: São Paulo 1765–1836.* Boulder, Colo.: Westview, 1986.

Lewin, Linda. *Politics and Parentela in Paraíba: A Case Study of Family-Based Oligarchy in Brazil.* Princeton, N.J.: Princeton University Press, 1987.

Mattoso, Katia M. de Queirós. *To Be a Slave in Brazil, 1550–1888.* Translated by Arthur Goldhammer. New Brunswick, N.J.: Rutgers University Press, 1986.

Metcalf, Alida C. *Family and Frontier in Colonial Brazil: Santana de Parnaíba, 1580–1822.* Berkeley: University of California Press, 1992.

Miller, Joseph C. *Way of Death: Merchant Capitalism and the Angolan Slave Trade, 1730–1830.* Madison: University of Wisconsin Press, 1988.

Peard, Julyan G. *Race, Place, and Medicine: The Idea of the Tropics in Nineteenth-Century Brazil*. Durham, N.C.: Duke University Press, 1999.

Reis, João José. *Slave Rebellion in Brazil: The Muslim Uprising of 1835 in Bahia*. Translated by Arthur Brakel. Baltimore, Md.: Johns Hopkins University Press, 1993.

Russell-Wood, A.J.R. *Fidalgos and Philantropists: The Santa Casa da Misericórdia of Bahia, 1550–1775*. Berkeley: University of California Press, 1968.

Schwartz, Stuart B. *Slaves, Peasants, and Rebels: Reconsidering Brazilian Slavery*. Urbana: University of Illinois Press, 1985.

From Colony to Republic (1800–1889)

Boxer, C. R. *The Golden Age of Brazil, 1695–1750: Growing Pains of a Colonial Society*. Berkeley: University of California Press, 1969.

Costa, Emília Viotti da. *The Brazilian Empire: Myths and Histories*. Chicago: University of Chicago Press, 1985.

Font, Maurício A. *Coffee, Contention and Change in the Making of Modern Brazil*. Cambridge, Mass.: Basil Blackwell, 1990.

Holloway, Thomas H. *Policing Rio de Janeiro: Repression and Resistance in a Nineteenth-Century City*. Stanford, Calif.: Stanford University Press, 1993.

Macaulay, Neill. *Dom Pedro: The Struggle for Liberty in Brazil and Portugal, 1798–1834*. Durham, N.C.: Duke University Press, 1986.

Maxwell, Kenneth R. *Conflicts and Conspiracies: Brazil and Portugal, 1750–1803*. Cambridge, England: Cambridge University Press, 1973.

Nabuco, Carolina. *The Life of Joaquim Nabuco*. Translated by Ronald Hilton. Stanford, Calif.: Stanford University Press, 1950.

Nabuco, Joaquim. *Abolitionism: The Brazilian Antislavery Struggle*. Translated by Robert Conrad. Urbana: University of Illinois Press, 1977.

Nizza da Silva, Maria Beatriz. "Divorce in Colonial Brazil: The Case of São Paulo." *Sexuality and Marriage in Colonial Latin America*, Asunción Lavrin, ed. Lincoln: University of Nebraska Press, 1989.

Schultz, Kirsten. *Tropical Versailles: Empire, Monarchy, and the Portuguese Royal Court in Rio de Janeiro, 1808–1821*. New York: Routledge, 2001.

Scott, Rebecca, Hebe M. Mattoso de Castro, Seymour Drescher, Robert M. Levine, and George R. Andrews. *The Abolition of Slavery and the Aftermath of Emancipation in Brazil*. Durham, N.C.: Duke University Press, 1988.

Stein, Stanley J. *Vassouras: A Brazilian Coffee County, 1850–1900: The Roles of Planter and Slave in a Plantation Society*. Princeton, N.J.: Princeton University Press, 1985.

Toplin, Robert Brent. *The Abolition of Slavery in Brazil.* New York: Atheneum, 1972.

Constructing a Nation of Free Laborers in the Late Nineteenth and Early Twentieth Centuries

Beattie, Peter M. *A Tribute of Blood: Army, Honor, Race, and Nation in Brazil, 1864–1945.* Durham, N.C.: Duke University Press, 2001.

Bethell, Leslie ed. *Brazil: Empire and First Republic, 1822–1930: A Selection of Chapters form Volumes III and IV of the Cambridge History of Latin America.* Cambridge, England: Cambridge University Press, 1989.

Borges, Dain. *The Family in Bahia, Brazil, 1870–1945.* Stanford, Calif.: Stanford University Press, 1992.

Chalhoub, Sidney. "Slaves, Freedmen, and the Politics of Freedom in Brazil: The Experience of Blacks in the City of Rio." *Slavery and Abolition* 10, no. 3 (1989):64–84.

Chandler, Billy Jaynes. *The Bandit King: Lampião of Brazil.* College Station: Texas A&M University Press, 1978.

Della Cava, Ralph. *Miracle at Joaseiro.* New York: Columbia University Press, 1970.

Graham, Richard. *Britain and the Onset of Modernization in Brazil, 1850–1914.* London: Cambridge University Press, 1968.

Lesser, Jeffrey. *Welcoming the Undesirables: Brazil and the Jewish Question.* Berkeley: University of California Press, 1995.

Levine, Robert M. *Pernambuco and the Brazilian Federation, 1889–1937.* Stanford, Calif.: Stanford University Press, 1978.

———. *Vale of Tears: Revisiting the Canudos Massacre in Northeastern Brazil, 1893–1897.* Berkeley: University of California Press, 1992.

Pang, Eul-Soo. *In Pursuit of Honor and Power: Noblemen of the Southern Cross in Nineteenth-Century Brazil.* Tuscaloosa: University of Alabama Press, 1988.

Stepan, Nancy. *"The Hour of Eugenics": Race, Gender and Nation in Latin America.* Ithaca, N.Y.: Cornell University Press, 1991.

Society and Politics in the First Republic (1890–1930)

Andrews, George Reid. *Blacks and Whites in São Paulo, Brazil, 1888–1988.* Madison: University of Wisconsin Press, 1991.

Butler, Kim R. *Freedoms Given, Freedoms Won: Afro-Brazilians in Post-Abolition São Paulo and Salvador.* New Brunswick, N.J.: Rutgers University Press, 1998.

Macaulay, Neill. *The Prestes Column: Revolution in Brazil.* New York: F. Watts, 1974.

Machado de Assis, Joaquim M. *Dom Casmurro*. Translated by Helen Caldwell. New York: Noonday Press, 1953.

From Getúlio Vargas to the Military Coup (1930–1964)

Alencar, José M. de. *Iracema: A Legend of Brazil*. Edited by Naomi Lindstrom. Translated by Clifford E. Landers. New York: Oxford University Press, 2000.

Amado, Jorge. *Gabriela: Clove and Cinnamon*. New York: Avon Books, 1962.

Andrade, Carlos Drummond de. *Traveling in the Family: Selected Poems*. Edited by Thomas Colchie and Mark Strand. New York: Random House, 1986.

Chilcote, Ronald H. *The Brazilian Communist Party: Conflict and Integration, 1922–1972*. New York: Oxford University Press, 1974.

Fischer, Brodwyn M. *A Poverty of Rights: Citizenship and Inequality in Twentieth Century Rio de Janeiro*. Stanford, Calif.: Stanford University Press, 2008.

Freyre, Gilberto. *New World in the Tropics: The Culture of Modern Brazil*. New York: Alfred A. Knopf, 1959.

————. *Order and Progress: Brazil from Monarchy to Republic*. Translated by Rod W. Horton. Berkeley: University of California Press, 1986.

Hanchard, Michael George. *Orpheus and Power: The Movimento Negro of Rio de Janeiro and São Paulo Brazil, 1945–1988*. Princeton, N.J.: Princeton University Press, 1999.

Landes, Ruth. *The City of Women*. With a new introduction by Sally Cole. Albuquerque: University of New Mexico Press, 1994.

Lispector, Clarice. *The Hour of the Star*. Translated by Giovanni Pontiero. New York: New Directions, 1992.

Mainwaring, Scott. *The Catholic Church and Politics in Brazil, 1916–1985*. Stanford, Calif.: Stanford University Press, 1986.

Skidmore, Thomas E. *Politics in Brazil, 1930–1964: An Experiment in Democracy*. New York: Oxford University Press, 1967.

Underwood, David Kendrick. *Oscar Niemeyer and the Architecture of Brazil*. Vol. 1. New York: Rizzoli International Publications, 1994.

Welch, Cliff. *The Seed Was Planted: The São Paulo Roots of Brazil's Rural Labor Movement, 1924–1964*. University Park: Pennsylvania State University Press, 1998.

Williams, Daryle. *Culture Wars in Brazil: The First Vargas Regime, 1930–45*. Durham, N.C.: Duke University Press, 2001.

From Military Dictatorship to Democracy (1964–2002)

Alvarez, Sonia E. *Engendering Democracy in Brazil: Women's Transition Politics.* Princeton, N.J.: Princeton University Press, 1990.

Boff, Leonardo. *Ecclesiogenesis: The Base Communities Reinvent the Church.* New York: Orbis Books, 1997.

Catholic Church, Archdiocese of São Paulo. *Torture in Brazil: A Shocking Report on the Pervasive Use of Torture by Brazilian Military Governments, 1964–1979.* Preface by Joan Dassin. Austin: University of Texas Press, 1998.

Jesus, Carolina Maria de. *Child of the Dark.* New York: E. P. Dutton, 1962.

Keck, Margaret E. *The Worker's Party and Democratization in Brazil.* New Haven, Conn.: Yale University Press, 1997.

Lesser, Jeffrey. *A Discontented Diaspora: Japanese Brazilians and the Meanings of Ethnic Militancy, 1960–1980.* Durham, N.C.: Duke University Press, 2007.

Levine, Robert M, and José Carlos Sebe Bom Meihy. *The Life and Death of Carolina Maria de Jesus.* Albuquerque: University of New Mexico Press, 1995.

Pereira, Anthony. *End of the Peasantry: The Rural Labor Movement in Northeast Brazil, 1961–1988.* Pittsburgh: University of Pittsburgh Press, 1997.

Weschler, Lawrence. *A Miracle, A Universe: Settling Accounts with Torturers.* New York: Penguin Books, 1990.

Popular Culture: Music, Sports, Television, and Cinema in Today's Brazil

Bocketti, Gregg P. "Italian Immigrants, Brazilian Football, and the Dilemma of National Identity." *Journal of Latin American Studies* 40 (2008): 275–302.

Brown, Diana D. *Umbanda: Religion and Politics in Urban Brazil.* New York: Columbia University Press, 1994.

Chestnut, R. Andrew. *Born Again in Brazil: The Pentecostal Boom and the Pathogens of Poverty.* New Brunswick, N.J.: Rutgers University Press, 1997.

Dunn, Christopher. *Tropicália and the Emergence of a Brazilian Counterculture.* Chapel Hill: University of North Carolina Press, 2001.

Fryer, Peter. *Rhythms of Resistance: The African Musical Heritage of Brazil.* Hanover, N.H.: University Press of New England, 2000.

Guillermoprieto, Alma. *Samba.* New York: Alfred A. Knopf, 1990.

Johnson, Randal. *The Film Industry in Brazil: Culture and the State.* Pittsburgh: University of Pittsburgh Press, 1987.

McCann, Bryan. *Hello, Hello Brazil: Popular Music in the Making of Modern Brazil.* Durham, N.C.: Duke University Press, 2004.

McGowan, Chris and Ricardo Pessanha. *The Brazilian Sound: Samba, Bossa Nova, and the Popular Music of Brazil.* New York: Billboard Books, 1991.

Parker, Richard G. *Bodies, Pleasures, and Passions: Sexual Culture in Contemporary Brazil.* Boston: Beacon Press, 1991.

Perrone, Charles A. *Masters of Contemporary Brazilian Song: MPB, 1965–1985.* Austin: University of Texas Press, 1989.

Pillitz, Christopher. *Brazil Incarnate: The Body Cult in Brazil.* Preface by Caetano Veloso. Text by Paul Theroux. Zurich: Edition Stemmle, 2000.

Brazil in the Twenty-first Century

Branford, Sue, and Jan Rocha. *Cutting the Wire: The Story of the Landless Movement in Brazil.* London: The Latin America Bureau, 2002.

Caipora Women's Group. *Women in Brazil.* London: Latin America Bureau, 1993.

Gay, Robert. *Popular Organization and Democracy in Rio de Janeiro: A Tale of Two Favelas.* Philadelphia: Temple University Press, 1993.

Hanchard, Michael, ed. *Racial Politics in Contemporary Brazil.* Durham, N.C.: Duke University Press, 1999.

Hecht, Tobias. *At Home in the Street: Street Children of Northeast Brazil.* New York: Cambridge University Press, 1998.

Marx, Anthony W. *Making Race and Nation: A Comparison of the United States, South Africa and Brazil.* New York: Cambridge University Press, 1999.

Patai, Daphne. *Brazilian Women Speak.* New Brunswick, N.J.: Rutgers University Press, 1988.

Ramos, Alcida Rita. *Indigenism: Ethnic Politics in Brazil.* Madison: University of Wisconsin Press, 1998.

Reichman, Rebecca, ed. *Race in Contemporary Brazil: From Indifference to Inequality.* University Park: Pennsylvania State University Press, 1999.

Revkin, Andrew. *The Burning Season: The Murder of Chico Mendes and the Fight for the Amazon Rain Forest.* Boston: Houghton Mifflin, 1990.

Scheper-Hughes, Nancy. *Death Without Weeping: The Violence of Everyday Life in Brazil.* Berkeley: University of California Press, 1992.

Silva, Benedita da. *Benedita da Silva: An Afro-Brazilian Woman's Story of Politics and Love.* As told to Medea Benjamin and Maisa Mendonça. Oakland, Calif.: Food First Books, 1997.

INDEX

Note: **Boldface** page numbers indicate primary discussion of a topic. Page numbers in *italic* indicate illustrations. The letters *c*, *g*, and *m* indicate chronology, glossary, and maps, respectively.